CLAY MODEL OF HOUSE

TERRA-COTTA MODEL OF WAGON

BATTLE AX WITH COPPER BLADE

SILVER JAVELIN HEAD

SILVER-HANDLED GOLD SWORD

HARPIST ON STOOL

SHELL GAMING BOARD

CHARIOT PULLED BY ONAGER

CUNEIFORM FROM HAMMURABI LAW CODE

STONE LIBATION JUG

DAIRYMEN POURING MILK

NOBLEWOMAN AND HAIRDRESSER

WOODEN COMB

PLUMB-SQUARE

MARKING CORD

SICKLE WITH FLINT TEETH

MAKING BRICKS WITH MUD

COPPER BIT BOW-DRILL

SEPARATING WHEAT FROM CHAFF

OBELISK AND PYLON

PHILISTINE WARSHIP

CANAANITE BLOWING RAM'S HORN

NECKLACE OF GOLD

GAMING DIE

HITTITE SLINGMAN

BRONZE SICKLE SWORD

GREECE–ROME Time of Christ

SURGICAL INSTRUMENTS

SCROLL BOX AND STYLUS

OIL LAMP

OLIVE PRESS

POSEIDON, GREEK GOD OF SEA

ROMAN ROUND SHIP

LEGIONARIES WITH STANDARD

ROMAN WRITING

WOMAN WITH LYRE

MODESIUM AED OF

Everyday Life in

BIBLE TIMES

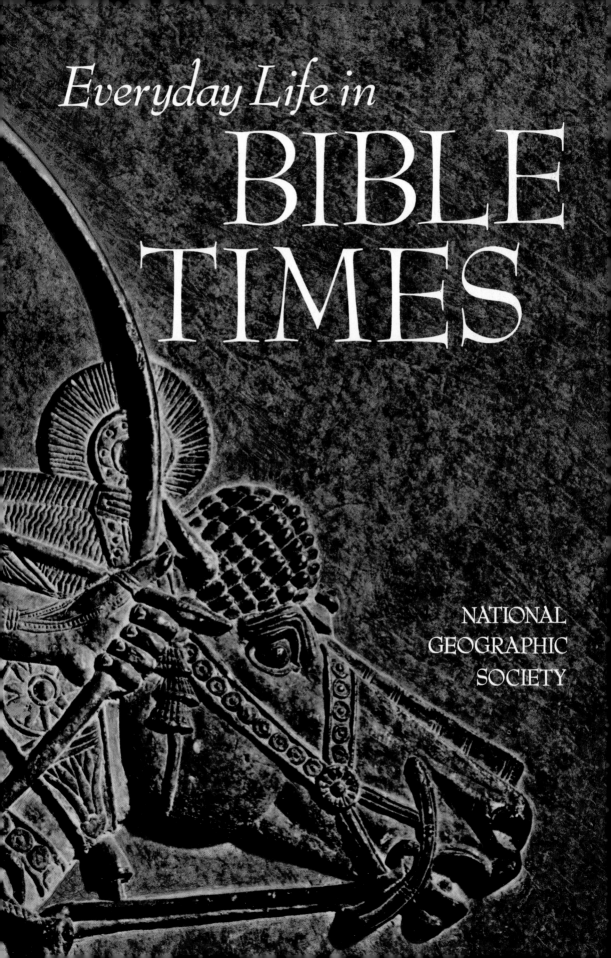

Everyday Life in

BIBLE
TIMES

NATIONAL
GEOGRAPHIC
SOCIETY

A VOLUME IN THE STORY OF MAN LIBRARY
PREPARED BY
NATIONAL GEOGRAPHIC BOOK SERVICE

PUBLISHED BY THE NATIONAL GEOGRAPHIC SOCIETY
MELVIN M. PAYNE, CHAIRMAN OF THE BOARD
ROBERT E. DOYLE, PRESIDENT

Foreword by
MELVILLE BELL GROSVENOR
Editor-in-Chief
National Geographic Society

Editorial consultant
JAMES B. PRITCHARD
Curator of Biblical Archeology, University Museum, and
Professor of Religious Thought, University of Pennsylvania;
excavator of Gibeon and Zarethan; author of Archaeology
and the Old Testament; *editor of* The Ancient
Near East in Pictures, Ancient Near Eastern Texts

Special Essays by
SAMUEL NOAH KRAMER
Former Curator of Tablet Collections, University Museum,
and Emeritus Professor of Assyriology, University
of Pennsylvania; excavator in Iraq; author of
History Begins at Sumer, The Sumerians

JOHN A. WILSON
Former Professor of Egyptology, Oriental Institute,
University of Chicago; former Director, Epigraphic
Expedition at Luxor, Egypt; author of The Burden
of Egypt, Signs and Wonders upon Pharaoh

G. ERNEST WRIGHT
Former Chairman, Old Testament Department, Harvard
Divinity School; excavator of Shechem; author of
The Old Testament Against Its Environment,
Biblical Archaeology; *co-author of*
The Westminster Historical Atlas to the Bible

H. W. F. SAGGS
Professor of Semitic Languages, University of Wales,
Cardiff, former visiting Professor of Akkadian, Baghdad
University; author of The Greatness That Was Babylon,
Everyday Life in Babylonia and Assyria

ROLAND DE VAUX
Director (1945-65), Ecole Biblique et Archéologique
Française, Jerusalem; excavator of Tirzah and Dead Sea
Scrolls at Khirbat Qumran; author of Ancient Israel:
Its Life and Institutions; *general editor of*
La Bible de Jérusalem

EMIL G. KRAELING
Former Professor of Old Testament at Union Theological
Seminary and Semitic Languages at Columbia University;
decipherer of Brooklyn Museum Aramaic papyri;
biographer of Paul and the Disciples; author of
Rand McNally Bible Atlas; *co-author of* Our Living Bible

First two printings 525,000 copies
Revised printing (1976) 100,000 copies
ISBN 0-87044-131-0
LIBRARY OF CONGRESS CATALOG CARD NO. 67-23392

Chapters by
JAMES B. PRITCHARD, A. DOUGLAS TUSHINGHAM,
Chief Archaeologist, Royal Ontario Museum;
and DAVID S. BOYER, HOWARD LA FAY,
KENNETH MACLEISH, *and* JOHN J. PUTMAN
of the National Geographic staff

Photographs by
THOMAS J. ABERCROMBIE, DAVID S. BOYER,
DEAN CONGER, LUIS MARDEN, WINFIELD PARKS,
JOHN J. PUTMAN, JOSEPH J. SCHERSCHEL,
HELEN *and* FRANK SCHREIDER, ROBERT F. SISSON, *and*
B. ANTHONY STEWART *of the National Geographic staff;*
JONATHAN BLAIR, CHARLES HARBUTT,
THOMAS NEBBIA, *and others*

Paintings by
PETER V. BIANCHI, H. M. HERGET, TOM LOVELL,
JOHN McDERMOTT, ROBERT W. NICHOLSON,
HENRY J. SOULEN, *and the Old Masters*

528 Illustrations,
412 in full color, 13 Maps

This book was prepared
under the editorial guidance of
MELVILLE BELL GROSVENOR
and FREDERICK G. VOSBURGH
by the following staff:

MERLE SEVERY
Editor and Art Director

SEYMOUR L. FISHBEIN, EDWARDS PARK
Associate Editors

JOHN J. PUTMAN
Project Editor

CHARLES O. HYMAN
Designer

ANNE DIRKES KOBOR
Picture Editor

THOMAS B. ALLEN, ROSS BENNETT,
BERRY L. REECE, JR., DAVID F. ROBINSON
Editor-Writers

JAMES P. KELLY
Production Manager

WILLIAM W. SMITH
Engraving and Printing

SUSAN C. ECKERT,
JEAN F. LEICH, *Editorial Research*

ANN MARTIN, *Picture Research*

WERNER L. WEBER, *Production*

LINDA L. MODLIN,
WILHELM R. SAAKE,
ESTELLE SADUSK,
EDWARD MARTIN WILSON, *Assistants*

ANDREW POGGENPOHL, *Art*

JOHN D. GARST, *Maps*

WERNER JANNEY, *Style*

DOROTHY M. CORSON, *Index*

W. E. ROSCHER, *European Representative*

Robed men and camels
photographed by Victor Englebert
evoke a caravan of Bible days

Foreword

ACROSS THE VALLEY OF KIDRON spread the massive walls and huddled houses, the towers and domes of Jerusalem. As I stood on the Mount of Olives, gazing upon this Holy City of three great faiths, I thought of its momentous past. Here, tradition says, Abraham prepared to sacrifice his son Isaac. Here rose the City of David, and here Solomon built his temple in days of Israel's glory. I could almost hear the tinkling of the Queen of Sheba's caravan—camels bearing "spices, and very much gold, and precious stones"—shuffling soft-footed into Solomon's resplendent capital.

Here Jesus walked during His last days. I saw the gleaming Dome of the Rock, site of Herod's Temple where Jesus scourged the money changers. Below me, gnarled olive trees in the Garden of Gethsemane reflected Jesus' agony. On Mount Zion, far to my left, stood the traditional Room of the Last Supper. In the distance ahead, I picked out the Church of the Holy Sepulcher, enshrining the place where He fulfilled His promise to "give his life as a ransom for many." I thought:

If only there were a book that could capture the power of this scene, that could bring Bible times to life as did my own journey to Bible lands!

So many ties link us to these desert-girt lands that arch through the Tigris-Euphrates valley, down the Levant coast, to the Nile's banks! Here in the Fertile Crescent man learned to harness oxen to his stick plow, to harvest grain and thresh it under the hoofs of cattle. He learned to save seed and plan for the river's seasonal retreat, when fields lay scorched and cracked.

Irrigation required community effort and helped weld clans into nations. Apportioning water taught man government. A steady food supply enabled him to build towns, gave him leisure to speculate on laws of the universe, to devise a calendar and a system of writing, to enrich life with arts. The words that I write, the paintings and sculptures of daily life that adorn these pages were rooted in Biblical soil. The ancestor of the giant map in the back of the book was incised on Mesopotamian clay 4,500 years ago.

How often my journey to Bible lands stirred memories of treasured Bible stories! In Damascus bazaars I rubbed shoulders with men in patriarchal robes and imagined Abraham coming to this Syrian oasis. On a cliff in Lebanon I gazed on 33 centuries of inscriptions—among them hieroglyphs marking the return of Ramesses II from a war against the Hittites. Ramesses! "Pharaoh of the Oppression" from whose bondage Moses led the children of Israel. In mountain snows I found a remnant of the cedars of Lebanon. They were shipped to Solomon from Byblos, which gave us our word "Bible." Amid the pagan splendors of Baalbek I sensed the power of Rome, whose legions rendered Palestine unto Caesar. At Tarsus, Antioch, Corinth, I felt the presence of Paul, whose message changed history's course.

To give readers the same rich experience, Book Service Chief Merle Severy and I planned *Everyday Life in Bible Times*. He too has traveled widely in Bible lands

SAMARITAN WOMAN *near Jacob's Well evokes Jesus' words: "whosoever drinketh of the water that I shall give him shall never thirst" (John 4:14). Scenes that span the centuries greet modern eyes in Bible lands.*

7

SCRIPTURES *became an open book when the famed Gutenberg Bible (left), first to be printed, appeared in the 1450's.*

Before then, monks in the scriptorium patiently lettered copies by hand; laymen seldom glimpsed the precious manuscripts. The invention of printing from movable type dramatically widened horizons. In five decades after publication of the Latin Bible named for Johann Gutenberg more than 100 editions appeared, many in common tongues.

At last everyman could read of "shepherds abiding in the field" near Bethlehem (opposite); "and the glory of the Lord shone round about them. . . . And the angel said . . . I bring you good tidings of great joy" (Luke 2:8-10).

and is deeply versed in their history. We sent National Geographic writers and photographers to trace the footsteps of Abraham, Moses, David, Solomon, Jesus, Paul. We commissioned artists to re-create Bible life in vivid detail. We turned to seven renowned authors whose researches have cast new light on the Bible world.

Our consultant during laborious months of production was Dr. James B. Pritchard of the University of Pennsylvania, both an ordained minister and a leading archeologist. Our eminent essayists likewise combine respect for the Bible with scientific inquiry. And I must salute the Book Service team for creating a volume that deepens understanding of the Bible by making its times live again.

We show how, in the 1,800 years between Abraham and Paul, the Old Testament's concept of a jealous God, guiding the destiny of one people, evolved into the New Testament's God of mercy and human brotherhood; how Bible lands spawned the first wars of conquest, and also gave rise to the ideal of peace on earth. We chronicle the Bible story as it unfolded in the context of its times, recording its moments of ruthlessness as well as its periods of grandeur.

Like many readers, I grew up with the ringing language of the King James Version, which so strongly influenced the literary heritage of English-speaking nations. Here we use its cherished phrases in quoted passages, except where clarity has led us to the Revised Standard Version.

We are proud that the first edition of *Everyday Life in Bible Times* won praise from such authorities as Dr. Norman Vincent Peale of Marble Collegiate Church in New York City, the late Richard Cardinal Cushing of Boston, and the late Dr. Nelson Glueck, archeologist and president of Hebrew Union College, Cincinnati. We are pleased, too, that enthusiastic reception by Society members has resulted in two printings totaling 525,000 copies. Now, in this revised third printing, we invite you to join us for an exciting journey into the living world of the Bible.

Melville Bell Grosvenor

CONTENTS

God begins the Creation

Temptation of Adam and Eve

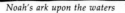

Noah's ark upon the waters

Abraham meets Melchizedek

Moses receives the Law on Sinai

David and Goliath

Jesus enters Jerusalem

The Crucifixion

Isabel Saul painted these miniatures from the famed stained-glass windows in England's York Minster; reproduced by courtesy of the Dean and Chapter

By James B. Pritchard

The Adventure of Rediscovery

W E HAD JUST FINISHED LUNCH when our chief pottery washer pulled a broken jar handle from his pocket. "I meant to show this to you earlier," he apologized. I glanced at it and forgot to reprove him. The fragment bore timeworn scratches—unmistakably four Hebrew letters: *[Hebrew letters]* . I read them, and nine weeks of toil under a scorching sun faded from memory. The characters spelled "Gibeon," the town of Biblical fame which our staff of nine and about a hundred laborers had been trying to find.

"This handle speaks to us," was all I could say at the moment. In my fingers I held the autograph of the city where Joshua led the children of Israel to a great victory, calling on the Lord for time to complete his triumph: "Sun, stand thou still upon Gibeon" (Joshua 10:12). Here, "by the pool of Gibeon" (II Samuel 2:13), David's men clashed with Saul's. Here "the Lord appeared to Solomon" and endowed him with "a wise and understanding heart" (I Kings 3:5, 12).

Under an olive tree, eight miles north of Jerusalem, Ibrahim the pottery washer and I were keeping a rendezvous in time with an unknown scribe of the seventh century B.C. This literate Gibeonite, a contemporary of Jeremiah the prophet, had inscribed a jar with a single word that enabled us to fit another stone into the arch that links us to the dim past.

Here in the Fertile Crescent, the strip of land between mountains and desert that loops past these hills of Palestine through Syria, then southward into Mesopotamia, civilization dawned. Man learned to farm, to group his dwellings into towns, to work metals. Our Land-Rover, jolting to the dig each morning, churned

GAZING ACROSS 43 CENTURIES, *a life-size head from Mesopotamia reflects a culture that predates the Bible. Scholars say it may portray Sargon of Agade, conqueror of the "land between the rivers." His Semitic descendants, fierce Assyrians, built Nineveh, where this bronze—once boasting jeweled eyes—came to light.*

13

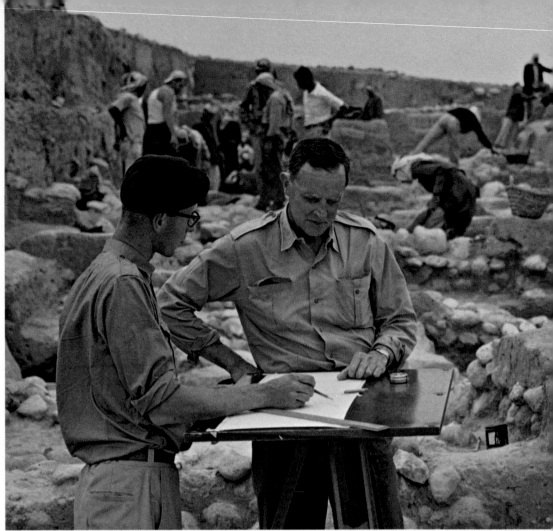

soil that might have been rutted by some of the earliest wheels. In this region, man invented writing and produced records of his story. One, the Bible, was once our only source of knowledge about vanished cities—Ur of the Chaldees, Babylon, Nineveh, Lachish—and such mighty rulers as Sargon of Assyria, Nebuchadnezzar, Cyrus of Persia. Generations of scholars have sought the Bible's full meaning. Our work, archeology, is simply a new method of inquiry into its pages.

New? For more than a century Biblical archeologists have been adding realism to the Bible story just as illustrations add interest to a book. Austen Henry Layard, an adventurous Englishman, and Paul Émile Botta, a French foreign service officer, found palaces of Assyrian rulers referred to in II Kings. Henry Rawlinson, a daredevil linguist, copied boasts of Darius the Great from a Persian cliff and worked out their meaning. At last the world could translate cuneiform writing, signs scratched or impressed on stones and clay tablets from more than a thousand years before Abraham to a century before Christ.

Suddenly, more than three millennia of records could be read. Kings who had been known only from the Bible—Omri, Ahab, Jehu, Menahem, Hoshea, Pekah, Hezekiah—came to light in cuneiform texts. In 1872, George Smith pieced together tablets in the British Museum, stirred with excitement as a familiar story unfolded,

SLICING THROUGH TIME'S LAYER CAKES, *archeologists in Bible lands sift secrets long locked in "tells," hills of debris where ancients built new cities on the ruins of old. Stairway to prehistory in an imaginary tell (below) yields artifacts—Stone Age to Byzantine— from Fertile Crescent sites; eras recede as steps descend.*

Author (opposite) and young assistant note finds at Tell es Saidiyeh in Jordan Valley. Shards of pottery—whose changing styles can date a town's rise and fall within half a century—place this walled city's heyday in the 10th century B.C. *Hoards of bronze vessels suggest it was Zarethan. Near that city, says I Kings 7:45, "the pots, the shovels, and the basins" for Solomon's Temple were cast.*

With patiently excavated minutiae—and chance bonanzas like the Dead Sea Scrolls (above)—scholars toil to awaken sleeping centuries.

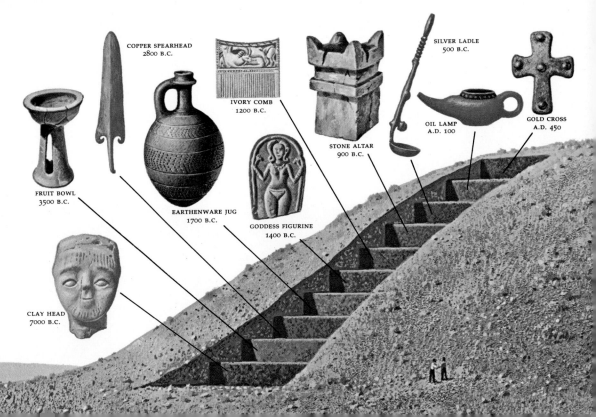

COPPER SPEARHEAD
2800 B.C.

IVORY COMB
1200 B.C.

SILVER LADLE
500 B.C.

OIL LAMP
A.D. 100

GOLD CROSS
A.D. 450

STONE ALTAR
900 B.C.

FRUIT BOWL
3500 B.C.

EARTHENWARE JUG
1700 B.C.

GODDESS FIGURINE
1400 B.C.

CLAY HEAD
7000 B.C.

FOCUS OF A FORGOTTEN FAITH, *Nippur emerges from the dust of Mesopotamia in this 1899 photograph. Chain of diggers carrying overburden to the dump heap conjures Sumerians who thronged here to worship at their chief temple 5,500 years ago. University of Pennsylvania expedition uncovered thousands of texts—among them tales of creation and a great flood.*

but found it incomplete. He journeyed to the ruins of Nineveh and there uncovered more tablets which fleshed out the story—the Epic of Gilgamesh, with its account of a great flood, strikingly similar to the tale of Noah.

In 1889, John Peters, Professor of Hebrew at the University of Pennsylvania, began to dig at Nippur, south of Baghdad. Here were found some 30,000 tablets relating to ancient Sumer. My colleague, Samuel Noah Kramer, is still translating them. And in the 1920's that prodigious worker, Sir Leonard Woolley, discovered the treasure-rich death pits at Ur. Here buried objects from homes and temples helped fill in the picture of everyday life 5,000 years ago.

NOT ALL GREAT FINDS were made by archeologists. On a hot day in 1880, a schoolboy playing near Jerusalem's Old City wandered into a tunnel, slipped, and splashed into a pool of water. Getting up, he noticed letters on the wall. They proved to be an inscription telling how Hezekiah, Biblical king of Judah, cut the tunnel to ensure a water supply during an Assyrian siege: "The quarrymen hewed the rock, each man toward his fellow, axe against axe," and so hacked the conduit through. Water still flows in it, and you can travel its course, armed with flashlight and garbed in hip boots. The Bible, too, tells how Hezekiah "made a pool, and a conduit, and brought water into the city" (II Kings 20:20).

Archeology's best-known amateur is Muhammad Adh-Dhib, the shepherd boy who tossed a stone into a cave and so discovered the first cache of famed Dead Sea Scrolls. Because of the impulse of a bored youth, scholars have gained profound new insight into the background of the New Testament and evidence that shattered theories about the Old Testament—texts from which it is translated have been backdated by at least a thousand years.

Perhaps the most famous of all texts came from Egypt. Soldiers under Napoleon found in the Nile Delta in 1799 a black basalt slab inscribed in three scripts. Scientists with the expedition puzzled over it. Jean-François Champollion, schoolmaster from Grenoble, deciphered the writing 23 years later. So this square yard of stone, named Rosetta for the village where it was found, opened wide the door to our knowledge of Egyptian hieroglyphics. Once understood,

BIBLE LANDS' VARIED FACES: *Greenery robes the Nile Delta (right), Moses' land of Goshen. Wind-etched sands of Jordan's Wadi Ramm (opposite) saw Solomon's caravans. Terraces stripe Samaria's hills. A Galilean seines the waters where Jesus drew "fishers of men."*

the carved symbols would trumpet the glories of pharaohs, including those who held the children of Israel in bondage.

Champollion inspired robust interest in Egyptology. Scholars flocked to the Nile to dig, collect, and ship relics to their museums. They found that tomb after tomb had been robbed. But in 1922, Howard Carter and his patron, Lord Carnarvon, broke the untouched seals of Tutankhamun, who died about 1350 B.C. Inconspicuous during his short life, "King Tut" became the world's most famous

Egyptian because of the treasures that surrounded him in death in his rock-hewn tomb in the Valley of the Kings.

In some ways the greatest treasure an archeologist can find is pottery. Written texts can stretch the truth. Broken pots cannot. The man who taught us to read them was Flinders Petrie, a rare genius who spent most of his long life in the field. He came out to Egypt from England in

SOIL OF SYRIA *yet tumbles from tree-limb plows the ancients knew. The Fertile Crescent, arching through Palestine and Mesopotamia, lured hunters and foragers to farming. Settling down, they developed wheel, plow, towns, writing—and faiths alive today.*

21

1880 to prove a remarkable theory, then current, that the dimensions of the Great Pyramid of Giza were somehow linked with Biblical history. Alas, Petrie's careful survey proved the pyramid's base 71 inches less than had been thought. Thus, in Thomas Huxley's words, "the slaying of a beautiful hypothesis by an ugly fact."

Petrie began work in Palestine in 1890. From then we date modern Biblical archeology. Instead of scooping treasures from the top of a tell, or mound, he sliced down through its layers. At Tell el Hesi, east of Gaza, a smallish mound rises some 100 feet above the plain. On its east side, winter rains had gashed it, exposing layers of ash—sure sign of occupation. Petrie sampled the strata, collected bits of pottery from them, and reported that the tell gave "at one stroke a series of all the varieties of pottery over a thousand years."

SCORES OF SIMILAR EXCAVATIONS have since shown us how ancient tells grew. The first settlers built houses near a spring and surrounded them with a wall. After the city eventually fell to plague, famine, or attack, new settlers moved in to take advantage of the water—always a priceless commodity in Bible lands. They found that the pile of debris left by their predecessors offered the security of height, so they built atop it.

Through centuries-long cycles of building and abandonment the tell grew, stratum by stratum. Drifting sand augmented its height in times when it was empty. Ash and refuse added bulk to it when it was occupied. The stubs of encircling city walls grew with it, serving to contain the mound.

Pottery, what Petrie called the "essential alphabet of archeology," dated the layers of a tell. Wood, cloth, and skin decayed; metal was costly and hence scarce; stone could not easily be fashioned into distinct shapes. Pottery did not decay, was common, and could take any form. It also broke easily in daily use. New pots often had new shapes since housewives liked to keep up with the times. From the broken pieces, thrown out on the dump heap long ago, we read the changes in form and decoration, and also the method of firing the clay. When an earth layer covers one kind of shards, we know that new settlers buried the rubble of the old. Shards in the style of a distant town indicate that trade flourished.

SCHOLARS WITH NAPOLEON'S ARMY *in Egypt probed ruins*
older than the Bible, collected antiquities, copied texts
none could yet read, and regaled the general with mummies.
"Soldiers," he exhorted his troops before a battle,
"from these pyramids forty centuries look down upon you."

BEFORE WORLD WAR I, archeologists trenched some of the best-known Bible cities: Gezer, Taanach, Megiddo, Jericho, Samaria. Between the wars Megiddo—the Armageddon of the Bible—proved to have no fewer than 20 layers, each a city with its own plan. At Beth-shan, south of the Sea of Galilee, excavators counted 18 separate strata. It was here that the body of Saul, Israel's first king, was displayed by the Philistines: "and they fastened his body to the wall of Beth-shan" (I Samuel 31:10). Treasures from this dig now lie on display in Jerusalem and Philadelphia.

In this period of exciting discovery I first went to Palestine on the team of William F. Albright, already a leading figure in Biblical archeology. What an experience for graduate students in their twenties! Night after night we would gather around Albright while he talked about our dig at Bethel—about the town's life in the Bronze Age, and its destruction by the Israelites.

Albright's unmatched enthusiasm kept our minds off dysentery. Also scorpions. "Never put your boots on in the morning without shaking them out," he warned. "Scorpions like the cool, damp place where your toes go."

G. Ernest Wright, a fellow contributor to this book, then drove the expedition station wagon. He, too, was in his

COCOONS OF SAND *saved many of Egypt's treasures, to dazzle modern eyes with ancient luster. Arab-garbed explorer Belzoni in 1817 dug into Abu Simbel, "one of the most magnificent of temples, enriched with . . . colossal figures" of Ramesses II, pharaoh of Moses' day.*

first season in the field. Once he had to rush one of the laborers to a hospital in Jerusalem—the man had been bitten by a huge viper.

Brushing pottery is always a chore, especially when you have some 20 baskets to go through. Albright made an offer: Whoever found an ostracon—an inscribed fragment—would have it named for him. Imagine the thrill for a young student

EANNATUM, KING OF LAGASH IN SUMER, DEFEATS THE NEIGHBORING CITY-STATE OF UMMA; PAINTING BY H. M. HERGET

on seeing his discovery published in a scholarly journal—an ostracon catalogued under his own name!

Albright was a legend in his time. At Tell Beit Mirsim, probably the Debir which Joshua "smote...and utterly destroyed" (Joshua 10:39), hundreds of shards were picked

WARFARE *45 centuries ago comes to light in texts and art from Mesopotamia. Tacticians formed phalanxes of overlapping shields; wild asses drew chariots in the birthplace of the wheel.*

up atop the mound before digging started. Glancing at them, Albright calculated that the tell had been inhabited from 2000 to 600 B.C. After four years of excavating he concluded that his estimate had been wrong. The proper dating should have been from 2200 to 586 B.C.!

Other archeologists helped fill in the map of Bible lands during these years: Nelson Glueck, crisscrossing deserts to search out lost cities, living with the Bedouin, writing of his explorations with rare verve; Claude Schaeffer, uncovering early Canaanite writings at Ras Shamra on the Syrian coast—the Ugarit where stood a palace-fortress complex and temples to pagan gods.

Since World War II, the profession has flowered. Yigael Yadin, career soldier, finally Israel's Chief of the General Staff, resigned in 1952 to devote full time to

PAUL VI, FIRST **POPE** TO MAKE A PILGRIMAGE TO THE HOLY LAND, ENTERS JERUSALEM'S DAMASCUS GATE IN JANUARY, 1964; BUNTE ILLUSTRIERTE. BELOW: THOMAS NEBBIA

FOUNT OF FAITHS, *Jerusalem preserves,
in remembrance and in stone, shrines holy
to Christians, Jews, and Moslems.
Jesus wept over it—"O Jerusalem, Jerusalem!"—
and ages wept at His Cross. Joy of Easter
lights a pilgrim's face (right); thousands
throng the streets on holy days. Men of war
fought over the City of Peace: Nebuchadnezzar,
Pompey, Saladin, 11th-century Crusaders,
soldiers in the Arab-Israeli war of 1967.*

*Hub of creation on early maps, it hailed
Pope Paul VI on a visit that echoed a Psalm:
"Pray for the peace of Jerusalem" (122:6).*

archeology. North of the Sea of Galilee he led a major dig at Hazor, destroyed by Joshua 33 centuries ago. Yadin, pipe-smoking, unhurried, enormously productive, organized his staff like an army unit. In the 1960's he dug at Masada on a bluff near the Dead Sea — last Jewish fortress to fall to the Romans, A.D. 73.

In Jordan, another fellow contributor, Père Roland de Vaux, patriarchal in beard and white robe, led expeditions at Tell el Farah, uncovering Biblical Tirzah, and at Khirbat Qumran, famed as the Essene community where the Dead Sea Scrolls were written. Every inch a Frenchman, this scholarly priest loved a good dinner (which he seldom got in the field) and drove with frightening abandon.

Jet travel now allows me to start an excavation in Palestine three days after walking out of my office in Philadelphia. But choosing a site remains a heavy responsibility. Once you stake a claim and begin work, ethics—and antiquity laws—allow a kind of permanent tenancy at the dig. The bond between an excavator and his tell is almost a marriage contract, not to be entered into lightly or unadvisedly.

Archeologists may choose a site to learn more about a people, such as the Philistines, or a historical event, such as the conquest of Canaan. Perhaps we are searching for a Biblical site, like Gibeon. An old clue led us there. In 1838 an American scholar, Edward Robinson, who had trekked from Cairo across Sinai to Damascus, theorized that names cling to places though languages change. He talked to Arabs, listened to conversations in bazaars and desert tents, and identified more than a hundred Biblical names. The Arabic name el-Jib seemed to Robinson an echo of Gibeon. Others contested this view, but we chose el-Jib as our site. Our findings proved Robinson right.

Moments of glamor come few and far between. Archeology is 99 percent drudgery—washing shards, filling out classification cards in triplicate, writing notes, drawing plans. Yet as I bend over the mats that hold the day's haul of broken pots I often wonder about their original owners. Some shards are smoke-blackened. What small domestic tragedy caused this? Did the family cooking pot, filled with hot pottage of lentils, break just as the family was ready for supper? Was a child stirring it when it fell? What did the father say when, like Esau, he returned home "from the field, and he was faint" (Genesis 25:29)? Archeology constantly reminds us that amid the debris of the past, love, hate, blame, disappointment, joy, kindness, cruelty—the whole range of human emotions—once flourished.

I N THE SUMMER of 1963, armed with a map by Nelson Glueck, I scouted the Jordan Valley looking for a tell that would picture life there in Bible times. I chose—for better or for worse—Tell es Saidiyeh, a mound big enough to have held a town of 5,000 to 10,000. Surface shards indicated at least 3,000 years of history.

The next step was to recruit a competent team, people with the stamina and sense of humor to cope with bugs, heat, and bad food. No prima donnas allowed. Picture, then, a Jesuit priest from San Francisco, a Canadian residing in Rome, a British architect, a Swedish teacher, professors from Ohio and Chicago, students from Paris, Munich, Pennsylvania, and Yale. One girl agreed to sail from New York to Beirut with considerably more personal baggage than a young lady usually carries: 12 brand-new wheelbarrows.

With staff and equipment ready, where do we take the first bite into the tell? We can only excavate about a quarter of an acre in a season, so which fraction of the mound should we choose?

ARTS OF MAN *adorn sites linked with the works of God. Christ, flanked by Elijah (left) and Moses, towers over kneeling disciples in the Transfiguration mosaic at St. Catherine's Monastery in Sinai. For 14 centuries pilgrims have trekked here, seeking the mount where Moses received the Ten Commandments.*

FRED ANDEREGG, MOUNT SINAI EXPEDITIONS

33

Plowman of Nablus in Samaria

Iraqi woman paces timeless Euphrates

Egyptian by the Nile Moses knew

Israeli villager near Acre, where Paul tarried
Left: Turkish women toil in Biblical Galatia

"So the Lord scattered them abroad...upon the face of al

Flinders Petrie had an answer: the northwest corner. Since Palestine's prevailing wind is from the northwest, rich residents would place their mansions upwind of a city's dust and stench. Twice I have begun on top of a tell, above the spring, since people must settle close to water. Surveying at Jericho one year, we climbed a mound overlooking a field of tomatoes and saw the plan of a building etched in yellow growth amid the plants. Shallow soil above the walls gave it away. We paid the owner for the tomatoes, and got a palace of Herod in exchange.

The first day of a dig is hectic: up at 5:30 for breakfast (my preference is green olives, goat cheese, Arab bread, and tea), then the drive to the tell. The surveyor stakes out five-meter grids for excavation. About two hundred local villagers line up, and I select a hundred who look strong and intelligent. Alas, later I must weed out my mistakes—the lazy, the mischievous, the dishonest. At el-Jib we

Street singer in Yemen, land of Sheba *Long-locked lads of Jerusalem hark to edict from Leviticus*

Matmaker in Iraq, cradle of civilizations
Right: Jordanian shepherd pipes as of old

Turkish madonna dwells where Hittites ruled

he earth" *Genesis 11:8*

HELEN AND FRANK SCHREIDER (SECOND, SIXTH, EIGHTH),
THOMAS J. ABERCROMBIE (FOURTH), B. ANTHONY STEWART
(FIFTH, SEVENTH), JOSEPH J. SCHERSCHEL (NINTH),
ALL NATIONAL GEOGRAPHIC STAFF; TOR EIGELAND, BLACK STAR
(FIRST); MARGARET DURRANCE (THIRD); THOMAS NEBBIA (TENTH)

offered bakhshish for inscribed jar handles. One workman produced a beauty—
except for a reversed letter. He had inscribed it himself with a screwdriver!

The laborers are split into groups of 12 to 15, issued equipment, and turned over
to the plot supervisors. By the 9:30 break, the crew has shaken down. Work is
under way with picks, hoes, baskets, and wheelbarrows.

The first encounter with the past may come quickly, as at Tell es Saidiyeh. A
pickman strikes a mud brick. The supervisor of his plot moves in with a trowel and
finds it is part of a wall, and that other walls join it to form a room. There must be a
door. Below, there is certainly a floor. We are eager to find it and preserve intact
what was crushed when the roof fell. The layer of debris on the floor will date the
destruction and tell whether it came suddenly, as by fire, or gradually, as by
abandonment and decay of roof beams. So now work slows and interest mounts.

35

We collect charcoal in a plastic bag to be flown home for carbon-14 tests. We uncover a crushed cooking pot beside a fireplace, also a jar that held oil, wine, or water. Olive pits, grain, a bowl, a knife, loom weights, and a spindle whorl emerge from the dust. Only six feet into the tell, we are sharing the daily life of 2,800 years ago.

At a lower level we were introduced to ancient high society. A breathless worker blurted the news: "Bronze vessels in the tomb!"

Moments later I was staring at the richest burial yet found in Palestine. I could see the rim of a caldron, the handles of a basin, part of a tripod, all the work of an artisan skilled in bronze. Several days of delicate brushing and loosening of objects revealed the scene as it had been 3,200 years ago, when an important Canaanite woman was luxuriously equipped for the afterlife. More than 500 gold and carnelian beads adorned her neck. A chain held decorated silver breastplates. Electrum pins fastened her garment. Cosmetic containers lay within easy reach: ivory bottles for unguent, makeup boxes, an ivory spoon in the form of a serving woman, a perfume juglet. Drinking set, lamp, incense bowl, all bronze, lined the brick-walled tomb.

Here lay a regal woman—proud, perhaps a little vain, surely religious, obviously wealthy. She had lived a mile east of the Jordan about the time Joshua crossed it. I wondered what she thought of the Hebrews, toughened by 40 years of desert wandering, who were to give to the world the Old Testament.

That find at Tell es Saidiyeh bolstered the theory that here stood Biblical Zarethan. These exquisite bronzes recalled Solomon commissioning Hiram to cast the bronze work for his temple in Jerusalem: "In the plain of the Jordan the king cast them, in the clay ground between Succoth and Zarethan" (I Kings 7:46). Once again an old story took on added dimensions.

This, then, is our job: To fill in the map of Bible lands; to link Bible times with world history. And finally to cast clear light on daily life, back through the ages, through the mists of the past, to the time of Abraham—and before.

GRANDEUR OF ANCIENT PERSIA *speaks across the centuries*
at Persepolis, where columns soar and griffins glower
over plazas that rumbled to chariots 25 centuries ago.
Sun-baked stones echo glories of Darius, the city's builder,
and Alexander the Great, its conqueror.

HELEN AND FRANK SCHREIDER, NATIONAL GEOGRAPHIC STAFF

By Samuel Noah Kramer

The World of Abraham

H IS CRY PIERCES the centuries: "My god . . . for me the day is
black. . . . Tears, lament, anguish, and depression are lodged
within me, Suffering overwhelms me. . . ." Four thousand years ago,
in a land called Sumer, a despairing man wrote these words
on a clay tablet—the earliest poem we have yet found on man's suffering
and submission to the will of his god. The poet's name we know not.
But his thoughts echo in the tormented eloquence of Job and in the agonized
silence of Abraham, poised to slay his son.

The domain of Sumer once encompassed what is now that part of Iraq from
the Persian Gulf to just above Baghdad. The hands and minds of its people
shaped the world of Abraham, whose journey from their great city of Ur
opens the Bible's epic story of a quest for God. History and, in a sense,
the Bible itself begin at Sumer, for here man learned to write, transforming
fragile speech into imperishable word.

For nearly 40 years I have spent countless hours hunched over bits of inscribed clay,
puzzling out the fascinating legacy of Sumer. From the strange symbols emerged
the story of an inventive and resolute people who developed remarkable
systems of government, law, commerce, and farming. The tablets also told tales
of man's creation, of a great flood inundating all humankind except one good man.

Yet this rich culture had vanished from history; until a century ago even the word
Sumer was unknown. Then scholars deciphered tablets bearing writing they called
cuneiform (from the Latin *cuneus*, wedge, for the shape of the characters).
In 1869 the French scholar Jules Oppert deduced the true location of Sumer
and opened the door to the lost world of the inventors of cuneiform.

"ABRAHAM, ABRAHAM.... *Lay not thine hand upon the lad*" (Genesis 22:11, 12).
*God's mercy stays the sacrifice of Isaac—a climactic moment in the spiritual journey
that began when Abraham's people heeded a divine call to leave the land of Sumer.*

"SACRIFICE OF ISAAC" BY ANDREA DEL SARTO, C. 1525; CLEVELAND MUSEUM OF ART

The Sumerians' clay writing tablets baked in civilization's dawning sun as it rose over *meso potamia*, "the land between the rivers." There, on the flood plain of the lower Tigris and Euphrates, the Sumerians began to arrive about 3500 B.C. They seem to have come from the east or northeast, and had close contact with Aratta, an ancient city-state possibly near the Caspian Sea. Like the American pioneers who also trekked westward, they found a land already inhabited. The earlier settlers, known as the Ubaid people, had learned to irrigate their dusty fields by channeling into them the silt-laden overflow of the rivers. We can deduce that the newcomers came upon a fairly advanced society, for the Sumerian language reflects a borrowing from the local tongue of such words as farmer, herdsman, fisherman, plow, metalsmith, carpenter, weaver, potter, mason, and perhaps even merchant.

In their many creation myths, however, the Sumerians portrayed themselves as the founders of civilization, men formed from clay to serve the gods who had made them. Aided by these deities, especially Enlil, "King of heaven and earth,"

they transformed a flat, dry, windswept land into a green and fertile realm.
Enlil called forth plant and animal from the earth. Without him, sang the bards,

> *No cities would be built, no settlements founded,*
> *No stalls would be built, no sheepfold erected,*
> *No king enthroned, no high priest born. . . .*
> *In field and meadow, the rich grain would not flower,*
> *The trees planted in the mountain forest would not yield their fruit.*

The Sumerians never forgot the purpose for which they were created. They
built great temples to their gods, and priests and priestesses burned incense,
offered daily sacrifices of animal and vegetable food, and brought libations
of water, wine, and beer.

By the third millennium B.C. the first known king of Sumer ruled the land.
Borne by trade and tablet, its culture spread over the entire Fertile Crescent
and as far east as India.

ABRAHAM'S WORLD LIVES ON *in southern Iraq.*
Marsh dweller tows a mashuf, *crescent-shaped canoe like those*
that plied the streams of ancient Mesopotamia. From giant reeds
men still fashion vaulted houses in a style set 6,000 years ago.
Along waterways such as this canal in the lower
Tigris-Euphrates region Sumerian civilization took root.

GAVIN MAXWELL

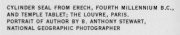

CYLINDER SEAL FROM ERECH, FOURTH MILLENNIUM B.C., AND TEMPLE TABLET; THE LOUVRE, PARIS. PORTRAIT OF AUTHOR BY B. ANTHONY STEWART, NATIONAL GEOGRAPHIC PHOTOGRAPHER

IN THE CLAY OF SUMER, *Dr. Kramer reads a 4,000-year-old hymn to "Ur, nourisher of all the lands . . . purest spot on heaven and earth. . . ."*

Sumerians invented writing. First they used cylinder seals, like the green jasper one at top, that impressed a stylized "signature" when rolled on wet clay. This label would identify the owner of property; on a temple gift, it would tell the gods who the donor was.

Then, some 5,000 years ago, scribes scratched pictographs representing men, cattle, houses, birds, plants, tools. A hand and cypress tree are easily recognizable on the temple tablet above. But already the symbols mean more: A hand and forearm may connote "side" or "with," ideas associated with this part of the body.

In time, pictographs were turned sideways, perhaps for ease in writing, then reduced to strokes of the wedge-pointed stylus (left). Now the symbol represented not only a word but a sound—and this syllable could be combined with others to form other words. Thus arose a versatile system of writing, employing some 600 cuneiform symbols.

$$36000 \times 2 + 3600 \times 4 + 600 \times 3 + 10 \times 5 + 6 + \tfrac{2}{3} = 88256\tfrac{2}{3}$$

Signs above show how Sumerians wrote numbers. They also solved equations, calculated square and cube roots and the areas of circles and rectangles. Their sexagesimal system lives on in our 360-degree circle and 60-minute hour.

Object shown				Sound and Meaning
Man's head and body				*lu*, man
Mouth marked on head				*ka*, mouth Also: nose, to speak, teeth, voice, word
Bowl of food				*ninda*, food, bread Also: thing, to place
Mouth plus food				*ku*, to eat Also: hunger
	3000 B.C. Early pictograph	2800 B.C. Pictograph turned	1900 B.C. Cuneiform symbol	

The Bible calls Sumer the land of Shinar. Its people, Genesis 11 tells us, "said one to another ... let us make brick. ... let us build us a city and a tower, whose top may reach unto heaven. ..."

Reading not Genesis but clay tablets, I see the Sumerians inventing the brick mold for shaping and baking the ubiquitous river clay. Humble villages grow into walled cities. A lofty, terraced ziggurat reaches toward heaven, an edifice fit for a god. Products of their keen minds—the wagon wheel, the sailboat—enliven their flourishing land. Canals dug by methodical plan stretch forth from the rivers, greening the plain. As their society becomes more complex, regional governments emerge. Bureaucrats bustle about, their open palms following citizens even to the grave. The petty official "who brought the dead to the cemetery," a chronicler of about 2350 B.C. tells us, has to be paid off with seven pitchers of beer and 420 loaves of bread. And the tax collectors lurk everywhere.

THE TABLETS RECORD the age-old conflict between herder and farmer. The rivalry is as old as Cain, "a tiller of the ground," and Abel, "a keeper of the sheep"— and as modern as the range wars between farmers and ranchers of the American West. Dumuzi the shepherd and Enkimdu the farmer both courted the goddess Inanna, patroness of love and procreation. Mocking Enkimdu as a mere "man of ditch, dike, and furrow," Dumuzi boasts of his wealth and wins the goddess.

Dumuzi usurped the throne of Sumer and married Inanna in a vain quest for immortality. Demons finally axed him to death, but he lived on in tale and song. His name endured as Tammuz in the Bible; the prophet Ezekiel (8:15) recoils at the "abominations" of seeing the women of Jerusalem still lamenting Tammuz's death.

The courtship of Inanna continued among Dumuzi's successors, for Sumerians believed the goddess brought fertility of womb and field to the realm of the king who married her. The ceremony usually took place in the king's palace, where attendants set up a couch for the goddess and purified it with pots of rushes and cedar. Great feasting and merrymaking followed, and the joyous crowds could look forward to thriving herds and granaries filled to overflowing.

Beneath the trappings of the sacred marriage ritual lay human passions. I discovered this one day in a back room of the Istanbul Museum of the Ancient Orient after weeks of poring over crammed symbols on crumbling clay. Such toil does not often induce exhilaration. But tablet No. 2461 did. Unearthed at Nippur, Sumer's religious center and site of a temple to Inanna, the tablet celebrates the marriage ritual of King Shu-Sin about 2000 B.C. Casually I began reading it. Then I read it again and again, enthralled by one of the oldest love songs written down by the hand of man:

Bridegroom, dear to my heart, Goodly is your beauty, honeysweet.
Lion, dear to my heart, Goodly is your beauty, honeysweet.
You have captivated me, let me stand tremblingly before you,
Bridegroom, I would be taken by you to the bedchamber. ...
Bridegroom, let me caress you, My precious caress is more savory than honey. ...

43

Sumerian schoolboys learned such poems in the "tablet house." We have found hundreds of their practice tablets, ranging from the sorry scratches of beginners to the elegant copybooks of young men about to "graduate." One delightfully human tablet tells of a boy's bad day:

"When I awoke early in the morning, I faced my mother and said to her, 'Give me my lunch, I want to go to school.' My mother gave me two rolls and I set out. . . . In school the monitor in charge said to me, 'Why are you late?' Afraid and with pounding heart, I entered before my teacher and made a respectful curtsy."

It did no good. A marked boy all day, he took canings for talking, for standing, for poor stylusmanship. We are quite sure of the rendering of *caning*, since the sign consists of *stick* and *flesh*.

We can imagine this lad of Ur—let's call him Abutab—a little older but obviously not wiser, as he tries to sneak home late one night. His father, waiting up for him, demands, "Where did you go?" And, in a classic teen-age response, he answers, "I did not go anywhere."

"Come now," his father chides, "be a man. Don't stand about in the public square, or wander about the boulevard. . . . Go to school. . . . I, night and day am I tortured because of you. Night and day you waste in pleasures. . . ."

Next morning, Abutab rises just after sunrise from the narrow wooden bed the servants set up nightly. He descends

ANXIOUS PUPIL, *lunch bag between his feet, shows the "school father" his practice stylus writing in this classroom of 2000 B.C. To erase, he balls the tablet, then flattens it. Student at left cribs from a benchmate. Teacher's assistant, dubbed "big brother," monitors in rear of the edubba, or tablet house. No girlish giggles disrupted Sumer schools, which trained well-to-do boys all year.*

PAINTING BY TOM LOVELL

from his small second-story room to the lavatory and washes in a copper basin. He dons his best chiton, or long skirt, and drapes over his left shoulder a large fringed shawl that leaves his right arm free. After a hasty breakfast of bread, dates, and milk, he rushes from the house.

Not far away, amid one-story mud-brick houses, stands a handsome 12-room home of plastered, whitewashed brick. Here we can picture a young girl we will call Innashagga, admiring herself in a polished bronze mirror held by a maid. Her black hair, braided and wound about her head, frames her face. Rouge reddens her lips; with a paint stick she has daubed black makeup on her eyelids. A tufted shawl enwraps her from her graceful neck to her sandaled feet, but leaves a shoulder fetchingly bared.

46

DEATH PITS AT BIBLICAL "UR OF THE CHALDEES" *startled the world with their 4,500-year-old cache of splendidly adorned courtiers, apparently buried alive to join fallen royalty in the nether world. In one chamber less than 27 feet square (left, foreground), Leonard Woolley unearthed 74 skeletons—women with "head-dresses of carnelian and lapis lazuli, silver and gold . . . chariots drawn by oxen or by asses, the drivers in the cars." One woman, perhaps late for her own funeral, left her silver hair ribbon, still coiled, in a pocket. While musicians played, Woolley surmised, the doomed drank cups of a potion and "composed themselves for death." Others came, slew the beasts, and filled the pit.*

Woolley (below, freeing a goddess from the earth) discovered the tombs in 1922; for four years he left them untouched, digging other sections while he trained helpers and won their loyalty. At one level he found a barren swath of flood-laid silt between strata studded with artifacts. Scholars later questioned his theory, but Woolley saw signs here of the Biblical Deluge.

After she leaves to meet Abutab on a "promenade street," her mother enters the room, sniffs disapprovingly at her daughter's exotic perfume, and smiles. Perhaps, she thinks, Innashagga and Abutab will marry. But it will take more than love's hot desire to get the marriage contract drawn up and "signed" with cylinder seals. Will the union benefit both families? Will the bridal gift from the boy's father suffice? In the end the fathers must decide.

She hoped Abutab would not take seriously old sayings like "Who has not supported a wife or child, has not borne a leash"; or "For his pleasure—marriage; on his thinking it over—divorce." Divorce comes easily here, but the wisdom of Sumer also acknowledges the bonds of family: "The wife is a man's future; the son is a man's refuge; the daughter is a man's salvation. . . ."

"Nothing like these things had ever before come from the soil of Mesopotamia"

From Ur's sepulchers of splendor, where golden ornaments lay "thick on the crushed and broken skulls," Leonard Woolley retrieved priceless treasures and restored their ancient glitter.

A bull with beard of lapis lazuli juts once more from the sound box of a lyre. On it cavort a Sumerian hero and mythical beasts made of conch shell.

Peering through a gilded tree (opposite), a shell-fleeced goat recalls the "ram caught in a thicket" that Abraham slew in place of Isaac. Sumerian artisans, hammering a wig-helmet from a sheet of gold, knotted the "hair" into a chignon at back. Alloying imported gold and silver into electrum, they cast an onager, or wild ass, on a silver rein ring.

The bier of one woman held rings for every finger, a golden garter for the knee. Woolley identified her as Queen Shubad from a cylinder seal that showed her raising a fluted cup like one (far right) that gleamed in her dust. Hands of an attendant lay on a moldering harp. Nine other women kept vigil, attired for eternity in lunate earrings, cascades of beads, and headpieces of golden leaves and rosettes (center).

In one tomb Woolley found an array of figures, their wood backing long vanished. Remounted, "The Standard of Ur" parades a tableau of war on one side, of victory on the other, at the British Museum (below).

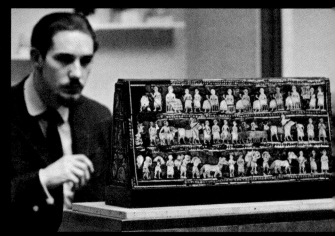

STANDARD, HEADDRESS, GOAT, AND REIN RING FROM BRITISH MUSEUM, LONDON.
BULL AND CUP FROM UNIVERSITY MUSEUM, PHILADELPHIA. HELMET FROM IRAQ MUSEUM, BAGHDAD

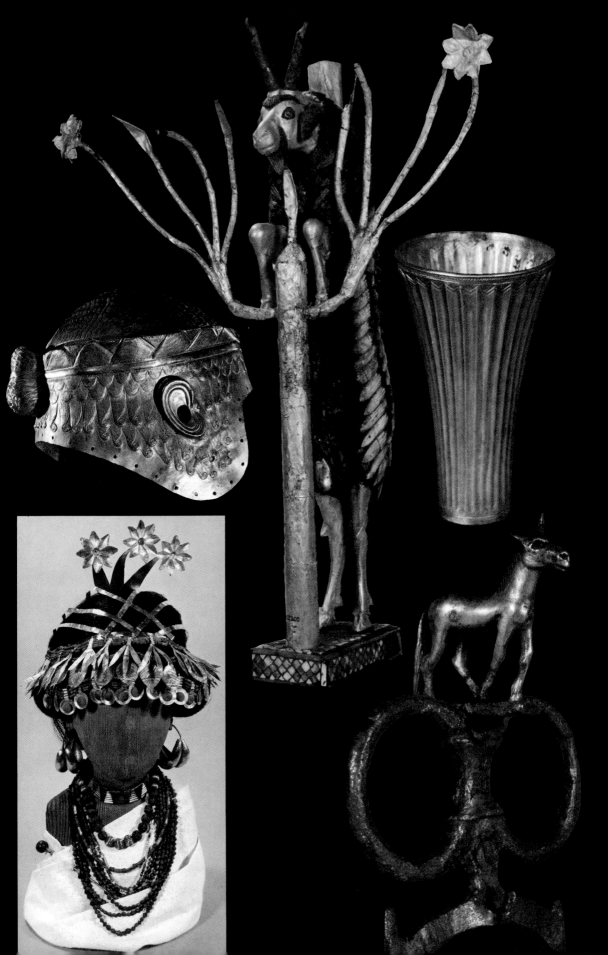

MORE THAN 90 percent of the excavated tablets of Sumer resemble our own
commercial documents: receipts, contracts of sale and exchange, deeds,
and wills. The rest bequeath to us Sumer's treasure of poetry, mythology,
and proverbs. Pieced together, these fragments can evoke Sumerians
who speak to us from the dull and lifeless clay. . . .

Ubar-Sin squats and picks up a handful of muddy soil, squeezes it, and
lets the damp earth sift through his fingers. The oxen have done their work well.
They have trampled and leveled the field, and precious water,
released from dikes, has given moisture to the earth. In his other hand
he holds a whip. The workers and slaves need to see it, and sometimes they need
to feel it. Slavery is a complicated affair here. A man can sell his entire family
to pay off his debts. The average price for an adult is 20 shekels — less than
the cost of an ass. Yet slaves have rights; they can engage in business,
borrow money, and buy their freedom.

Squinting up at the morning sun, Ubar-Sin recalls a hymn to Inanna:

> *May the watered garden produce honey and wine,*
> *In the trenches may the lettuce and the cress grow high,*
> *. . . May the holy queen . . . pile high the grain. . . .*

He walks now to a grove of trees he has planted to shield his garden from
the withering sun and the dry winds that carry the dust of the mountains.
Lentils and onions grow here, chick-peas and turnips, mustard and leeks.
Beyond, shallow pools glint in the fields, awaiting the oxen's oozing trample.
Ubar-Sin's thoughts drift from gods and watery fields to Ziusudra and the Flood.

MARCHING IN MOSAIC *on the Standard of Ur,*
Sumerians celebrate a victory. Porters haul
booty and grooms lead captured onagers (left).
For the feast, servants bring a bullock, fish, and
goats (below). The king, bigger, more ornately
skirted than his guests, toasts the triumph
(lower) while a musician plucks a bull-headed lyre.

Adhesive bitumen held the engraved shell figures,
as well as decorative chips of lapis lazuli.
The Standard's purpose puzzles scholars;
its pieces lay near a man's shoulder,
as though he had held it on a pole.

The ancient tale dwells deep in the minds of all who live near the river plains.

The gods decreed the destruction of the seed of mankind and all that grew
upon the earth. But some of the deities demurred and decided to warn one pious
man, Ziusudra. He built a great boat; then "all the windstorms, exceedingly
powerful, attacked as one." For seven days and seven nights the flood swept over
the land, but Ziusudra safely rode it out. Then "Utu [the sun-god] came forth"
and "brought his rays into the giant boat." Ziusudra sacrificed an ox and a sheep
to the gods, who awarded him immortality. And the seed of man once more
flourished on the earth.

Of all mortals, only Ziusudra was saved from dread Kur, the dark and dreary
nether world to which the spirits of men descended at death. Instead he achieved
the Sumerian paradise of Dilmun, a divine garden where neither sickness nor

51

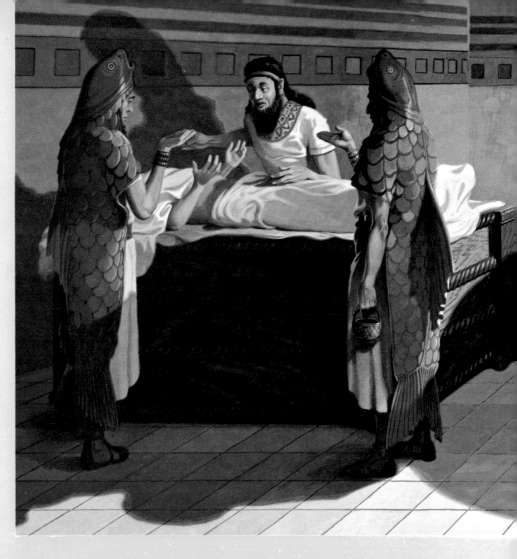

death entered. But when the water god Enki devoured eight sacred plants in Dilmun, the angered mother goddess Ninhursag cursed him with death. Stricken in eight parts of his body, Enki would have died had not a clever fox persuaded Ninhursag to relent. She restored Enki by creating a healing deity for each ailing part. One was Nin-ti, "the Lady of the rib."

GILGAMESH, Sumer's greatest hero, reigned about 2700 B.C. from the throne of the city-state of Erech. When the ruler of Kish, a city-state to the north of Erech, demanded that Gilgamesh submit to its power, he summoned into session the first "congress" recorded in history. From epic poems written much later we learn that Gilgamesh consulted two "houses" of this congress—first "the convened assembly of the elders of his city," then "the convened assembly of the fighting men of his city." He took the warriors' advice: "Do not submit to the house of Kish; let us smite it with weapons."

Gilgamesh, son of a "wild man" (probably a barbaric nomad), really existed, but his biographers were bards whose songs transformed him into legend. So appealing did their hero become that others began to sing of him in

MESOPOTAMIAN MEDICINE MEN, *clad in fish garb in homage to a water god, invoke magic against demons who enfeebled a youth. Seeking a prognosis, another priest in this 16th century* B.C. *sickroom ponders an inscribed clay sheep's liver (also above). Texts on the model, along with minute study of a fresh sheep's liver, enable him to divine the patient's chances. Widely consulted in Bible times, diviners drew the wrath of the Hebrews' God.*

Sumerians could practice the healing arts without magic. Their tablets record numerous medicines, though none indicates the ailment it would remedy. One prescription of about 2000 B.C. *reads: "Pulverize . . . the dried vine, pine tree, and plum tree; pour beer over it, rub with oil, fasten as a poultice."*

a tongue we today call Semitic. These strangers had marched into Sumer from the west, led by Sargon the Great (page 12). He founded a resplendent capital called Agade, from which derived their name, Akkadians. Semitic-speaking Akkadians came to be called Babylonians by the Hebrews and Greeks of a much later day. Borrowing and modifying Sumerian tales of Gilgamesh, Babylonians molded them into what we know as the "Epic of Gilgamesh."

Ceaseless warfare among Sumer's city-states weakened the land and opened it to Sargon's conquest. With arrow and sword and battle-ax he carved an empire that probably ranged from Ethiopia to India. His dynasty ended in less than a century. About 2200 B.C. the Gutians—"the snake and scorpion of the mountain"—swept down from Iran and "covered the earth like the locust." But the Sumerian civilization survived. Gudea, an *ensi*, or governor, of Lagash, kept alive the old traditions. He also commissioned so many statues that to us his somber face has become the best known of all Sumerians.

After barely a century of Gutian rule, King Ur-Nammu rose to power at Ur
and founded Sumer's last great dynasty. He built the towering ziggurat
of Ur, renovated canals, and "made straight the highways." And he drew up the
oldest law code yet known to man. I was privileged to copy and translate a tablet
inscribed with part of the code, promulgated about 4,000 years ago.
In a prologue Ur-Nammu boasts of removing grafters from office, of regulating
weights and measures, of protecting widows and orphans. His laws deal
with divorce, runaway slaves, slave girls who presume to be the equals of their
mistresses, and damage to person and property. Hammurabi, in his famed code,
borrowed from Ur-Nammu, as did the Israelites when they drafted their laws.

SURROUNDED by aggressive enemies, torn by internal strife, Sumer fell.
Semitic nomads—the Amorites of the Bible—pressed in from the western deser
The Elamites struck from the east, sacking Ur. The raiders carried off Sumer's
last king, Ibbi-Sin. In a pathetic appeal for help, he wrote an epitaph to his land:
"Lo, in the assembly of the gods, Sumer has been prostrated."

For the next two and a half centuries the Semitic rulers of vanquished
Sumerian city-states fought each other. Finally, about 1750 B.C., from the northern
city of Babylon, the great Hammurabi emerged. His law and his sword reigned
over a united kingdom stretching from the Persian Gulf to the Khabur River
north of Mari. With Hammurabi, Sumer's history ends and Babylonia's begins.

By the time of Abraham, the streets of Ur rang with the guttural speech
of the city's conquerors. But Ur's temples and schools still resounded to the sober,
placid tones of the ancient Sumerian language. For the victorious Babylonians
had succumbed to Sumerian culture, which would prevail long after
Babylonia's glory faded. Sumerian thought still paces our daily lives—from
the 60-second minute to the solar year. Whether citing a proverb or a code of law,
we draw on forms that took shape on tablets of clay in Sumer—
"great mountain, country of the universe, filled with enduring light."

Yet, Genesis informs us, Abraham saw a greater light beyond Sumer. Though he
wandered far from Ur, the legacy of his native land went with him and lingered
with his people. Sumerians conceived of covenants with many gods; he covenantec
with the one God. Sumerians nurtured the written word; the people of Abraham
would ever cherish literacy.

When the Patriarch's forebears journeyed from the east to the plain of Shinar,
they cried, "Let us make us a name!" In our Bible the name of Sumer has vanished
into a linguistic thicket only scholars can hope to penetrate. But we know
that when the Biblical scribes recorded the psalms, proverbs, and lamentations
of the Hebrews' heritage, they enriched and ennobled ideas and themes first
set down in Sumer—a land that truly made a name for itself.

"DAY OF DARKNESS" *dims sere hills east of the River Jordan. But sunshine warms camels
setting out to graze in the Promised Land. On his trek from Ur, Abraham probably
followed a caravan route, "the King's Highway," which parallels the Jordan Valley (center).*

DEAN CONGER, NATIONAL GEOGRAPHIC PHOTOGRAPHER

In the Footsteps of Abraham

JOURNEY
UNTO CANAAN

From the plains of the
Euphrates to the hills of Judah,
National Geographic's Kenneth MacLeish
follows the "Friend of God"

THE NIGHT TRAIN from Baghdad pulls into Ur Junction at about three o'clock in the morning, if the roadbed is in good shape. No one gets off. At that hour there is no sound of human life at the lonely station in the Iraq delta. The train rumbles away toward the Persian Gulf. When its clamor fades in the desert stillness, other sounds replace it. A nesting stork clatters its beak, a bat shrills, a wolf howls, and a sheep dog answers. The voices of the Mesopotamian night have not changed since Ur began, more than 5,000 years ago.

Ur Junction is the last living expression of Ur—capital of Sumer, earth's first great civilization—whose ruins lie a mile and a half to the west. In the cold light that follows night, the topless hulk of its ziggurat tower, called "Hill of Heaven" by its builders, looms on the dead-level horizon.

At just such an hour we approached Ur, bouncing along baked ruts in an elderly dust-drenched sedan. We had come 6,000 miles over the curve of the world to this spot. For tradition holds it to be the birthplace of a man named Abram, son of a herdsman from the upper Euphrates and destined to be known in later life and forever after as Abraham, the Friend of God.

Here at Ur began the epic journey of this wayfarer who lived as long before Christ's coming as we live after it. Abram walked with his clan up the sun-ridden valley of Mesopotamia to what is now Turkey. Later, in obedience to a divine command, he led his people to the Judaean highlands. He grazed his flocks in the Negev. Once, in a time of drought, he went down into the lush lands of Egypt.

The ziggurat of Ur; Dean Conger, National Geographic photographer   57

National Geographic photographer Dean Conger and I would follow the course of this inspired pilgrimage, pursuing a legend that is history, a folktale that is truth, a folk hero who never aspired to wealth or power. This modest person became one of the most venerated human beings who ever lived. For in his wanderings Abraham the Patriarch became dedicated to a great and simple idea: the idea of a single, almighty God.

Half the world now cherishes that concept: Judaism, then Christianity, then Islam espoused it, the last two deriving from the first, and the first nurtured by the old man's dream.

STAIRWAY FOR THE GODS
climbs the ziggurat of Ur.
Trees shade a sacred garden below
the summit shrine, whose blue
enamel suggests the azured realm
of Sumerian deities. A merchant,
his wife, and daughter prayerfully
watch a New Year's procession
restore the moon god Nanna-Sin
to his temple. Cymbals clash,
ram's horns blare, pipes shrill,
tambourines jangle, lyres twang,
and drums thunder "louder than

PAINTING BY JOHN McDERMOTT

the storm." The god's gilded statue bears symbols of authority: a ring and an architect's tools. Hebrew prophet Ezekiel (40:3) saw similar instruments in his vision of a man who "was like bronze, with a line of flax and a measuring reed in his hand."

The "ladder" in Jacob's dream may have referred, in early accounts, to a ziggurat stairway. On it he beheld angels "ascending and descending" (Genesis 28:12).

For the God of Abraham became the God of his Hebrew descendants, worshiped in spoken prayers and doctrines handed down through the generations. Centuries later, scribes put these sacred oral traditions into writing.

Thus we read in Genesis 11: "Now these are the generations of Terah: Terah begat Abram, Nahor, and Haran; and Haran begat Lot. And Haran died before his father Terah in the land of his nativity, in Ur. . . ."

I stared at the ziggurat, thinking that no journey could have a more imposing point of departure. Beside the ziggurat stood a little barracks, home of the two government

59

guards who kept treasure seekers out of the vast ruin field. Here our driver Hamid stopped and let go a skull-splitting blast of his big horn.

In a moment the guards came out, small brown men with heavy rifles, dressed in the corded headcloths and robes of desert Arabs. Mr. Hatin, our escort from Iraq's Department of Antiquities, explained our presence. The guards offered us all Ur in a generous gesture of welcome.

"The steps themselves are not old," Mr. Hatin said as we climbed the main stairway. "The ziggurat was built more than 4,000 years ago. But the steps were retreaded by Nabonidus of Babylon, who ruled in the sixth century B.C."

At the top of the steps lay the rubble of what had once been a second level, on which had stood

60

With mud and tar men raised a "Hill of Heaven"

In a land lacking timber and stone, men mold clay and mud into bricks as their forebears did in Abraham's time. Sumerians, yearning for a holy mountain, built one at Ur with millions of bricks, each about a foot long. Sun-dried for the inner mound, burned for the thick façade, the bricks were bonded with "slime" from bitumen pits. Those at Hit (left) supplied Babylon's builders. Rifle-toting guards (below) now protect Ur's ziggurat ("mountain top"), which once soared some 70 feet from a base spreading 30,000 square feet.

a third. Here had rested the temple of Ur's special deity, Nanna-Sin, the moon god. Weather, brick thieves, and amateur archeologists had laid waste the upper levels.

From this ruined eminence the land that was Sumer stretched away like the sea to a horizon as flat as an ocean's. Laid down by the twin rivers, Tigris and Euphrates, its soil gave the country's first farmers their first crops. But here, where cultivation first fostered civilization, no fields remain. The old plantations have vanished into the desert as the city they supported has vanished into the earth. A few foundations show. Low mounds, smooth with age, hide fallen walls. This is all the eye sees of the dead capital.

No WRITTEN RECORD, of the many found at Ur, tells, as Genesis does, of "Abram, son of Terah." But Terah and his clan were not people of Ur. Probably Semitic herdsmen from far up the valley of the two rivers, they were sojourners who spoke a strange tongue and lived outside the city wall. This was to be the pattern of the life of Abram, to use his original name. Not until the day he died did he lie in land of his own.

What kind of city was this Ur in which Abram grew to manhood and married? In our time a generation of archeologists has dug the answer from the ancient earth. Inscribed clay tablets by the tens of thousands have revealed the history of their day. We know more now about the age of Abram—he lived in the early 18th century B.C., as nearly as scholars can fix his date—than anyone has ever known before, including the Hebrew priests who first wrote down the sacred spoken stories of the Patriarchs.

Ur was old when Abram was young, a bustling, prosperous commercial center somewhat past its prime. Priest-ruled and merchant-ridden, it offered luxury to the privileged and subsistence to its slaves and peasants. Artisans plied their crafts with skills unequaled in all the world save Egypt. Astrologists applied the mathematics invented here by their ancestors. In temple rooms scribes practiced another art which Sumer had created: writing.

Narrow streets ran crookedly between windowless buildings of baked and unbaked brick. In each, the street entrance led to a court into which opened six or seven rooms. They were pleasant houses, well suited to the life in the sun-seared delta country—so well suited, in fact, that their like can still be found in the towns of Iraq.

The Euphrates lay along the western side of the wall that circled the city. Ships up from the sea unloaded goods of India and the East on crowded quays where merchants traded surplus grain for gold, copper, and ivory. Canals carried smaller vessels to other centers and water to fields which felt rain only during the winter months.

"How it has changed," said Mr. Hatin, beside me on the broken ziggurat. "No people, no fields, no trees. Even the river has gone away."

In truth, where the great Euphrates had held the shipping of the Eastern world, there was only a grassless plain, salt-poisoned and sterile. The river had made itself a new channel, three miles to the east. Beyond, on the dust-dimmed horizon, the sun rose dull as a counterfeit coin. Our friends the guards led us into their barracks, put before us oiled, sugar-sprinkled flat bread and powerful coffee, then watched us consume what was to have been their breakfast.

Before the sun rose high enough to scorch the shadeless plain, we, like Abram, headed for Haran, almost 600 miles away in the southern edge of Turkey. Genesis tells us nothing of the route. But men bound from Ur to Haran would set off before

THE MIGHTY TIGRIS *(below) and the Euphrates bring life to the land of two rivers. Men long ago learned to channel the priceless waters, extending the rivers' domain to distant fields and orchards. The rivers, says Genesis 2, branched from one that "went out of Eden to water the garden." Where they pour into the Persian Gulf, marshes sustain the Madan, whose bloodline mingles Arab, Sumerian, Babylonian, and Persian. Water buffaloes' need for new grazing land uproots this Madan herdboy's family each year.*

DEAN CONGER, NATIONAL GEOGRAPHIC PHOTOGRAPHER
INSET: GAVIN MAXWELL

"And Terah took Abram his son... and they went forth... from Ur"

Genesis 11:31

the coming of the nine dry months that would strip every blade of grass from the land, and would probably follow the Euphrates. We too took the river route.

The modern Euphrates road, rough and partially unpaved, serves as the main highway through southern Iraq. From Baghdad to the Persian Gulf, railroad, powerline, irrigation ditches, and auto tracks run side by side.

The towns along the road reflect the past; the villages perpetuate it. Here in the delta, now as in antiquity, mud and date palms are the only building materials. The date groves that make Iraq the world's first-ranking date producer supply leaves for matting, frond stems for framework. Clay pits provide adobe.

These materials dictate the form of a house such as Abram might have known: thick-walled, almost windowless, opening into an enclosed court and roofed with mats laid over arches of frond stems. Water pots stand in ring frames beside each doorway, and domed ovens smoke in the yards. Add donkeys, dogs, frisking lambs, cavorting children, and straight-backed women balancing burdens on their heads, and you have a scene that met the eyes of Abram.

We stopped at one such village and stood at a respectful distance waiting to be invited in. One does not approach a village of the fellahin (peasants) or the black tents of the Bedouin without proper welcome and escort. The people would resent it; the dogs would prevent it. Soon the village sheik came up to us. After an exchange of greetings, he led us to the village guesthouse. On the way a teacher in Western dress turned to me and asked: "Why do you take pictures here? This is only a village of poor people living in the old way. Do not show old ways."

"But the old ways interest people in our country. Besides, the old ways are the ways of the man we follow," I told him. And when he asked what man we followed, I said: *"Ibrahim Khalil*—'Abraham the Friend.' The Friend of God.'"

In the guesthouse court our host offered us a big bowl of fermented sheep's milk and watched with pleasure as we drank deeply from it. Arab hospitality is both formal and genuine, and is not to be refused.

Between villages, few people appeared in the land. A file of women bearing brush bundles five times their size. Half a dozen cultivators directing irrigation water into fields of

TREKKING WESTWARD, *Terah leads his clan up the Euphrates Valley, destined for Haran. A strapping young Abram takes his place beside his father and other elders. Abram's dark-haired bride Sarai admires the infant of a friend riding beside her. The slap of a stick guides the bridleless mount.*

On donkeyback, they might travel 20 miles a day. But many walk. On a similar trek, in Genesis 33, Jacob leads on "softly" so that "the children be able to endure."

A slave girl tags behind Sarai. Other servants bear a water jar, provisions, and the few belongings needed by the nomadic herders. Lot, Abram's nephew, tends a mixed flock of goats and sheep.

65

green wheat. A solitary horseman, rifle in hand. A herdsman leading camels to pasture. A tribe of gypsies in tattered splendor, mocking us with reckless grins. A dusty wolf trotted over the wasteland, and an eagle circled, watching.

When Terah and Abram passed through central Mesopotamia, Babylon ruled the land. It was one of the greatest walled cities ever built and the seat of Hammurabi, scion of a dynasty of Semitic nomads, called Amorites in the Bible, who had swept into power. Following the west bank of the Euphrates, Terah would not have entered the city, which lies across the water. But he would have marveled at the eight-storied ziggurat, greater than Ur's. Warfare and weather razed the ziggurat. The ruins that remain today are those of the Babylon built by Nebuchadnezzar more than a thousand years later. The city's name recalls the famous story in Genesis 11 of divine judgment upon presumptuous men who tried to build a tower that would reach unto heaven: "Therefore is the name of it called Babel; because the Lord did there confound the language of all the earth: and from thence did the Lord scatter them abroad upon the face of all the earth."

SINCE "ALL ROADS MEET AT BAGHDAD," according to ancient tradition, ours turned briefly away from the Euphrates at Babylon and headed for Baghdad, which straddles the Tigris where it and the Euphrates come closest together. With more than a million people, it is Iraq's major city and contains most of the nation's industry. But Baghdad, a scant 1,200 years old, does not relate to Abram's day or route, and so we resumed the Euphrates road.

The level lands along the river look much as they did in the time of Terah's travels—green with wheat and barley in the early spring, or red-brown from recent

DEAN CONGER, NATIONAL GEOGRAPHIC PHOTOGRAPHER

BENT UNDER BRUSH, *women trudge along a road between Ur and Baghdad. Gleaned from a stark land, their burden kindles fires, feeds camels, reinforces adobe, casts a cooling shadow.*

Shy daughter of Ishmael unloads skins of water (above), relieving Bedouin men of the indignity of manual labor. Thus do these desert roamers— sired, tradition says, by Abram's firstborn— divide responsibilities. Seeking a wife for Isaac, a servant waited by a "well of water at the time of the evening . . . that women go out to draw water." And, says Genesis 24, the fair maid Rebekah came out "with her pitcher upon her shoulder."

plowing. They are called Al Sawad, meaning "the dark lands," contrasting them with the pallid desert on whose edge they lie like elongated oases.

At Hit, 400 miles upstream from the sea but less than a hundred feet above sea level, the delta of the Euphrates ends. Here the bluffs close in. Here, too, an oddity must have caught the eyes (and nose) of Abram as it did ours: a natural tar pit, stirred by a bubbling flow of noxious gas, from which bitumen was gathered. A well-thrown match will set the gases afire.

Hit's antique water wheels, arranged in pairs, are set in a stone dike which projects into the stream from a glade as green as Surrey in spring. These ingenious machines, turned by the river's force, lift the river's water in pottery jars lashed to their rims. As the ten tall wheels turn, they empty jar after jar into an aqueduct, from which high point water flows ceaselessly, and at no cost, to the gardens of Hit.

Above Hit the river narrows and hurries, cocoa-colored, between high banks. Forced up out of the constricted valley at times, the road cuts across a broad, steppelike upland. In this rock-studded country, too high to irrigate and too dry for rain-fed crops, are clusters of the black tents of the Bedouin. We drove cross-country to a small encampment. The sheik came forward, beating back his dogs, and escorted us to his dwelling. Here men stood at ease and watched small, powerful women carrying water.

The women eyed us bashfully. They would not address us, nor would we appear to notice them. When their work was done, they would disappear, leaving the men to entertain the strangers. And this the men would do as naturally as they would mount a raid or repel attackers. The Arab world is a man's world, and nowhere so much so as among the Arabs of the desert. Of all earth's present people, none are so close in customs to the Patriarch as are these nomad herdsmen.

A man who would follow Abram's route today needs formal authorizations to cross half a dozen frontiers. As we approached Syria it occurred to me that the situation was not greatly different in the Patriarch's day, when kings and chiefs jealously guarded their borders. At the checkpoint of Abu Kamal we had to interrupt our journey for several frustrating days to assure Syrian security men we were not spies but simply followers in the footsteps of Abram.

A FEW MILES northwest of Abu Kamal I found archeologist André Parrot excavating, as he has for 30 years, the site of Mari, the greatest city of northern Mesopotamia in the time of the Patriarchs. Here, in a magnificent 300-room palace, Professor Parrot found scrupulously kept stewards' records that evoked scenes of regal banquets: beef, mutton, and fish; local beer, imported wines, pastries oozing with date syrup or honey, bread made from barley flour.

Low mounds and mud-brick foundations evoke no picture of the Mari that young Abram and his father saw. When

Route of the Patriarch threads "a dry and thirsty land"

The song of the Psalmist (63:1) still echoes along the river valleys that form the Fertile Crescent. Wielding strings like puppeteers, farmers near Basra in southern Iraq draw water from a well and toss it into an irrigation ditch.

Civilization burgeoned here when Sumerians toiled together to web their land with canals— and thus bound themselves into a society. To them, water flowed from the gods' goodness, and deities bore "pickax and basket," symbols of the irrigating art. When a god tamed "the high water" grain gilded the fields, "vineyard and orchard bore their fruit," and "everything on earth rejoiced."

Traveler bargains for supplies in the bazaars of Damascus

Egyptian women lament plagues sent by God

Herder tends flock near beehive huts of Haran

Farmer of ancient Mesopotamia lifts water into an irrigation ditch

Abraham laid to rest in the cave of Machpelah at Hebron

Nomad crosses the vast desert toward Egypt

Mediterranean Sea

TURKEY

Haran

Halab (Aleppo)

Al Hammam

CYPRUS

Hamath (Hamah)

Homs

SYRIA

Mari

Abu Kamal

Orontes

Euphrates

MESOP

LEBANON

Beirut

Lebanon Mts. Anti-Lebanon

Damascus

Hit

Sea of Galilee

Dara

CANAAN

Shechem

Nablus

(Baytin) Bethel

Ai

Amman

ISRAEL

Uru Salem (Jerusalem)

Dead Sea

Gerar

Hebron (Al Khalil)

Beersheba

Jordan

SAUDI ARABIA

Negev

JORDAN

Nile

Tanis

GOSHEN

Gerar

Cairo

EGYPT

Suez

U.A.R.

SINAI

Abraham's World
of 3,700 years ago

Biblical and ancient names in brown
Modern names in black
Brown line shows Abraham's probable route
∴ Ruins
Drawings based on ancient bas-reliefs and wall paintings

0 — 100
STATUTE MILES

IRAN

• Baghdad

AKKAD
∴ Babylon

Priestess of Ur offers a libation before
ziggurat of Nanna-Sin, the moon god

∴ Nippur

Susa •

Lagash ∴

S U M E R

∴ Erech

Ur ∴ • Ur Junction

ham begins his wanderings

Basra •

Tigris

E L A M

Euphrates

DRAWN BY LISA BIGANZOLI AND ELIE SABBAN
COMPILED BY LEO BOBERSCHMIDT
GEOGRAPHIC ART DIVISION

Kuwait • Persian
Gulf

guards on Mari's walls looked down on Te-rah's caravan, the city was ruled by sophisti-cated Babylonian Semites. Many generations out of the desert, they spoke the refined Ak-kadian tongue. But many western Semites, seminomads, lived in the city and its lands. These recent arrivals were of Abram's kind and spoke his language.

The Mari dig has yielded more than 20,000 clay tablets inscribed with cuneiform writing. Some of them describe the doings of the troublesome westerners and fix the date of their stay (and Abram's) in northern Meso-potamia, a region which then included Haran. Among the wandering groups, the tablets tell us, were the Habiru—the original Hebrews, some scholars believe, and thus not only Ab-ram's kind but his kin.

I watched Professor Parrot directing a crew of chanting Arabs as they hauled dirt from the excavations. A workman hurried to him with a tablet he had just unearthed. Parrot looked at it eagerly, but did not touch it.

A HERDSMAN *of Lagash cradles a stray kid in his arms. In Dilmun, the paradise of the Sumerians, "the wolf snatched not the lamb" and "unknown was the kid-killing dog."*

Ancient scenes come alive in Bible lands today. Sheep graze in green pastures, led by the shepherd over safe trails—"the paths of righteousness" in the 23d Psalm. He watches for serpents lurking in the rocks as his flock threads a shaded wadi—"the valley of the shadow of death."

TERRA-COTTA FROM LAGASH, LATE THIRD MILLENNIUM, B.C.; THE LOUVRE, PARIS. PHOTOGRAPHS AT RIGHT BY DEAN CONGER, NATIONAL GEOGRAPHIC PHOTOGRAPHER

A CRAFTSMAN *of Erech, sighting down his adz, shapes wood with skill divinely endowed. For it is written that Inanna, queen of heaven, herself brought to this Sumerian city "the arts of wood-working, metalworking, writing, toolmaking, leatherworking."*

The metalsmith of Biblical days might feel at home in Baghdad's copper market today: "The noise of the hammer and the anvil is ever in his ears, and his eyes look still upon . . . the thing that he maketh. . . ."

TERRA-COTTA FROM ERECH, EARLY SECOND MILLENNIUM, B.C.; THE LOUVRE

A PEASANT *of Babylonia whips on his zebu, or humped ox. Old Testament law stressed the value of the beasts that carried man and cleft the soil of a hard land. The ox and the ass must share the reward of Sabbath rest. An ass fallen under its load must be helped, even one of "him that hateth thee. . . ." And the Decalogue commanded that "thou shalt not covet thy neighbour's wife . . . nor his ox, nor his ass" (Exodus 20:17). Both still toil, the surefooted ass bearing goods and travelers along timeworn paths.*

TERRA-COTTA FROM DIYALA REGION, EARLY SECOND MILLENNIUM, B.C.; ORIENTAL INSTITUTE, UNIVERSITY OF CHICAGO

"This is the first of the season," he said. "It is only raw clay, you see, and must be dried for several days. Then we can brush it clean and read what it has to say."

H ARAN IN TURKEY is a living town as well as a dead city. Of the two, the former relates more closely to the age of Abram than the latter. The town's beehive huts are not very different from dwellings of 4,000 years ago, while its ruins are those of an Islamic citadel no more than 1,000 years old.

The hill of Haran is man-made, a layer cake of human habitation. Its lower levels have never been exposed, but scientists believe that a temple to the moon god Nanna-Sin, contemporaneous with Ur's ziggurat, lies under the wasted walls of the old Moslem fort. Merchants, as well as worshipers, came to the city, for it lay at the crossroads of two great trade routes. One linked the settlements of Syria and Palestine with the Anatolian Plateau; the other bore caravans toward India.

The administrator of Haran led Dean and me around the ruins of the fortified palace. From its walls we looked out over the rolling plain the Patriarchs called Paddan-aram, meaning "Field of Aram," and the small streams that gave it its other name, "Aram of the Two Rivers."

Here Abram stayed until his father died, living perhaps as he had at Ur, outside the walls. Haran was not a Semitic town, but one founded by Hurrians, a little-known people from the northern hills — the Horites of the Bible. As a cosmopolitan center,

FINE MARTS AND MINARETS *grace Baghdad, capital of Iraq and a city of wares and prayers. Bowls of yogurt, made from water buffalo's milk, ride to market on the heads of migrant Madan. The women wear black shrouds, or abas, but leave faces bare, disdaining Islam's veil.*

A stork, bird of good omen to Moslems, walks the rail of the Maradiya Mosque, where the muezzin's call summons the faithful to prayer five times a day.

73

"And they came unto Haran, and dwelt there" Genesis 11:31

Abram spoke of this region and its folk as "my country...my kindred." Here he prospered, perhaps as a caravaneer; the name of this Turkish village near the Syrian border— "caravan city"—recalls Haran's role as a junction of trade routes.

Boy and his sheep (right) look down from a ruined Islamic citadel whose stones helped build beehive houses Abram would recognize. Genesis 31 recounts Jacob's years tending flocks near Haran. His words limn the shepherd's age-old lot: "in the day the drought consumed me, and the frost by night." Piebald markings on lambs and kids intrigued men of Biblical times; they saw omens in the odd coloring.

KENNETH MACLEISH AND (LEFT) DEAN CONGER, BOTH NATIONAL GEOGRAPHIC STAFF

Haran was a place where people of different races lived together in peace. The Mari tablets tell us that the Benjaminite tribe, possible relatives of Abram, "signed a treaty with the King of Haran" in the moon god's temple there. Hurrian ways became part of Abram's cultural heritage.

Sinuhe, an Egyptian official who lived long in exile, left us a record of what the Haran region was like around the time of Terah. "It was a good land," Sinuhe noted. "Figs were in it, and grapes. It had more wine than water. Plentiful was its honey, abundant its olives. Every fruit was on its trees. Barley was there, and emmer [a hard, red wheat]. There was no limit to any cattle...."

For a few days we explored and photographed Haran, followed by larger and larger crowds of noisy youngsters whose horseplay grew rougher and rougher. We sought peace in the guesthouse, where grown men sat each morning in quiet conclave. Here we sat too, backs to a windowless wall, on strips of carpeting.

Coffee was served from long-spouted pots heated over charcoal. In a precise ritual we were each given a minuscule cup into which a splash of bitter black fluid was poured. Should we refuse to drink, the cup would be emptied on the ground. Coffee is costly, but pride is priceless; and a man

75

cannot accept that which another man has rejected. To accept three servings was proper, showing appreciation but falling short of greed. After the coffee ceremony, there being no common words between us, Dean and I smiled politely and the others sat back for a long, interested stare.

UPON THE DEATH of Terah, family leadership fell to Abram. When the call came to move on to an unknown land, he unhesitatingly forsook stability and security. With his acceptance of God's order, the foundation was laid for the covenant between God and man on which great

NEW MEN OF AN OLD RACE, *villagers of Al Hammam, Syria, forsake the footloose ways of their Bedouin forebears. They have folded their tents, settled in homes, and become fellahin, tillers of the soil. But strangers in their midst still enjoy the desert-bred tradition of welcome at the guesthouse (above). Sumerians knew the nomad as a man "who has no house in his lifetime."*

religions of the future would be based. Abram mustered his clan, and they went forth from Haran "to go into the land of Canaan; and into the land of Canaan they came" (Genesis 12:5). The Bible tells us nothing of their itinerary, but we can make some valid assumptions.

As a trader and stockman, Abram would know the routes available and their conditions in various seasons. He would likely leave in spring, when the high pastures ahead would still be green from winter rains. He would cross the Syrian border, turn up the Euphrates Valley, then head cross-country toward Aleppo. From there, he would follow the southward swing of the Anti-Lebanon mountains in order to water his flocks in streams that flowed from them.

We re-entered Syria and with a new escort, Mr. Saqr, took up our trail. Mr. Saqr was well qualified to aid us in our pursuit of Abram. Even his given name suited his assignment: Ibrahim.

The lands along the Euphrates, like most of Syria's arable lands, were owned until recently by wealthy landlords who

HELEN AND FRANK SCHREIDER AND (LEFT) DEAN CONGER, ALL NATIONAL GEOGRAPHIC STAFF

SWIFT HANDS AT AN OLD TASK, *Syrian women flatten dough at Apamea. A wafer-thin disk of bread clings inside the oven. Sumerians and ancient Hebrews similarly plastered dough—made of wheat flour or barley meal—on the sides of their ovens. Lot "did bake unleavened bread" for his angelic visitors in Sodom, and Bedouin eat it thus today. Keeping a timeless custom, Arabs break, rather than cut, bread.*

WIND AND WATER *faithfully serve the people of this ageless region. Silhouetted on a Lebanese plain, a woman winnows grain in a way unchanged since Biblical times. "The wind," says the first Psalm, "driveth away" the chaff; the grain cascades into a sack. Beyond grazes a sheep, fat-tailed like its ancestors, whose slaughter gratified gods and honored guests.*

From the parched plain rise the snow-crowned Anti-Lebanon mountains, where the Orontes River flows. At Hamah in Syria (opposite), nine giant water wheels lift the waters of the Orontes to fields and gardens. Already old when Abram trekked south from Haran, Hamah marked the northern border of the land later promised to the people of Israel in the Old Testament.

treated the fellahin like serfs. Today that picture is fading. Great holdings have been broken up. Agrarian reform has begun. The average fellah may not yet have land, but he has hope.

Tractors were readying the fields for small grain and cotton. Farmers sat at ease on the fresh-tilled earth, eating their lunch of boiled wheat, bread, and onions washed down with fermented milk from greenish goatskins.

Power-driven pumps throbbed in every adobe village, raising water from the river to the fields. We stopped at one such village at sundown and were welcomed by the sheik of a clan of big brown-haired, blue-eyed men. No labor-loathing Bedouin, this man was a cultivator and proud of it.

ALEPPO EXISTED in Abram's day. Like Haran, it straddled a caravan route and doubtless catered to the caravan trade. But the buildings of that time cannot be seen in modern Aleppo. The huge citadel, riding a rock in the city's center, commemorates the relatively recent drama of the Crusades. Ironically, the conflicting philosophies that sparked the bloody battles between Christian and Moslem both grew from the revelation that the herdsman of Haran was to receive in the high places of Canaan.

Although Genesis makes no mention of Aleppo, an Arab legend says Abram passed through the town and found its inhabitants ill and underfed. He milked his white cow and gave the milk to the poor, restoring them miraculously to health. From this act comes the city's Arabic name, Halab Shahba. It means "to milk the white cow."

From Aleppo the modern road, like the ancient caravan track, turns south. On the right are the Anti-Lebanons and other mountains, some snow-capped even in summer, that separate the Syrian plateau from the Mediterranean coastal plain. Where the mountains end, in northern Israel, the Great Rift Valley deepens and runs southward to form the Sea of Galilee, the Jordan Valley, and the Dead Sea. The Bible calls this caravan route the King's Highway.

How far down the King's Highway Abram traveled before crossing the Jordan to go up into Canaan, we do not know. The best guess is that he turned westward between the Sea of Galilee and the Dead Sea. But he must first have come close to Damascus, a sizable city at that time. And on his way to Damascus, he may have camped on the cool Orontes River where Hamah now stands.

Near Aleppo the peasant villages are of the ancient beehive form, functional, handsome, and wonderfully distinctive. Where wood is scarce, what better way to get a roof

over one's head than to make a dome of bricks? The rows of smooth-contoured plastic shapes seem like natural outgrowths of the Syrian earth. The young lieutenant who administered one village led us to a well-kept beehive. "You might think that such a place would be ugly inside, but it is lovely. You will see."

The house consisted of two white-painted rooms. Rugs covered the floors; cushions and bolsters served as furniture. Small windows let in light, and holes at the top let out smoke.

"These are warm in winter because of the thick earth walls and cool in summer because of the high dome. They keep out the dust that comes on the wind and they are easy to repair. Also," the lieutenant added, "they cost nothing."

I was saddened to hear Mr. Saqr boast of government plans to replace these beehives with "nice little square cement houses."

Evening brought us to Hamah, where the wonderful water wheels that make the place a fresh-smelling oasis snored and splashed through the night. In the morning we drove on to Damascus.

Every traveler on the ancient north-south

MERCHANT OF MARI *pleads with Sarai, but the haughty beauty leaves the haggling to her slave girl. Fruit stall offers melons and grapes; at left a carpenter shapes a board and an instrument maker plays a lyre. Abram's way along the Euphrates passed this royal city.*

High-born Elamite woman (below) spins while a servant fans her in a relief unearthed at Susa in southern Iran.

"She seeketh wool, and flax, and worketh willingly with her hands. . . . She perceiveth that her merchandise is good. . . . She layeth her hands to the spindle. . . . She looketh well to the ways of her household. . . ." So lives the good wife of Proverbs 31.

PAINTING BY TOM LOVELL. BELOW: THE LOUVRE, PARIS

caravan route knew Damascus for its arts and crafts—and its beautiful women. Its snow-fed, seven-branched Barada River gave it greener fields than any to be found for hundreds of miles around. Its groves were legendary along the dusty trail. Its very name—Esh Sham—connoted loveliness: It means "beauty spot."

Abram, trail-weary and no doubt curious, might well have gone into the rich bazaars of Damascus to trade or tarry. We learn from Genesis 15 that in his later years Abram had a servant, a sort of honored lieutenant and majordomo, who appeared also to have been an adopted son, for he was to inherit all Abram's wealth should Abram die childless. This man was called Eliezer of Damascus. "And Abram said, Lord God, what wilt thou give me, seeing I go childless, and the steward of my house is this Eliezer of Damascus . . . mine heir." Perhaps Abram acquired Eliezer on this, his only visit to the town.

D AMASCUS, the oldest continuously inhabited city in the world, wondrously links present and past. As elsewhere, even at ancient Mari, the walls that stood when Abram passed this way are buried under later levels. But for all its modern buildings and clamorous traffic, a feeling of antiquity pervades this sprawling, slope-climbing city of half a million, whose population reflects as many succeeding cultures as do its structures. Mosques and monuments, even whole streets, present the patterns of a thousand years ago. Here and there a foundation or a tomb or some other vestige harks back to a still earlier time.

Damascus handicrafts perpetuate the traditions if not the patterns of the distant past. Glass and mosaics are worked with rare skill. Woodworking has reached a level of intricacy unrivaled elsewhere. Copper and brass are etched, inlaid, and engraved to produce pieces famed throughout the world. Native silk and threads of silver and gold are woven on foot-powered handlooms into rich brocades. Indeed, the patterned silk called damask bears the name of its place of origin.

To us, as no doubt to Abram, the empty, unbroken plain south of Damascus stretched in dreary contrast to the life and color of the city. We crossed it in two hours, passing into Jordan at Dara. Abram would have journeyed a week or more, if he followed the King's Highway well south of the Sea of Galilee before turning westward down one of the many wadis to the low-lying Jordan River.

We ourselves, bound by the road's present course, crossed at the head of the Dead Sea, 1,296 feet below sea level, and came up to the warm golden limestone and dark cedars of

At the desert edge,
a golden city
delights the weary ey

Crowning a 150-square-mile
fertile plain, Damascus cheers
dusty travelers with city comforts
architectural beauties, and
fabled bazaars. The prophet Ezeki
hailed its "multitude of all riches,"
especially wine and wool.
A modern quarter of Syria's capit
climbs sun-bathed Jebel Kasyun,
topped by a TV tower.

From this famed caravan center
camel-borne pilgrims journeyed
to Mecca, whose sacred shrine—
the Kaaba—was built by Abraham
and his son Ishmael, according
to Islamic tradition.

Damascus elder (above) counts
prayer beads of his tasbih, *or*
rosary, that recall 99 Islamic name
expressing the attributes of God.
Laffe-*wrapped tarboosh marks hir*
as a dignitary of the Moslem faith

Old Jerusalem at the edge of the hill country, 2,000 feet above. We stood now in Canaan.

Centuries before Abram reached the new-found land, Canaan boasted flourishing cities with rich pottery and imposing temples. Then the Amorites pushed into the land, causing upheavals like those that rocked Mesopotamia. Abandonment and destruction depopulated the towns. But the nomad invaders soon settled down; new walled cities rose. Tribal chieftains lived within their fortresses; tribesmen clustered in surrounding huts or tents except when danger drove them inside the citadels. Little distinguished their ways from those of the wandering herdsmen.

"And Abram passed through the land unto the place of Sichem [Shechem], unto the plain of Moreh." The fine sweeping valley of Shechem remains, accented by recently excavated ruins whose walls were standing when Abram entered the valley from the depths of the gulch called Wadi al Fariah. They are thick walls, stone-built, for the hill country is a country of stones. But probably they never sheltered Abram's clan, for here as elsewhere he pitched his tent in the open, built an altar to his one true God, and lived at peace with those who were there before him.

Abram was no hot-eyed fanatic but a tolerant man, respectful of the gods of others. In Ur and Haran he doubtless worshiped Nanna-Sin, the moon god. In Canaan, he shared with the Canaanites the practice of sacrificing living animals, and probably followed the form if not the spirit of Canaanite religion, whose chief god was El.

Yet there was a vast difference in Abram's faith. His God was personal, demanding, forgiving, jealous, and generous—omnipotent and omnipresent. The El of the Canaanites was impersonal and too lofty to be approachable. He required only a modest payoff in burnt offerings to assure his benevolence.

SYRIAN SUQS *span centuries of style and taste.*
Amid the fragrance of incense and roasting lamb
the bustling marketplaces offer radios and electric shavers,
jewelry and antiques. Shoppers in high heels contrast with
a man wearing a kaffiyeh—traditional desert headdress—
in the stall-lined arcade of Hamidieh Bazaar, Damascus.

HELEN AND FRANK SCHREIDER, NATIONAL GEOGRAPHIC STAFF

"And whatsoever Adam called every living creature, that was the name"

WHEN God let man name the animals in Genesis 2, this symbolized man's dominion over them. For to name a thing meant to know its character and destiny.

Abraham's twin grandsons received descriptive names. Esau's refers to his hairy body. Jacob denotes "seize by the heel," for he was born holding his brother's heel. It also translates as "supplanter," heralding Jacob's purchase of Esau's birthright for a mess of pottage.

Just as God changed Abram's name to Abraham, so did Jacob receive a new name—and a new destiny. He wrestled with God, who called him Israel, "may El persevere." El, the basic Semitic word for deity, stems from "power." It appears in Elijah, Nathaniel, and 111 other personal Hebrew names in the Bible.

In *Hallelu-yah* we hear the cry—"Praise Yah!"—that early Hebrews raised to their God. In time, God's name became so awesome that they dared not utter it. They wrote it as four letters—יהוה or YHWH. Reading scriptures, they substituted *Adonai,* "Lord." The original pronunciation of YHWH was lost. Medieval scholars, using vowels of *Adonai,* rendered it "Jehovah." Today many favor "Yahweh."

Joshua means "Yahweh is salvation." Deborah denotes "bee" and Caleb "dog." Even today Bedouin hope that a girl named Deborah will be busy as a bee, and a boy called Caleb will be as fierce to foes as a dog.

Nimrod remains the synonym for "mighty hunter." Hamites and Semites recall the names of Noah's sons Ham and Shem. The Hebrew word for horn resounds in Jubal, "father of all those who play the lyre and pipe." His name echoes in "jubilee."

Numbers also hold symbolic significance in the Bible. When a Hebrew swore an oath, he invoked 7. The 7th day of the week was the Sabbath, the 7th year the Sabbatical; the Israelites marched 7 days around Jericho with 7 priests blowing horns. Twelve, signifying fullness, is the number of months, tribes of Israel, and apostles. And 4, from "the four corners of the earth," multiplied by 10, the sum of the fingers, became the measure of many Biblical events: 40 days of the Deluge; Moses' 40 years, and Jesus' 40 days, in the wilderness; the 40-year reigns of David and Solomon. Our "quarantine" originally meant 40 days.

"Get thee out of thy country...
unto a land that I will shew thee" Genesis 12:1

"Northward, and southward, and eastward, and westward" — thus did the Lord bequeath
this fertile land to Abram and his seed. Then, as now, olive groves and vineyards
mantled the vales and hills of Canaan. Long-trod roads and wisps of cloud
wind among the wadis. Villages near Nablus bestride this valley in Samaria.

THOMAS NEBBIA

But Abram was a wise and wondering man, a god-hungry man who sought something more worthy of his devotion than a celestial source of guaranteed good luck. Somewhere in Canaan he found what he sought. This revelation was the concept of "covenant" — a binding commitment between God and man. No such idea evolved in the religion of Canaan.

The hill country of Canaan was not only a land of revelation, where the elemental forces of nature confronted the searching mind; it was also the only part of Canaan where a seminomad could move freely with his flocks. In the Jordan Valley to the east and the coastal plain to the west, planted fields would have blocked his way.

We do not know how long Abram camped at Shechem, but only that in time he left to pitch his tents in a spot with "Bethel on the west, and Hai [Ai] on the east."

SCARRED STONES, *scaled with ease by children, once girded mighty Shechem, "uncrowned queen of Palestine." Guarding a strategic pass between Mount Ebal and Mount Gerizim, this hub of ancient highways loomed in Hebrew traditions long before Jerusalem. Here "the Lord appeared unto Abram," who built an altar, as did Jacob. Centuries later Joshua "gathered all the tribes of Israel to Shechem," to renew the covenant with God. In the time of the Judges, Abimelech "beat down" the rebellious city and "sowed it with salt."*

Archeologists read the city's story in its artifacts. Jug below probably held funeral offerings for a child buried in an urn around 1725 B.C., when Egyptian customs flourished in Canaan. The ram's head lay in the ruins of Israelite Shechem, conquered by Assyrians in the eighth century B.C. Romans slaughtered some 10,000 people here around A.D. 67 and renamed the town Neapolis. This name lives on in nearby Nablus.

DREW-McCORMICK
ARCHAEOLOGICAL EXPEDITION
LEFT: DEAN CONGER, NATIONAL
GEOGRAPHIC PHOTOGRAPHER

The place has never been precisely located. Archeology proved Bethel to be the modern village of Baytin. The ruins of Ai are thought to lie under the houses of Et Tell, about two miles southeast of Baytin. Both are hilltop sites. Natural points of reference, they serve even today as local landmarks.

We left our car at Baytin and walked east through a fig grove. Ahead were hills, red-earthed and littered with pale rock, where sheep and goats grazed. Abram had built an altar on a high place, surely the highest place in the vicinity. From one high hill we could see many miles in all directions. Jerusalem stood within the circle of our sight. Bethel lay to the west, Ai to the east.

Stones were piled in rows to expose a little earth on the leveled hilltop. Had some of them once formed a rough altar? In the quiet of this place, with a long

view of the land about me, I felt closer to the questing wanderer than I had at any point along his trail.

"Come now to my house," said a small boy who had followed us up the hill. "Drink milk. Is only small house made of "—he pointed to a goat cropping a nearby shrub—" his hair. But good milk."

We came down the slope of the hill that could have been Abram's and approached the black tent. A blanket was spread for us. A pretty young woman in brilliant reds and blues milked the ewes, peeking shyly over their backs. A cheerful crone with tattooed chin and a headband of gold coins watched us with frank fascination.

The boy brought hot sheep's milk and stood before us, ragged and wonderfully courteous, proud to act out the tradition of hospitality which Abram also honored.

"AND ABRAM JOURNEYED, going on still toward the south. And there was a famine in the land: and Abram went down into Egypt to sojourn there." Where in Egypt? We are not told. But since he was going there to escape the drought, he would go no farther than was necessary. The eastern delta country would provide fodder and water. And it was this same region, known as Goshen, that Abram's descendants frequented a century or two after his death.

Abram came out of Egypt a rich man, a fact which Genesis attributes to his own human frailty and the loyalty of God to His friend. We read in chapter 12 that "[Abram] said unto Sarai . . . thou art a fair woman . . . Therefore . . . the Egyptians . . . shall say, This is his wife: and they will kill me, but they will save thee alive. Say, I pray thee, thou art my sister: that it may be well with me. . . ."

As a result, Pharaoh took Sarai into his harem and enriched her "brother." God, instead of punishing Abram, "plagued Pharaoh and his house with great plagues." Pharaoh then sent Abram away, wife, wealth, and all.

The meaning of this episode has puzzled many. But here again scholars of our time have new-found knowledge with which to interpret Abram's behavior. The late Professor E. A. Speiser, one of the leading authorities on the Old Testament and Middle Eastern civilization, did so by studying recently discovered tablets.

Dr. Speiser points out in his brilliant volume on Genesis in the Anchor Bible series that, in Hurrian society, men sometimes conferred special status on their wives by adopting them as sisters. Genesis 20 notes that Sarai was actually Abram's half-sister, and this alone, Dr. Speiser writes,

Graven images, frenzied rites conjure Canaan's erotic gods

Masked votaries of an unknown deity dance in a Jordan Valley shrine of about 3500 B.C. Beyond the *tannur,* a hearth oven, the mud-brick wall glows with colorful frescoes archeologists unearthed at Teleilat el Ghassul, near Jericho. Ghassulians made pottery, wielded flint knives and copper axes in the twilight of the Stone Age.

Later Canaanites worshiped sensuous Astarte, a fertility goddess, and Baal, a storm god. Celebrants re-enacted the erotic frenzies of lascivious deities, mutilated themselves, revered snakes, sacrificed children. Such rites tempted the Hebrews, whose leaders since Abraham had condemned their neighbors' idolatry.

Artisans shaped Astarte with her sacred creatures— rams, snakes, and a lion—in beaten gold (opposite) and incised royal deeds on ivory. Warriors (above) return with bound captives, while a Canaanite king celebrates his victory with wine and song.

DEAN CONGER, NATIONAL GEOGRAPHIC PHOTOGRAPHER

would make her eligible for sistership status under the customs of a Hurrian city like Haran, Abram's old home. Since this relationship was a point of prestige for Sarai, Abram would have stressed it in presenting her to so important a personage as Pharaoh.

When Abram left Egypt, he went by stages back to Bethel, where he and his nephew Lot separated, for their herds and followers were increasing. "And Abram said unto Lot, Let there be no strife . . . between me and thee. . . . Is not the whole land before thee?" Lot, given first choice, chose the rich-looking Jordan Valley and followed it down to Sodom, south of the Dead Sea.

When he had gone, God said to Abram, "Lift up now thine eyes, and look from the place where thou art. . . . For all the land which thou seest, to thee will I give it, and to thy seed for ever. . . . Then Abram removed his tent, and came and dwelt in the plain of Mamre, which is in Hebron, and built there an altar unto the Lord." Later translations of Genesis 13 change "plain" to "terebinth" or "oak."

The grove became the closest thing to a permanent home Abram had ever known. Despite God's gift, he owned no land in the eyes of other men, or any house. But he spent much time in his camp at Mamre.

From here Abram went out with 318 retainers to conquer the Kings of the East who had sacked Sodom and carried off his nephew Lot. He received the blessings of Melchizedek, the King of Uru Salem (Jerusalem), on his return. In the narrative of these events — Genesis 14 — he is called "Abram the Hebrew," a term no Hebrew writer would use,

Abram "armed his trained servants" and smote his foe

Genesis 14:14-15

suggesting that this famous chapter was not set down by Hebrew priests but by a foreign source reporting on a truly historical individual.

Though favored by God, Abram lacked what he wanted most: a son to ensure his succession. Sarai, being barren, gave him her Egyptian maid Hagar as concubine—another Hurrian custom mentioned in the tablets of the times.

Hagar became pregnant and proud. Harassed by the jealous Sarai, she fled. But an angel ordered her to return, saying: "Thou art with child, and shalt bear a son, and shalt call his name Ishmael. . . . And he will be a wild man; his

hand will be against every man, and every man's hand against him" (Genesis 16:11, 12). Thus the first Bedouin.

When Abram was 99 years old, God spoke to him and promised him a second son, to be born of his wife Sarai, who was 90. Abram smiled at this thought and the forthright Sarai laughed when she heard of it. "After I am waxed old...?" she asked. But God expanded his covenant with Abram: Through this second son, to be named Isaac, he would become a "father of many nations." And this covenant was to be symbolized by circumcision.

God changed Abram's name to Abraham, which, according

IN SWIFT VENGEANCE, *Abram storms a marauders' camp. His enemies, led by four kings, had sacked Sodom and carried away booty and prisoners, including Lot.*

Pursuing them north "unto Dan," Abram strikes by surprise, breaching the chariot barricade before some can don armor. Spears flash; ox-gut bowstrings twang. Abram, swinging a duck-bill ax, routs the invaders and brings back "all the goods... and the people."

to Professor Speiser, means "the father is exalted," and Sarai's to Sarah, which means princess.

Abraham apparently migrated often into the Negev, for it was there, near Beersheba, that Sarah again grew jealous of Hagar and said to Abraham: "Cast out this bondwoman and her son: for the son of this bondwoman shall not be heir with my son, even with Isaac" (Genesis 21:10). Sarah had her way. But "God was with the lad," and Ishmael too became a father of nations, for the Arabs are his get.

I rode past orange groves and fields of ripe wheat to Beersheba, a new industrial community on the edge of the desert in Israel. Raw-looking, hard-striving and efficient, Beersheba suggests nothing of the place Abraham knew.

A day's donkey ride to the northwest—or half an hour by car—lies a mound called Tel Abu Hureira, thought to contain the ruins of Gerar, a town well known to Abraham. We found the mound north of the desert line where orchards and vineyards shone in the glow of evening. I made my way up the brushy side of the hill to its level top, where galaxies of flowers bloomed in response to recent rain. A small half-ruined Arab shrine stood empty and forlorn.

As I passed the old tomb, I glanced into its dim interior and froze. Fresh green branches formed an altar beneath a white headcloth. Congealed blood smeared a corner of the building. The embers of a recent fire lay nearby. Here on

96

DEAN CONGER, NATIONAL GEOGRAPHIC PHOTOGRAPHER

FIRE FLICKERS in a Bedouin camp
by the Dead Sea as dusk glows
above Judaean hills climbing toward
Jerusalem. These wanderers live,
as Abram did, in a tent of woven
goat hair—the sackcloth
of the Bible. The coarse, heavy fabric
keeps out sun, sand, and wind.
Curtains form compartments,
one for family, the other for guests.
Status-conscious sheiks
count their tent poles much as
suburbanites count rooms—
bigger tents need more poles.

Genesis 25 contrasts the hunter
Esau with his brother Jacob,
"a quiet man, dwelling in tents."
To poets of old, cut tent cords
betokened desolation. To nomads,
"pulling out" meant moving on.

A woman in Hebron (left),
face hidden by a gay veil,
clutches her white headdress—
badge of a successful pilgrimage
to Mecca. Women toiling in
desert and farmlands today find
that simply averting their faces
to avoid the gaze of men
works just as well as the veil.

97

the mound of Gerar I saw the age-old elements of a burnt offering: altar, blood, fire. The Bedouin had not forgotten the old ways.

Abraham knew the ritual well. Often he had set up an altar to his God, killed an animal upon it, and burned its flesh. And it was here in the northern Negev, perhaps at Gerar, perhaps at Beersheba, that God said to Abraham: "Take now thy son, thine only son Isaac, whom thou lovest, and get thee into the land of Moriah; and offer him there for a burnt offering" (Genesis 22:2).

No greater trial could have been conceived by God to measure His friend's faith. Abraham saddled a donkey, took two servants, some split wood, and his son, and traveled for three days to "the place of which God had told him." Tradition puts it on Mount Moriah in the Old City of Jerusalem—present site of the Dome of the Rock. Abraham left the servants and walked in silence to the hilltop. Isaac carried the wood and Abraham the knife. After a time the boy asked his father, "Where is the lamb for a burnt offering?" Abraham replied that God would see to it.

As Dr. Speiser puts it, "The boy must by now have sensed the truth. The short and simple sentence, 'And the two of them walked on together,' covers what is perhaps the most poignant and eloquent silence in all literature." At the last moment—but only at the last moment—an angel stayed Abraham as he raised his knife to destroy his son and all his hopes. The awful ordeal was over (page 38).

UNWORLDLY GUESTS, *welcomed in the grove of Mamre at Hebron, startle Abraham with the message: "Sarah thy wife shall have a son" (Genesis 18:10). These three are no ordinary men, he realizes.*

God had pledged to Abram: "Thy name shall be Abraham; for a father of many nations have I made thee." Now, eavesdropping in the tent, the Patriarch's 90-year-old wife, rechristened Sarah, chuckles at the idea of bearing a child.

"Wherefore did Sarah laugh. . . ? Is any thing too hard for the Lord?" demands the spokesman, now recognized by Abraham as the Lord himself.

Sarah conceived. "And Abraham was an hundred years old, when his son Isaac was born unto him."

PAINTING BY TOM LOVELL

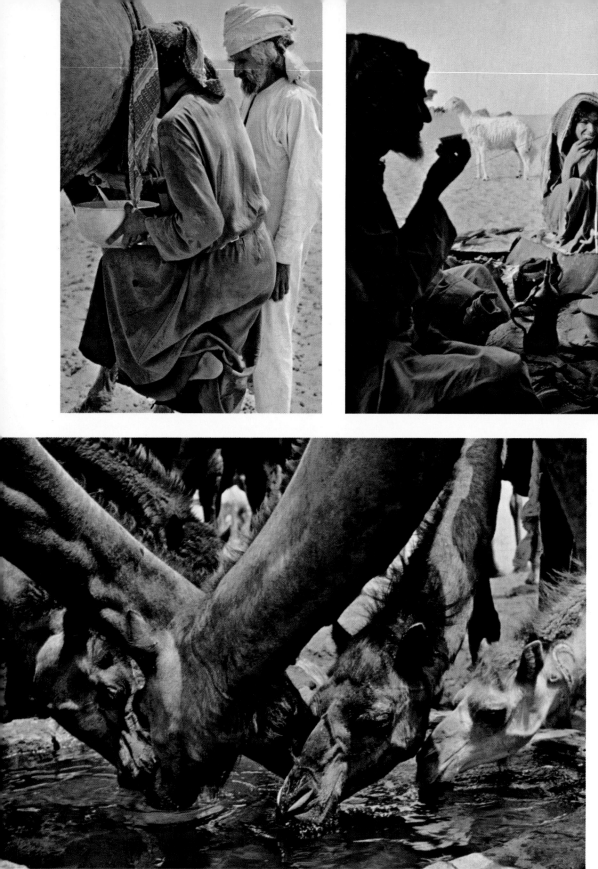

PHOTOGRAPHED IN ARABIA'S "EMPTY QUARTER" BY THOMAS J. ABERCROMBIE, NATIONAL GEOGRAPHIC STAFF

Welcome flows at a Bedouin well

"My house of hair! Come home and eat with me!" The familiar cry calls the wayfarer to share the shade of a tent and a repast of delicious dates and bowls of milk freshly drawn from camels. To quench their own thirsts, the beasts quaff the well's smelly, brackish water, unfit for humans. Pouring from a long-beaked pot, the host serves coffee spiced with cardamom and ginger root.

In this sun-scorched world, where outcasts must die, men have lived by the cherished rules of hospitality since the time of Abraham. The desert code, which would give asylum even to a father's slayer among his victim's kin, treats a stranger as a "guest of God" — inviolable when he has eaten his host's food. "There is salt between them," says an ancient proverb.

The Dome of the Rock is a sight to delight the eye. But as I looked at this storied mosque, the magnificence around me faded, and I saw only an old man and a boy standing in silent despair on a lonely hill in Canaan.

Soon after his torment on the heights of Moriah, Abraham went back to his home at Hebron. "And Sarah died in . . . Hebron in the land of Canaan: and Abraham came to mourn for Sarah, and to weep for her." For the first time in his life, Abraham purchased a piece of property — the cave of Machpelah — as a tomb in which to bury his dead.

"The living," as Dr. Speiser has observed, "could get by as sojourners; but the dead required a permanent resting ground." In time Abraham himself joined Sarah in death. He was "old, and well stricken in age: and the Lord had blessed Abraham in all things" (Genesis 24:1). The Patriarch was laid beside his wife in the cave.

The cave exists. Covering and concealing it is a mosque whose foundations date from Herod's day. Later portions were built by Byzantine Christians, still later ones by Arabs. The surrounding town, called Al Khalil — The Friend — in honor of Abraham, is Moslem. The mosque itself is one of the most sacred shrines of Islam. Until recently, no non-Moslem was permitted to set foot in it.

Six cenotaphs, or symbolic tombs, stand on its floor, representing those whose bones are believed to lie in the

101

cave below: Abraham and Sarah, Isaac and his wife Rebekah, Jacob and his wife Leah. Abraham's cenotaph and Sarah's stand in enclosures behind silver bars, draped in green silk.

In the cool gloom pilgrims moved silently on bare feet over carpeted floors. Some knelt immediately to pray, but others, particularly women, approached the cenotaphs to caress their corners or kiss them.

Nearby an old man prostrated himself over a brass grate set flush with the floor and looked into the cave itself through the only aperture. He bowed and moved away and I knelt in his place. A current of moist air rose from the darkness where an oil lamp, suspended far below, revealed no feature of

THEN THE LORD RAINED *upon Sodom and upon Gomorrah brimstone and fire" (Genesis 19:24). Lot and his daughters flee the holocaust, but his wife looks back and "she became a pillar of salt." Lot lived, helped by two angels he had shielded from the frenzied lusts of his Sodomite neighbors.*

Abraham pleaded with the Almighty: "Wilt thou also destroy the righteous with the wicked?" Had but ten guiltless people been found in Sodom, the Bible relates, God would have spared it.

Sin haunts the cities' names, mystery shrouds their sites. Scholars believe they stood in a valley now submerged under the Dead Sea, across from the Mount of Sodom (right). Sawtooth barrens little resemble the "well watered" land where Lot brought his flocks; earthquakes and underground gas explosions may have changed it.

"THE DESTRUCTION OF SODOM" BY CAMILLE COROT, C. 1857; H. O. HAVEMEYER COLLECTION, METROPOLITAN MUSEUM OF ART, NEW YORK. RIGHT: ORIENT PRESS PHOTO

Abraham's resting place. Monks who inhabited the shrine in the Crusader period, when the building was a Byzantine church, claimed to have discovered the mortal remains of the Patriarchs on the 7th of July, 1119. Since no archeologist may enter the cavern, this claim cannot be confirmed.

But perhaps it doesn't matter. The darkness beneath the brass bars in the floor of the mosque is enough. Here the long voyage ended. And here we latter-day followers of the half-hidden trail from Ur to Egypt felt sure, for the first time, that our paths and Abraham's had met.

The people of Abraham journeyed on. A time of famine brought them to Egypt and a joyous reunion with Jacob's beloved son Joseph, grown mighty as vizier of Pharaoh's domain. They prospered in the fruitful land of the Nile. Then their fortunes tumbled and they bent to the bitter yoke of slavery. And once more a great leader would be summoned to lead the children of God.

GRIEVED AND TOTTERING, *Abraham leans on Isaac as father and son lay Sarah to rest in the cave of Machpelah at Hebron. Kin and servants bear mortuary wine, food, ointment, and jewelry. Ephron the Hittite sold the cave to the landless wanderer for an exorbitant 400 shekels of silver, taking advantage of a mourning widower. Today it lies under the great Mosque of Abraham, with square minarets (below). Padlocked gate of silver protects the cenotaphs of Abraham and Sarah.*

By John A. Wilson

The World of Moses

W HO AM I, that I should go unto Pharaoh. . . ?'' The lonely shepherd
Moses draws back in anguish when he hears the dread command of
God on the heights of Sinai: Go to Egypt and rescue the enslaved
children of Israel. Slow of speech, uncertain whether his own people
would support him, Moses must defy the mightiest monarch on earth.
Small wonder that he hesitates.

But Moses has the might of his God behind him. And before his sands run out
at the age of 120, he will humble Pharaoh, lead the Hebrews through a hostile
wilderness to the homeland promised since Abraham's time, and forge bonds
between them and the Almighty that will endure for 3,000 years. It is a great epic,
beautifully told in the Books of Exodus, Numbers, and Deuteronomy.

The memory of those experiences never left the people of Israel. They carried
with them also the lasting influence of Egyptian culture, a heritage that touches us
today. For, with the Sumerians, the Egyptians opened the door to civilization.
They left us institutions we still take for granted—family life, education, law,
writing, the beginnings of science and engineering. They gave us chairs and tables,
metal tools and weapons, and a formal art. They followed a faith that dared
to deny death, and organized the world's first great empire. And they raised
monuments in stone that are immortal.

The Egypt Moses knew was not the squarish land on today's maps but mainly
a strip of green—the "gift of the river"—lining the Nile for some 600 miles.
The river drew scarcely a drop of rain from the bright skies; in Egypt no tributary
brought it waters. The burning sun and thirsty sands drank its moisture.
Yet here in this valley men had settled thousands of years earlier when grasslands
withered on the plateaus and game became scarce. For the Nile's surging summer
floods enriched Egypt's soil with layer upon layer of alluvium from the heartland of
Africa. Even today a man can stand with one foot on the fruitful black soil laid down

"AND MOSES . . . WENT DOWN FROM THE MOUNT . . . . *and the writing was the writing of God"*
(Exodus 32:15, 16). Sinai and the Ten Commandments marked a spiritual milestone
as the great prophet and lawgiver led his people out from bondage in Egypt.

by the river and the other on the lifeless sand of the desert. Proud Egyptians called their home the "black land" and themselves "the people." Sea and desert walled off their land from enemies. They were favorites of the gods, surrounded by Nubians, Libyans, and Asians, who lived like beasts in the highlands.

But the caprice of the Nile could spell famine as well as feast. Even in good years the floodwaters must be captured and retained, for the soil quickly dries out. One still sees the back of a peasant bending and lifting all day at the well sweep; one sees men mending the channels that carry water to outlying fields. Fortunately, Egypt has always been crowded with strong backs.

People in the south lived close to the great river, hemmed in by desert cliffs. But downstream—to the north—the Delta fans out in green field and marsh. As irrigation and the animal-drawn plow revolutionized agriculture, life became more specialized. Men became potters, weavers, smiths, merchants, sailors. From Mesopotamia came the cylinder seal and perhaps the idea of representing objects and concepts through pictorial symbols—the beginning of writing.

As Stone Age farming villages grew into cities, then provinces, separate kingdoms of Upper and Lower Egypt gradually emerged. About 3000 B.C. the kingdoms combined into a single nation under an all-powerful god-king. Thus began the first of the 31 dynasties that ruled Egypt until the conquest by Alexander the Great in 332 B.C.

WORSHIP OF THE GOD-KING and obedience to him held the long land together. The vibrant nation flourished, the riches of its soil buttressed by lodes of gold and copper in nearby mountains. Slaves filled Egypt's kitchens and weaving rooms, swelled her army, toiled on her shrines. One pharaoh boasted of carrying off 232 Asian princes, 323 princesses, and 270 court women in one campaign, and 89,600 warriors in another. Nile-built ships ventured to Crete and Phoenicia, or southward to a land Egyptians called Punt for incense, myrrh, gum, and ivory.

To an explorer in the south bringing back a dancing pygmy, the boy king Pepi II wrote an urgent letter: "When he goes into the ship . . . have careful men who will be around him . . . so that he does not fall into the water. . . . My Majesty wants to see this pygmy more than all the products of Sinai or Punt."

During the early dynasties great pyramids rose, wonders of the world in any age, symbols of the yearning for immortality, and of the power, skill, and organization of the Egyptian state under its kings.

WALL PAINTING FROM TOMB OF KHNUMHOTEP III AT BENI HASAN, 19TH CENTURY B.C., COPIED BY C. R. LEPSIUS IN "DENKMÄLER AUS ÄGYPTEN UND ÄTHIOPEN," 1849-56

But though the Egyptians built for eternity, the world would not stand still. Foreign peoples chafed under her yoke and worried away at the borders. Officials gained independent power. Around 2200 B.C. the Old Kingdom fell and two centuries of chaos ensued. With the XIIth Dynasty came the Middle Kingdom; strong rule returned. But feudal nobles did not yield their powers lightly. Statues of XIIth Dynasty pharaohs show care-lined faces, unlike the serene visages of the Old Kingdom.

About 1700 B.C. Egypt suffered a great shock— conquest by the Hyksos, Asian overlords whose identity still puzzles us. Out of the east they swarmed with horses and chariots, body armor, improved bows. Neither Pharaoh's lightly equipped army nor the land's natural barriers could prevent this humiliation.

Established in the Delta, the Hyksos tolerated weakened Egyptian rulers at Thebes. One of these, Ahmosis I, pushed a war of liberation and, about 1567 B.C., drove out the Hyksos. Thus began the XVIIIth Dynasty and the New Kingdom. A new spirit swept through Egypt. Gone was the complacency of former times. A great king, Thutmosis III, felt it necessary to conquer the world. Around 1470 B.C. he nearly succeeded. His armies ruled from the Fourth Cataract on the Nile, deep in Nubia, to the great bend of the Euphrates in Syria.

Mediterranean Sea

Alexandria

LOWER EGYPT

Lake Manzala

Tanis (Raamses)

GOSHEN

Pithom Succoth

GREAT SPHINX

Heliopolis
Cairo

Pyramids of Giza
Saqqara *Memphis*
Dahshur

STEP PYRAMID

EL FAIYUM

Sinai

Nile

Gulf of Suez

QUEEN NEFERTITI

Beni Hasan

Tell el Amarna

UPPER

EGYPT

TEMPLE OF HATHOR

Abydos

Dandara

Valley of the Kings
Western Thebes *Thebes*
Luxor

Idfu

HORUS THE FALCON

Ombos

Elephantine Island *Aswan*
1st Cataract

Dandur

El Dakka NUBIA

Nile

Abu Simbel

0   50   100
STATUTE MILES

DRAWN BY ROBERT C. MAGIS AND VICTOR J. KELLEY
GEOGRAPHIC ART DIVISION

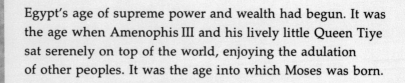

Egypt's age of supreme power and wealth had begun. It was the age when Amenophis III and his lively little Queen Tiye sat serenely on top of the world, enjoying the adulation of other peoples. It was the age into which Moses was born.

*I*F EGYPTIAN SCRIBES recorded the Hebrews' escape on papyrus, the scroll has not survived. And the thousands of inscriptions on Egypt's temples and tombs emphasize triumphs, not defeats. So we cannot identify from Egyptian records the pharaohs of the Oppression and the Exodus. Traditionally, we regard Ramesses II, who ruled from about 1304 to 1237 B.C., as the oppressor. His son Merneptah should then be the pharaoh of the Exodus.

One of Merneptah's inscriptions boasts of a campaign in which "Israel is laid waste"—the only reference to Israel in ancient Egyptian literature. The hieroglyphic sign refers to a people, not a place, indicating the presence in Canaan at that time of an unsettled group called Israel.

In this period of the XIXth Dynasty, Egypt continued to press its far-sweeping claims to domination. Royal couriers drove their flimsy chariots all over the Near East, carrying clay tablets inscribed with Akkadian cuneiform, the diplomatic language of the day. Foreign princes, hostages to the conduct of their fathers, crowded Pharaoh's court.

The two great powers were Egypt and the Hittites, bold warriors from Anatolia who first mastered ironworking. Between them lay the little peoples of Palestine and Syria. From somewhere to the north the "Sea Peoples" sailed to the edges of Pharaoh's empire, raiding on land and sea.

Moses was no stranger to the grandeurs of Pharaoh's court when, during his exile, he received the divine commission to confront the king. An alien foundling in Egypt, he had been reared as a prince.

With the royal princes he surely "sang the writings" at school and copied texts on papyrus and fragments of stone. The words for *teaching* and *punishment* were identical, and a teacher grimly remarked that "the ear of the boy is on his back, and he listens when he is beaten."

"A SMASHER OF FOREHEADS IS HE... *he spares not." This ancient inscription befits King Narmer of Upper Egypt as he conquers Lower Egypt (the Delta), uniting his white crown with the red one of the northern kingdom. Scholars identify Narmer with the legendary Menes, who welded "the Two Lands" into one nation about 3000 B.C.*

PAINTING BY H. M. HERGET

111

Surviving texts give us a delightful peek into the hearts and minds of Moses' day. Schoolmasters continually praised the life of a scribe and scorned lesser crafts: "I have seen the metalworker . . . . he stank more than fish-roe. . . .

The weaver in the workshops, he is worse than a woman, with his thighs against his belly. . . . The embalmer, his fingers are foul, for the odor thereof is corpses. . . . Behold, there is no profession free of a boss—except for the scribe: he is the boss."

"Wisdom" texts—advice of a father to his son—were popular. If you dine with a great man, "take what he may give, when it is set before thy nose. . . . speak only when he addresses thee. Laugh after he laughs, and it will be very pleasing to his heart."

Young Moses doubtless would have known such sayings. Some of the documents, hymns, and tales used in the schools were more than 700 years old. One letter might have reminded him how his forebears came to Egypt. An old border report, it tells how guards let nomadic "tribes of Edom pass the Fortress . . . to the pools of Per-Atum . . . to keep them and their cattle alive." We may imagine him copying these prophetic words from a letter about runaway slaves: "Which patrol found their tracks? What people are following them? Write me all that has happened. . . ."

Ancient Egyptians called their writing script "speech of the gods." Later Greeks called it "sacred carved letters," *hieroglyphika grammata.* Hieroglyphic was the only proper writing for temples or tombs; scribes furnished the texts, sculptors or painters applied them to stone.

For routine records and communications, scribes devised a cursive form of hieroglyphic and wrote it on sheets of papyrus, made from the pith of the sedge stalks which abounded in the Nile marshes. Often the scribe carried the tools of his trade on a string slung across his shoulder— a palette with cakes of ink, a water jar, and a pen case. He wrote with a reed pen, its tip pounded into a brush or cut to a tiny chisel edge. Documents were dated by reign and regnal year. The civil calendar had a 365-day year—12 equal months with 5 days tacked on at the end.

SKIRT FOR A DESK, *a scribe unrolls papyrus and pinches a long-lost pen of frayed reed. Knowledge of writing set men on the path to high office; its power verged on magic. Food and clothing lists in tombs meant real bread and beer and linen garments for the departed. Each of some 700 signs stood for an object, sound, or clarifier of another sign. Hieroglyphs opposite praise Hatshepsut, calling her "Son of Re." Oval ring encloses the royal name. Cartouche above denotes Ramesses II. While sculptors carved "the god's words," affairs of state and trade called forth a script called "hieratic." Line above, read from right, orders "one oxhide of good quality."*

FOWLING *in a fish-filled papyrus pool, the noble Nebamun grasps throwing-st* and *heron decoys. Wife and daughter join in the outing; cat retrieves. Nobles sought to surround themselves in death with scenes they knew in life. Reliefs in the lord Ti's mastaba at Saqqara (left) portray his world of 4,300 years ago.*

For a child of the court like Moses, the drudgery of writing practice would be lightened by outdoor games, which the Egyptians always loved. Princes probably had little training in running an estate. Stewards, and possibly a few Asian slaves, would manage things under the noble's direction.

The noble might take business in leisurely stride, inspecting his estates, hearing reports of his overseers, sitting as local magistrate, acting as lay priest in the temple. Only the call of duty to country could bring a hard chore—serving at some remote post, supervising a quarry, crossing the dreaded sea on a royal errand. Back at last, he would value his carefree rounds all the more.

How different was his life from that of the Asian chieftains he had met on Pharaoh's business in Palestine. The Asian wore a beard, a heavy fall of hair, a long woolen garment, gaudily colored and belted at the waist. He lived in a rude stone shelter, and probably ate and sat on the floor. In contrast, the Egyptian noble shaved, bathed frequently, and sometimes put on a ceremonial wig. He wore a white linen skirt and sandals, and at times threw a light shawl over his shoulders. With jeweled collars, ear studs, and fly whisks, he and his wife expressed sophisticated elegance. Their manor house was designed for light and airiness. They sat on chairs and dined at a table. They could take their leisure in an arbor of the garden, listening to a blind harper chant a love song or an old heroic tale. Wearing their finest regalia and cones of sweet-smelling ointment on their heads, they would attend gala dinner parties where each guest was assigned a servant. They were plied with food and drink to the full. The high point in the entertainment came with the acrobatic dancers — scantily clad girls specializing in the high kick.

Court sessions had their tedious moments, with fixed places and procedures for everyone. Pharaoh sat enthroned on a little platform, while courtiers stood stiffly

around the edges of the room. No one looked directly into the god-king's face; an official who had a report to make prostrated himself before the throne. So awesome was the royal power that Egypt did not develop a written law code. Officials decided cases on the basis of custom, and sought to reflect the king's own characteristics of Hu, Sia, and Maat—authority, perception, and justice.

For the Egyptian gentry, death held no fears. They believed they could ensure an abundant life for all time. As soon as a noble gained the means and authority, he started on his tomb and its furnishings. Quarrymen roughed out the rooms in Thebes' western hills. Stonemasons smoothed the walls, then artists decorated them with scenes of the owner's fields and servants, so that his pleasant life might continue in the afterlife. Models of workers, *ushabtis*, were included to perform manual labor. Magic texts such as the Book of the Dead enabled him to proclaim his worthiness: "I have not killed. . . . I have not been covetous."

*F*OR MANY YEARS I have studied ancient Egyptian monuments. In the glare of the desert sun I have copied their inscriptions, the basis for much of what we know about Egypt's past. The shrines are silent and lonely places, looming in battered and crumbling ruin. There is no loneliness like the loneliness of a mighty place fallen out of its proper service.

Because it emphasized eternity, Egyptian art seems flat and lifeless to many. The statues, carvings, and paintings were presented in solid repose, so that the people they depict would not tire out. Children, servants, and animals could be shown in action, but even they had to conform to a pattern. A line of cows might be as regimented as soldiers, all stepping off on the same foot. To me this mingling of dignity and a strong sense of humor is a delight.

Only once has the spade revealed the dazzling luxury of a pharaoh's life. For more than 3,000 years Tutankhamun, a weak boy king of the XVIIIth Dynasty, lay in silent majesty in the Valley of the Kings at Western Thebes. Robbers of the 12th century B.C. and archeologists of the 20th century A.D. had missed his burial chamber, for ancient workmen, tunneling another royal tomb in the same hillside, had heaped a great pile of stone on the sepulcher.

When Lord Carnarvon and his skilled excavator Howard Carter took up the search in 1914, many feared the site was exhausted. By 1922 Carter, too, was ready to give up. But three days after the dig resumed that year, his workmen discovered steps leading down to a sealed doorway. Carter summoned Lord Carnarvon from England. On November 26, a lower door was breached and Carter peered through a small hole. His own words capture the scene: "As my eyes grew accustomed to the light, details of the room within emerged

"I WAS STRUCK DUMB WITH AMAZEMENT." *The richest treasure of a pharaoh ever found lay before Egyptologist Howard Carter when he discovered Tutankhamun's tomb in 1922. For weeks he removed from the antechamber furnishings he would be years cataloging. Then, beyond a sealed door, he dismantled a nest of gilded shrines, reached through the innermost (right) and found the young king's sarcophagus—intact after 3,300 years!*

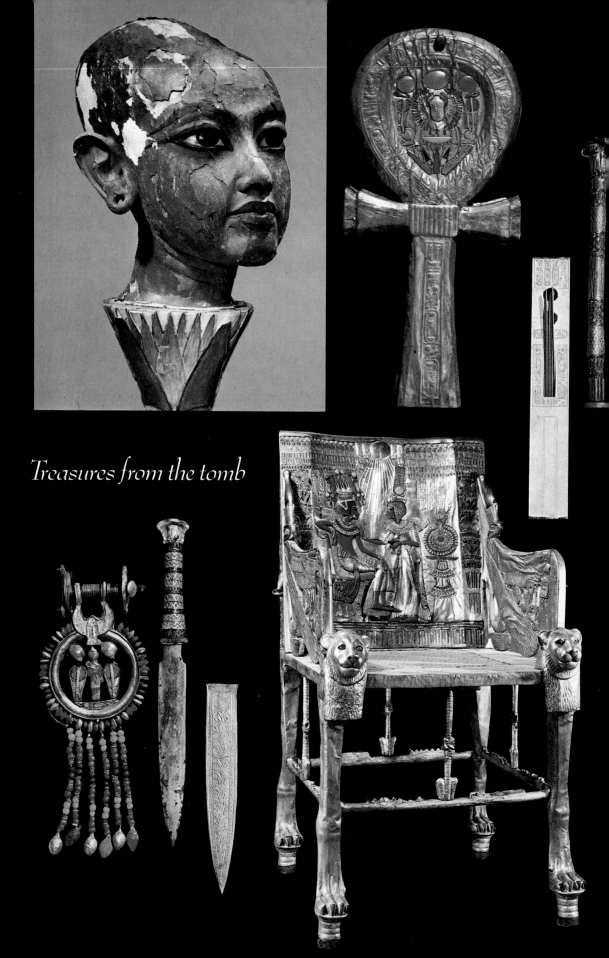

Treasures from the tomb

"**MAYST THOU SPEND** millions of years . . .
sitting with thy face to the north wind,
and thine eyes beholding felicity."
Hieroglyphs on the alabaster cup proclaim this
wish for Tutankhamun. Other objects herald
his rebirth: cylindrical pen box; writing reeds
and ink cakes; mirror case in the crosslike shape
of the ankh, symbol of life.

The boy king's head springs from a lotus,
as did the sun on the first day of creation;
pierced ear could hold the tasseled gold earring.
Iron dagger and sheath ensured protection against
enemies such as the bound Nubian carved in ebony
on a royal cane. Scorpion goddess guards
the king's viscera, encased in a gilded shrine.
Lions on his throne symbolize power.

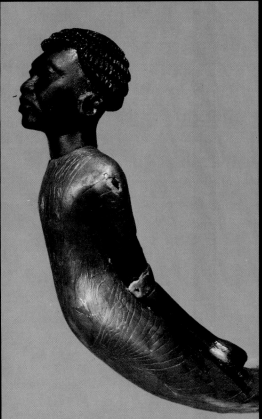

slowly from the mist, strange animals, statues, and gold—everywhere the glint of gold. For the moment . . . I was struck dumb with amazement, and when Lord Carnarvon, unable to stand the suspense any longer, inquired anxiously, 'Can you see anything?' it was all I could do to get out the words, 'Yes, wonderful things.'"

Every room of the small tomb was packed to the ceiling with treasure: furniture, jars, statues, chariots, walking sticks, bows and arrows, scarabs, bouquets, clothing. Today the fabulous hoard in the Egyptian Museum in Cairo awes visitors, as does Tutankhamun's mummy in its gilded coffin entombed in the Theban hills.

*I*N ANCIENT EGYPT the gods ruled everything. The Nile flooded because a god willed it, or fell off because a god was displeased. There were gods of the cosmos, like Re of the sun or Geb of the earth. There were deities of function, like Thoth, the god of learning, and Hathor, the goddess of love. Some might take on additional duties. And some might merge, so that three became one, like Amon-Re-Harakhte. But the two greatest were Re—in the brilliant light of Egypt, sun worship was always primary—and Osiris, the ruler of the dead. Egyptians who had led virtuous lives merged at death with Osiris and might live forever.

A few generations before Moses, Pharaoh Akhenaten swept away the old pantheon in favor of a kind of monotheism, worship of the life-giving sun disk— the Aten. After Akhenaten's death, Egypt returned to old gods, but the tendency to focus on one remained. Was this the origin of Hebrew monotheism? Surely not. Moses' religion was anti-Egyptian. It opposed his unseen God, Yahweh, against the Egyptians' seen gods. Yahweh set forth rigorous law; Aten had been a benevolent nature god.

But in other ways Egypt did influence the foreigners. Compare Akhenaten's praise of the sun disk—"How manifold are thy works! They are hidden from man's sight. O sole god, without thy peer, Thou hast made the earth

TUTANKHAMUN'S QUEEN *anoints him with perfume in this scene adorning his throne. Hand-tipped rays of the Aten, or sun disk, caress the crown of cobras balancing sun disks that tops his wig; her crown holds disk and horns of Hathor, goddess of love. Tut's child queen was the daughter of lovely Nefertiti (right), whose name means "the beautiful one is come." Her brother-husband Akhenaten sought to place Egypt under the benevolent rays of one god, the Aten (far right).*

HEAD AND BALUSTRADE RELIEF FROM TELL EL AMARNA, 14TH CENTURY B.C.; AUDRAIN-SAMIVEL OPPOSITE: F. L. KENETT © GEORGE RAINBIRD LTD. ALL IN EGYPTIAN MUSEUM

according to thy desire!"—with Psalm 104:24: "O Lord, how manifold are thy works! in wisdom hast thou made them all: the earth is full of thy riches." One group of proverbs, displaying the new humility Egypt learned after its empire fell apart about 1100 B.C., bears striking similarities to the Book of Proverbs. Egyptian love songs have parallels in the passionate Song of Songs.

In one heroic tale an Egyptian demigod refuses the advances of his brother's wife, recalling Joseph's experience with Potiphar's wife in Genesis 39. Like Joseph, he suffered for his nobility but ended in triumph. Much else in the Joseph story can be matched from Egyptian sources: the interpretation of dreams, the seven years of famine, and Joseph's death at the ideal age of 110. After the lean years Joseph's people stayed on in the Delta. Cuneiform and Egyptian texts of these times refer to an apparently alien people called Habiru.

We have little information of the Hebrews' daily life during the harsh servitude in Goshen. But we know a great deal about the labor gangs who built the tombs upriver at Thebes. They lived under the eyes of guards in a walled village— a hot little place with tight-packed adobe houses and hardly any light or air. Their staples were bread and beer, both made from grain. Once when the officials failed to supply grain on time, the workmen went on strike!

Since Egypt had no caste system, peasants and slaves might rise to high position, as Joseph did, and thus be freed of the overseer's lash. Skilled craftsmen could become royal sculptors or artists. Nobles might well prefer slaves as household attendants; as personal property the foreign servant could be trusted.

If the lot of the work gangs was hard, there were feast days when they enjoyed handouts of meat and all the beer they could drink, and shouted themselves hoarse as a god passed by in procession. The Hebrews would remember those feasts, "when we sat by the flesh pots, and . . . did eat bread to the full" (Exodus 16:3).

"FOR I WILL PASS through the land of Egypt this night, and will smite all the firstborn . . . and against all the gods of Egypt I will execute judgment: I am the Lord. . . . And this day shall be unto you for a memorial; and ye shall keep it a feast to the Lord throughout your generations" (Exodus 12:12, 14).

One reason why the story of Moses appeals to us so strongly is that the little man with his one God defeated the great king with his many gods. On the night Hebrews would celebrate as Passover, their God passed over their houses and smote the Egyptians only. Over and over the Bible recalls how God delivered His own people from the land of bondage. The wonder of it was never dying.

Yet Moses had to do more. The prophet must now become the leader. Moses had to hold the uprooted tribes together in a terrifying wilderness, teach them the Law of God, give them dignity, courage, and a sense of high destiny. Long after Moses' time, his message would light a fire in men's hearts.

BREEZE AND BRAWN *inch broad-beamed naggars along Nile-filled canals that net the Biblical land of Goshen. Ancients hymned the Nile "who makes a ship to prosper." Building irrigation canals and dikes demanded group effort, spurred civilization's rise.*

DEAN CONGER, NATIONAL GEOGRAPHIC PHOTOGRAPHER

GOSHEN, LAND OF BONDAGE

WE SPED north from Cairo in the early morning darkness, past sleeping villages and strings of laden camels. Now and then we braked before the flickering lantern of a police checkpoint. Each time a drowsy sentry waved us on. As we entered the old caravan town of Bilbeis, a Land-Rover roared out of the darkness and blocked our way. Men in desert robes leaped out. In the glare of our headlights I saw the glint of pistols and cartridge belts. I listened to the staccato exchange between

Thou living Aten,
the beginning of life!
When thou art risen on the eastern horizon,
Thou hast filled every land
with thy beauty....
Thou drivest away the darkness
and givest thy rays.

Pharaoh Akhenaten's hymn to the sun befits this dawn scene in Tanis photographed by the author

Sojourn in Egypt's Delta
with National Geographic's
John J. Putman. Here Hebrews toiled
and life still moves to the
ancient rhythms of sun and Nile

the men and Salama, my driver. But the only phrase I made out was "San el Hagar," our destination. The men flung open the doors, searched the car, probed my camera bag. Then the leader grunted. They piled into their car and drove off.

Salama whistled. "Police. Looking for hashish!"

Smugglers still ply the ancient caravan routes over which Ishmaelite traders carried Joseph into slavery. They come from the east across the Sinai Peninsula, the narcotic hidden in the folds of their camel saddles. The police had suspected us of picking up a shipment.

Though our mission was far different, the hint of danger, the sudden confrontation with the authorities, seemed strangely appropriate. I had come to Egypt to trace the footsteps of Moses, the towering "servant of the Lord" who led his people from Pharaoh's bondage to freedom and a new

covenant with God. I would journey from the lush Nile Delta to the barren wilderness of Sinai, from Moab's lonely highlands to the deep cleft where the Jordan River cuts the Promised Land. I would travel by jet airplane, train, desert car, felucca, camel, donkey, and on foot. Somewhere along the way I hoped to discover some still-vibrant echo of the Exodus—that searing experience that welded the children of Israel into a nation—and of Moses, its leader. I was not confident. The trail was more than 3,000 years old.

It began here in the Delta, the great fertile wedge of Egypt formed by the spreading mouths of the Nile. To the Delta's eastern edge had come Joseph's brothers with their families and flocks to dwell in time of famine. In this land the Bible calls Goshen they prospered until "there arose up a new king . . . which knew not Joseph" (Exodus 1:8). Fearful that the aliens in his border lands might join his enemies, this Pharaoh decided to "deal wisely" with the Hebrews. He ordered every son born to them "cast into the river." And one of these sons—saved, ironically, by Pharaoh's daughter —was the man whose path I pursued.

Salama pointed, "San el Hagar!" The tranquil village draws its name—"preserver of the stone"—from the great mound that rises beside it. Here as elsewhere in the Fertile Crescent an ancient city had been built, destroyed, and rebuilt again and again, its tell growing layer by layer.

BASKET-BURDENED WOMEN *on a misty Delta road recall the poignant Bible scene: To save her "goodly" son from Pharaoh's death sentence, a desperate Hebrew mother set him in an "ark of bulrushes" at river's edge. There a princess found the basket and rescued the babe (right). "And she called his name Moses: and she said, Because I drew him out of the water." In Hebrew the name means "to draw out"; in Egyptian, "to beget a child."*

Pharaohs of the Hebrew sojourn ruled Egypt from the lush Delta, whose palm-fringed fields stretch away to hostile desert.

127

We drove to its crest. Upon seeing my permit from the Department of Antiquities in Cairo, the two sleepy guards stepped aside and I scrambled down the slopes into the bowels of the ruins.

I saw utter desolation. The granite eyes of a fallen colossus stared blankly skyward. Shattered obelisks and tumbled columns lined a dusty avenue. Dark steps led down to an old city well, scummed and silent. On a fragment of stone two severed hands held tight an ancient embrace. The only sound was the chirp of swallows that nest in the mounds of decayed brick. Was this the Biblical city of Raamses? Was it here that young Moses lived?

For centuries the mound kept its secret, the winds off nearby Lake Manzala whipping the bare soil over shattered Tanis, last of the cities to stand here. Peasants hauled away decayed refuse, or *sibakh*, for fertilizer. Children romped among protruding columns. Then, in the early 19th century, French savants sketched the site; one speculated that it was in "*cette ville que Moise....*" In this city that Moses...!

Before the century ended, Flinders Petrie, beginning a brilliant career, came to San el Hagar, "the marsh village reeking with old fish." Tenting through weeks of storm, he dosed himself with quinine and strychnine to avert fevers. To read inscriptions, he levered stone after stone. At times he had to dodge: "The sound of crushing granite was the signal for motion...."

In 1929 a young Frenchman, Pierre Montet, began to dig. In campaigns spread over 37 years he brilliantly brought to light the history of the tell and called it the Raamses of the Bible, one of two store cities built by the Hebrews for Pharaoh.

The city flourished first under the Hyksos, the Asian kings who invaded Egypt in the 18th century B.C. Many scholars believe it was during the reign of these "rulers of foreign countries" that Joseph rose to high position and his kin were allowed to settle in Goshen. In time the Egyptians regained strength and besieged the Hyksos here—breaching fortifications which still stand—and drove them back into Asia. For centuries the city slept while Egypt was ruled by New Kingdom pharaohs from Thebes.

THEN RAMESSES II rose to the throne of Egypt. Hungry for conquest in Asia, he moved his capital here—near the sea and land links to the east. Even today fishing vessels of San el Hagar sail north over the same watercourses that bore Ramesses' ships to the Mediterranean.

Many scholars consider Ramesses II as the Pharaoh of the Biblical Oppression who forced Joseph's people into great work gangs under harsh taskmasters. Ancient Egyptian texts tell how the vainglorious Ramesses

PHARAOH FACES THE HEBREWS—*a Biblical theme of welcome and woe that marked the generations from Abraham to Moses. Here, during the first encounter in the Delta, Pharaoh commands Abraham: "behold thy wife, take her, and go thy way." Punished with plague for taking the beautiful Sarah into his harem, he sends her forth to rejoin her people. The Patriarch prospered in the Delta, as did his descendants: "ye shall eat the fat of the land," a king promised Joseph (Genesis 45:18). By Moses' time the Hebrews' fortune had ebbed and the Delta became a land of bondage.*

PAINTING BY JOHN McDERMOTT

THREE-MAN BUCKET BRIGADE (left) taps
the lifeline of Egypt. Lowest shadoof
dips into the Nile; a stone or mud
counterweight lifts the brimming bucket
to the next level. Topmost fellah hauls
the precious water field-high. Simple rigs
like these moistened New Kingdom
gardens (opposite). Creaking saqiah
(above) came later. Often turned by
animals, its meshed wheels deliver
more than triple the shadoof's trickle.

Moses' people knew the yearly struggle
to capture the bounty of the Nile flood.
Leading them to freedom, he promised
a land which "drinketh water of the rain
of heaven"—unlike Egypt, "where thou
sowedst thy seed, and wateredst it
with thy foot" (Deuteronomy 11:10).

JOSEPH J. SCHERSCHEL AND (OPPOSITE) WINFIELD PARKS, NATIONAL GEOGRAPHIC PHOTOGRAPHERS

conscripted laborers, including Asian nomads, to build his new capital and other cities in the Delta.

On papyrus, poets marveled at Raamses, the new seat of Pharaoh: "His majesty . . . has built himself a castle. . . . Its granaries are so full of barley and emmer that they come near to the sky. . . ."

Professor Montet has described Ramesses' show-place city as Moses would have known it: "Snarling human-headed lions of black granite and sphinxes in roseate granite confronted each other all along the narrow basalt-paved alleys, while crouching lions kept watch in front of the gates. . . . The palace blazed with gold, lapis lazuli and turquoise, and the whole scene was gay with flowers."

In my mind's eye the deserted avenues and

COPY OF WALL PAINTING IN TOMB OF IPUI AT THEBES,
13TH CENTURY B.C.; METROPOLITAN MUSEUM OF ART, NEW YORK

131

crumbled ruins came alive with ghosts of the past—black Nubians of the army, Sardinians of the royal bodyguard, Libyan diplomats, Bedouin traders, Phoenician sailors from ships tied up along the river banks, perhaps the seed of Jacob among the hapless Asians of the labor gangs. I imagined too, standing among the men of the palace, a favored Asian, the young Moses.

The Bible recounts little of Moses' early life. We read that Pharaoh's daughter adopted him and he "was learned in all the wisdom of the Egyptians" (Acts 7:22). In this privileged station he would have studied at the scribe school, joined the hunt in desert and marsh, listened to girl harpists at dinner parties, practiced archery and chariot driving.

But as I walked to the very top of the tell, I wondered if Moses ever stood here and looked east across the barren flats toward the land of his fathers, Abraham, Isaac, Jacob. Did he yearn to go there in quest of his origins? The Bible doesn't say. Perhaps he heeded only the song of the poets of Raamses: "So dwell content of heart and free, without stirring...."

The guards of the tell asked us to tea. A tiny alcohol stove sputtered and flamed. In a few moments I held a scalding

TIME-TESTED COMBINE—*man and beast and primitive sledge— trudges a threshing floor near the Delta hamlet of Salamant, rubbing new-mown wheat against the earth to separate the grain from the stalks.*

In days of yore, music and merrymaking enlivened harvest toil, farmers even had cheering words for their animals. "Tread it for your own good," urges an inscripti "Your masters get the grain and you can eat the straw." The law of Moses forbade the muzzling of oxen on the threshing floor so they could nibble while they worked.

Early Egyptian farmers hacked the soil with crude hoes made of tree limbs or lashed sticks; they reaped with flint sickles. By the time of the New Kingdom metal blades were common; they still serve the fellahin today.

132

glass of dark, sugary tea between thumb and finger, and cheerfully added to the medley of approving slurps. One guard blew dust from a register and handed it to me. As I signed I noticed that the last visitor had been here weeks before—an archeologist assigned to the dig. We said good-bye in the traditional way: *"Ma' assalama"*—"Go with safety." *"Allah yisallimak"*—"God preserve you."

As we left Tanis, the sun was well up and the land vibrantly alive. Black-gowned women scurried along beneath earthen jars; camels staggered by, almost hidden by loads of sugar cane; donkeys pranced before carts laden with fellahin, lettuce, or manure. In the fields children goaded

"Grain in great abundance,
like the sand of the sea" *Genesis 41:49*

oxen and water buffaloes to turn pot-rigged water wheels. A primordial joy seemed to grip the people of Goshen.

I recalled a peasant song from an ancient tomb:

A good day — it is cool.
The cattle are pulling,
And the sky does according to our desire....
Let us work as our hearts may be bound!

But for the Hebrews, captives in an alien land, there could be no such satisfaction. To them Goshen was a "house of bondage" where their lives were made bitter with hard work "in morter, and in brick, and in all manner of service in the field." Salama and I set out to watch work in the fields.

COTTON RULES the Delta today. In Moses' time, grain held sway. Fields of wheat and barley stretched unbroken from the northern marshes to the First Cataract. The year began with *akhit,* the season of the flood, from June through September. The Nile rose, creeping over fields, making islands of villages, depositing moisture and rich African soil. During the next four months — the season of *perit,* the "going out" — the river receded. Fellahin cried: "Let us prepare our team of oxen for ploughing, for the waters have uncovered the earth, and the ground is ready...."

Sowers planted seed and plowmen with shallow shares turned the damp earth. Sometimes planters scattered seed and let herds of animals tamp it in. After sowing came months of irrigating and tending the growing plants. I joined fellahin on a Nile-side farm as they broke the crusted

WALL PAINTING, 15TH CENTURY B.C., FROM "THE TOMB OF NAKHT AT THEBES" BY NORMAN DE GARIS DAVIES

IN TOMB OF MENNA AT THEBES

134

CHAFF *freights the breeze as Delta farmers winnow grain with wooden forks, ending an arduous season often depicted by ancient artists. Plowman and men with hoes and mallets break the soil at far left; sowers rain seed. Harvester in panel at right leaps to force overflow into bin. Thresher (center) goads his team while a helper forks shocks under oxen's hooves.*

135

earth of February and heaped the dark, moist soil around potato sprouts. Ahmed, the overseer, approached me. Would I take his picture? Of course. Snap! We clasped hands and Ahmed said, "You have made me a happy man."

In the spring harvest season of antiquity, *shemou,* labor gangs worked their way north from Luxor and Memphis, hurrying to gather the crops before locusts or hail laid them waste. From dawn to nightfall they labored, sometimes bantering, "Beer for the man who cuts barley" and "Don't stop for a drink today before you have done something worth doing." Cut, threshed, forked, and winnowed, the grain was measured, recorded by scribes, and stored in silos.

Even as they fled Pharaoh's bondage, the Hebrews would longingly recall the bounty of the Delta—"the fish, which we did eat in Egypt . . . the cucumbers, and the melons . . . and the onions, and the garlick" (Numbers 11:5). I saw the Delta's bounty displayed on market day at Zagazig. Sheep filed between rows of carts piled high with tomatoes, turnips, eggplant. Women haggled while merchants adjusted brass weights on balance scales. Salama and I bought sandwiches: thick slices of fish in heavy brown sauce ladled on a flat, floppy piece of bread. Egyptians still relish garlic. As the "chef" looked on, I managed a smile— "*qwayyisa, qwayyisa*" . . . "good, good." We washed it down with steaming tea.

WHILE PEASANTS TOILED, *the gentry sported in columned country villas (below, left). Palms and sycamore fig trees, jasmine and chrysanthemums flank a shallow lotus pool. Only fish swim in it; Egyptians could swim but seldom did for sport. Here lads roughhouse and girls toss baseball-like spheres of sewn hide stuffed with barley husks. Fond parents watch from a high veranda's shade.*

The ideal estate reflected the nobleman's love of orderliness and symmetry, of nature and his family. He might relax with his wife in a game like backgammon, or tour his acres with lunch and retinue to watch serfs tend his fields and herds. Musicians and dancers kept his banquets gay with flute, lute, and harp (below). He cherished his mate. Sculptors and artists portrayed couples close together (left) to symbolize family affection. "Love thy wife at home as is fitting," counsels an ancient text. "Fill her belly; clothe her back. Ointment is the prescription for her body. Make her heart glad as long as thou livest."

WALL PAINTING IN TOMB OF NAKHT AT THEBES, 15TH CENTURY B.C.
UPPER: STATUES OF PRINCE RAHOTEP AND HIS WIFE NOFRET FROM HIS TOMB AT MAIDUM, 27TH–26TH CENTURIES B.C.; EGYPTIAN MUSEUM, CAIRO. LEFT: PAINTING BY H. M. HERGET

137

Meketre, "Great Steward and Governor of the Six Great Tribunals," inspects his herd

Enthroned in wood 40 centuries ago, the official sits on the portico as long-haired cowherds clout his cattle into line and scribes with shorn heads keep tally. Servants in tomb models, ushabtis or answerers, answered for the noble when the gods summoned him to toil in the afterlife. Stockmen of old worked with lasso and brand, called prized beasts by pet names such as "Golden" and "Brilliant." Egyptians dedicated herds and temples to Hathor, goddess in guise of a cow. Sacred bulls munched in sacred stalls amid mooing harems. When Joseph interpreted the "fatfleshed" and "leanfleshed" cows in Pharaoh's dream as omens of plenty and famine, the awed king "set him over the land of Egypt" (Genesis 41:33).

MODEL FROM TOMB OF MEKETRE AT THEBES, 21ST CENTURY B.C.; EGYPTIAN MUSEUM, CAIRO

Market day also brought out the militia. Grim-faced villagers pedaled in on bicycles, rifles strapped across their backs. I recalled ancient tensions in the Delta: Hyksos threatening from Asia, Ramesses preparing to march eastward.

I visited a village of doorless mud-brick houses jammed together into one big cocoon. Pigeons spiraled up from a sugarloaf-shaped dovecote and goats skittered off at my approach. In one home I found a bare floor with a bench piled with straw that served as a bed. A naked child stared at me. His pregnant mother smiled; arm bracelets rattled as she brushed the hair from her face. Such crude dwellings have scarcely changed since the Hebrew sojourn.

In the same village I was startled to see two men in loincloths shower golden straw onto mounds of black mud. Pharaoh's harsh command echoed down the ages: "Ye shall no more give the people straw to make brick . . . let them go and gather straw for themselves" (Exodus 5:7).

"Bow thy back to thy superior, thy overseer"

Patient hands and vigilant eyes made estate workshops hum. Portly brewmaster wields his scepter of authority (below) as the worker on his right cracks grain on a stone mortar and a woman grinds it to flour. In back men knead dough and bake loaves on a low oven, then tread them in jars with water. Men in center strain mash into vats whose midriff spouts draw off beer, leaving barm at top, dregs on bottom. Strenuous work, as the

*thrusting arms of a tomb figure
show (below), but the end product
slaked the national thirst.
Scribemasters railed at tippling
students: "you trail from street
to street, smelling of beer. . . .
you are like a broken rudder,
good for nothing. . . ."*

*Second in popularity only to
beer, wine was easier to make.
Pickers stripped the vine (bottom
right), then treaders pressed
the grapes. Wine aged in huge
jars labeled, as today, to show
the year and estate of origin—
but for tax men, not gourmets.*

*Clay vessels came from Qena,
where potters still favor age-old
styles (right)—but not the slow,
hand-turned wheels of antiquity.
Modern foot-powered wheel can
"throw" a pot in two minutes.*

*Early carpenter (center) tugs
at copper saw with both hands;
teeth cut on the pull. Weighted
stick keeps wood bound tight
to anchored post. Other workers
chisel grooves. They also worked
with adz, ax, scraper, bow drill.
Timber fleets from Phoenicia
brought cypress, cedar, fir, pine
to augment meager local woods.
Hardwood pegs and skillful
joinery made articles strong and
rigid; many remain so to this day.*

WINFIELD PARKS, NATIONAL GEOGRAPHIC PHOTOGRAPHER. OPPOSITE: PAINTING BY H. M. HERGET

TOMB RELIEF FROM SAQQARA, 26TH CENTURY B.C.; UNI-DIA VERLAG. LEFT: MODEL FROM SAQQARA, C. 26TH CENTURY B.C.;
EGYPTIAN MUSEUM, CAIRO. BELOW: WALL PAINTING IN TOMB OF NAKHT AT THEBES, 15TH CENTURY B.C.; HASSIA

GILDED HOUR OF DAWN *lights the way for a donkey-borne traveler in the Delta (below). Canal-side hamlets of adobe (from ancient* tobe, *or brick), each with its minaret, dot this thickly populated region between Cairo and the Mediterranean— a land of honey since Biblical days*

Up the Nile in El Ballas (The Po a potter takes a smoke break as children peer in his doorway.

Near Salamant, women bake stacks of thin bread called battaw. *The New Kingdom knew 40 kinds of baked goods. In those days bread sustained the dead as well as the living; nobles wished for "thousands of loaves" to supply their needs in the next world.*

The brickmakers worked the straw into the mud as a binder, shaped the bricks in wooden molds, and set them out to dry in the sun. They were proud men, well muscled. They asked me to tea, but I saw that they had no more time to pause for tea than to gather their own straw. I thanked them, then asked what their brick was for. The older man spread his mud-caked arms, embracing the entire village.

On our last day in Goshen, a banana truck blocked our narrow road. While Salama strove to get by, I watched young girls bringing up the green bunches on their heads. When two paused to gossip, the overseer tapped them with his stick. My thoughts turned to the event which wrenched Moses' life into a new direction.

"And it came to pass... when Moses was grown, that he went out unto his brethren, and looked on their burdens: and he spied an Egyptian smiting an Hebrew.... he slew the Egyptian, and hid him in the sand" (Exodus 2:11-12). Fearing retribution, Moses fled southeast to the land of Midian and began a new life as a shepherd. In that wilderness God would summon him to return and confront Pharaoh with the stirring demand, "Let my people go...."

I planned to follow Moses' trail. But first I would head south to survey landmarks of the great civilization which had nurtured him.

In the Footsteps of Moses: Part II

SPLENDID REALM OF THE PHARAOHS

Ascend the Nile to temples
and tombs that mirror
the lost world of god-kings.
John Putman shows the way

W E CLIMBED for 30 brutal minutes under a blazing sun, scuffing against massive sandstone blocks. Finally, gulping for air, I grasped my guide's outstretched hand and stepped atop the Great Pyramid of Cheops, 450 feet above the Giza plain. "You see, sair," Mohammed smiled, "there is no sight to match it in all Egypt."

Agreed. Eastward, green loops of the Nile snaked across the desert. Beside the river sat Cairo, a blue haze. Southward, lesser pyramids marched along the bluffs like toy figures. To the west, only sand.

Here began Upper Egypt, a desert-squeezed realm stretching 500 miles from Giza south to Nubia. If Moses came this way, the Bible does not record it. But the pharaohs of his time, even when they reigned from Tanis, came south to ancient shrines and cities to celebrate national festivals and build monuments. Many of their temples and tombs still stand; inscriptions on them speak from Moses' day:

"I have enlarged thy house in Memphis . . . with gold and genuine costly stones. . . . It is equipped with priests, prophets, peasant-slaves. . . . cattle beyond limit. . . . the fat thereof, it has reached heaven." Thus spake Ramesses II to Ptah, god of Memphis, creator of the world. No king rivaled the

VULTURE AND COBRA on *Tutankhamun's splendid mask symbolize Upper and Lower Egypt. Lifelike features of beaten gold fitted over his face. Forty years after the young king's death, Ramesses the Great, "Pharaoh of the Oppression," came to rule the Two Kingdoms and rekindle Egypt's imperial glory.*

F. L. KENETT © GEORGE RAINBIRD LTD.

145

*"Hail to thee,
O Nile....
making verdant
the two banks"*

traditional persecutor of the Hebrews as a builder. Of himself, he ordered it inscribed: "Lo, the Good God inclined his heart to make monuments; sleeping or waking, he ceased not seeking to do excellent things."

At Memphis, Egypt's most ancient capital, his statue, originally some 40 feet tall, sprawls in a shed. Outside, an alabaster sphinx smiles benignly on passing fellahin, while stately palms whisper of past glories. The rest is dust. Jeremiah's prophecy, issued long after Moses, has come true: "Memphis shall become a waste, a ruin, without inhabitant."

But the pyramids, already 1,300 years old in Ramesses' day, still stand in mystery and majesty, proclaiming the Old Kingdom pharaohs who built these "houses of eternity." The pyramids still wore white casing stones when Ramesses

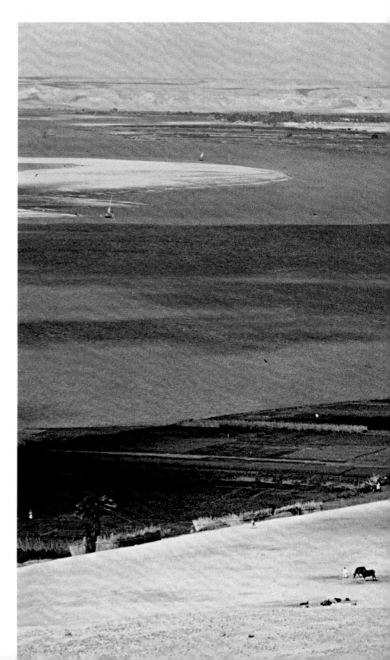

MARGARET DURRANCE. RIGHT: WINFIELD PARKS,
NATIONAL GEOGRAPHIC PHOTOGRAPHER

saw them, and reflected the rising sun like great mirrors. Not even Ramesses dared despoil them, as he did lesser monuments, taking their stone to build his own edifices. His son Khaemwese, a priest, haunted the tombs—restoring some, studying others, perhaps searching for lost wonders. For had not Thutmosis IV uncovered the Great Sphinx in the sands of Giza only a hundred-odd years earlier?

I could imagine Khaemwese leading his illustrious father, as Mohammed had led me, on a pyramid tour. Chariots would whisk them from Memphis up the bluff to Saqqara, where stands the Step Pyramid of Djoser, oldest free-standing stone structure in the world. They would have remembered its architect, legendary Imhotep, who "discovered the art of building with hewn stones, and occupied himself with

BEARING WATER *precious as blood, a daughter of the river (opposite) mirrors the ancients' hymn to the Nile: "When he rises, then the land is in jubilation . . . every backbone takes on laughter, and every tooth is exposed." For the river's fertile fringe makes "man and cattle to live!"*

Village of Beni Hasan and its beehive tombs in foreground stand on desert to save arable land for crops. Fellahin stride from sere to sown in one step. Cliff tombs here and ruins at nearby Tell el Amarna yielded knowledge of Pharaoh's realm.

So that Pharaoh might live forever
thousands toiled under the Egyptian sun
to raise man's mightiest monument in stone

HUMAN ANTS reared tombs for titans at Egypt's dawn. Early lords lay under mud-brick "mastabas," so named because they resemble benches. Then, about 4,600 years ago, the vizier Imhotep built one of stone for King Djoser, topping it with smaller ones to create a "step" pyramid. A century later, the true pyramid of Cheops (Khufu) dwarfed all others. Here is how experts believe the IVth Dynasty pharaoh organized his realm for the generation-long task of building his Great Pyramid:

Planners pick a site on bedrock. Entry must face north, so they make star sights. Crews box the base with a water-filled trench for a level. Stonecutters sink a crypt; others quarry nearby limestone outcrops. Upriver, gangs with names such as "Vigorous" and "Enduring" cut blocks, boat them to within three miles of the site. Massed muscle sledges them up a stone causeway, then up the tomb on spiraling earth and rubble ramps (shown in cutaway view) over planks cooled by water, possibly slicked by the butterfat in milk. At top, men lever stones into place, build in galleries and granite sarcophagus as they go, fitting joints with copper chisels. Twice Cheops redesigns: Crypts in base and bedrock go empty; instead an upper crypt with five stress-relieving chambers and two air vents awaits his mummy.

Jubilant crews top the 206-layer "Mountain of Pharaoh" with a gilded capstone. Removing ramps as they work down, they case the core's stepped sides in smooth white limestone and flank the pyramid with temples, tombs for kin and court, pits for funerary boats to buoy Cheops through eternity. After the god-king's awesome funeral, workers knock props away; huge blocks crash down to seal his tomb. Entry vanishes behind a final casing slab. The Great Pyramid covers 13 acres, contains 2,300,000 blocks averaging 2½ tons. Yet conscripted laborers and farmers idled by flood reared it without iron tools, the wheel, or the horse!

DRAWINGS BY WILLIAM H. BOND, GEOGRAPHIC ART DIVISION. BRONZE STATUETTE OF IMHOTEP IN THE LOUVRE, PARIS

IMHOTEP BUILT FIRST PYRAMID

MASTABA STEMS FROM BURIAL MOUND

SIX MASTABAS FORM STEP PYRAMID

SLOPES OF GREAT PYRAMID SHIELD MAZE OF CORRIDORS AND CRYPTS

enthusiasm in writing." Scribes of Ramesses' day often spilled drops of water in his honor. Later, Egyptians and Greeks worshiped him as a god of healing. Pilgrims flocked to his tomb, leaving in the honeycomb tunnels mummified ibises—sacred birds representing Thoth, god of magicians and scribes. As I strolled the 4,500-year-old temple complex, workmen hauled sand from a great pit where archeologists sought the great scribe's tomb.

Inscriptions in the nearby pyramid of Unis reveal the motive for building these great piles: "O King . . . thou hast not at all departed dead, thou hast departed living! For thou sittest upon the throne of Osiris, with thy scepter in thy hand, that thou mightest give command to the living. . . ." At death the king spiritually became one with Osiris, god of the afterlife. For the well-being of the spirit the body must be preserved and equipped with life's needs. In valley temples, richly endowed during life, priests daily chanted prayers and made offerings of food.

It was also written that the king's *ba*, or soul, sailed with the sun god, vanishing each evening into the western hills and the underworld below. For these journeys planks of precious cedar of Lebanon—shaped and prepared for assembly into heavenly barks—lay in pits beside Cheops' Great Pyramid.

The idea of immortality was pleasing. Yet if Ramesses ascended the great gallery of Cheops' tomb to the small chamber at its heart and glimpsed its empty sarcophagus, he may well have sensed the pang expressed by a poet of an earlier day:

> *The Gods that were aforetime rest in their Pyramids. . . .*
> *None cometh from thence that he may tell us how they fare,*
> *That he may tell us what they need, that he may set our hearts at rest,*
> *Until we also go to the place whither they are gone.*

MAN-MADE MOUNTAINS *jut from seas of sand at Giza. "Nowhere are there so many marvelous things . . . so many works of unspeakable greatness," wrote Herodotus about Egypt. The pyramids were as ancient to the Greek historian of the fifth century* B.C. *as he is to us. Yet wonder remains as we gaze on the Great Pyramid of Cheops (right), rising 450 feet. Nearness enlarges smaller tombs of Chephren (center) and Mycerinus. All three lost limestone facing to later builders; a remnant clings to apex of Chephren's pile. "All the world fears Time," say Egyptians, "but Time fears the pyramids."*

JOSEPH J. SCHERSCHEL, NATIONAL GEOGRAPHIC PHOTOGRAPHER

PYRAMIDS BESPEAK the dead; Cairo proclaims the living. Yet even here I could not escape Ramesses. One of his obelisks pierces the sky above Gezira Island in the Nile. In the Egyptian Museum, crowded with the treasures and images of pharaohs and nobles, he stared at me from giant pink granite heads and a colossal statue. In the museum's Mummy Room, I gazed on his very face—shrunken, cracked with age (page 162). X-rays indicate he was plagued with toothache. He had teeth missing, abscesses, cavities, receding gums. Still, a hint remains of the good looks and the vigor that marked his early years.

His granite image towers even at the railway station. Around it, like Nile floodwaters, swirl workbound streams of humanity. How I love this city, half modern, half medieval, totally Egyptian.

In the covered bazaar of Khan el Khaliili, children hammered arabesque designs into brass trays and gnome-like men inlaid cedar boxes with mother of pearl, reminding me of ancient arts. In tiny shops I sipped Turkish coffee while bargaining for attar of roses or tiny scarabs and mummy beads. I joined evening strollers along the fashionable

ETERNAL PYRAMIDS *nick a gilt-edged horizon (below); glow of modernity bejewels Cairo, Egypt's capital by the Nile.*

Medieval pilgrims called the pyramids "Joseph-barns"; inside, they said, Joseph stored grain against the seven lean years.

Of the nearby Sphinx (left) —seven stories high, nearly a football field in length—they saw only a head above drifted sand. Workers cleared it in 1926. So did Thutmosis IV in the 15th century B.C., *says a stela found near its paws. He thought it a sun god. Experts now say the lion-bodied statue, carved from an outcrop 4,500 years ago, portrays Chephren and guards his tomb. The centuries have battered his face*

Treasures of the pharaohs awe visitors to the Egyptian Museum (right); mirror gives top view of Tutankhamun's solid-gold coffin.

GEORGE HOLTON, PHOTO RESEARCHERS. RIGHT: HELEN AND FRANK SCHREIDER, NATIONAL GEOGRAPHIC STAFF
OPPOSITE UPPER: WILLIAM EPPRIDGE

Kasr el Nil, lingering at Groppi's to sample delicate pastel candies fashioned into flower-bud shapes.

In the twisting, poorly lit streets of the old quarter below the citadel of Saladin, I heard the wail of Arab music, the clip-clop of donkey carts, the shouts of vendors. Here the smells of living animals and roasting lamb mix with city dust and Nile mist—and men eye you sharply, for life is lived on the edge. Here I felt some sense of ancient Egypt's crowded cities. The poor hauled straw mats out into parks and gardens to sleep in the cool night air.

THE CAIRO-LUXOR SPECIAL rattled through the night, hot, sticky, jammed. Traveling third class, I had only Egyptians for companions. We sat four abreast, swaying, staring straight ahead as a thickening layer of dust settled on window sills and passengers. One woman nursed a baby. A fat man in a red fez flicked a whisk back and forth.

On an earlier trip aboard the Special I had sat with a young police official and his wife, a beautiful woman with the features of Nefertiti. They were bound for his first major assignment. Like so many Egyptians, he regarded his ancient heritage as personal property. "I've read Breasted," he announced, and went on to discuss the classic history of Egypt by the American scholar James Henry Breasted.

NIMBLE FINGERS *have woven bright threads of artistry through 7,000 years of Egyptian life. Village girl near Luxor weaves colorful place mats of bamboo, which sprouts along the Nile. Mat maker, squatting in his mud-brick home, uses local reeds.*

Ancients wove the papyrus plant, source of primitive paper, into mats, ropes, and sandals. Bundles of the sturdy seven-foot stalks served as skiffs, also supported roofs. These pillars evolved into the colossal papyrus columns, carved in stone, that uphold many New Kingdom templ

Abundant flax, woven into linen provided the clothing, shrouds, and sails of Pharaoh's realm. Then history records garments of about 550 B.C. embroidered with "wool from a tree"—cotton. In time it replaced linen, calling to mind Isaiah's prophecy: "The workers in combed flax will be in despair" (19:9). Today cotton leads Egypt's industry.

JOSEPH J. SCHERSCHEL, NATIONAL GEOGRAPHIC PHOTOGRAPHER

SACRED LAKE *at Karnak reflects a*
remnant of the glory that was Thebe
Two thousand years of building,
two thousand more of siege, fire,
earthquake, and decay mark the
world's largest columned temple.
Pharaohs raised it to honor Amun,
patron-god of their capital.

They spiked the sky with obelisks
monoliths barged from Aswan on th
largest ships the world had seen.
Two shafts still stand: that of
Thutmosis I and a taller one on
which daughter Hatshepsut lavished
"bushels of gold, as though I had
been pouring out sacks of grain."

First pylon, largest of a
dozen monumental gateways, hulks
to left (above) — beside the pillared
hypostyle hall. Boasts of Ramesses I
encircle the mighty columns (left),
134 in all. This hall could swallow
Notre Dame cathedral in Paris;
but no congregation gathered here.
Egypt's temples were fortresslike
palaces of the gods, who dwelt in
dim inner chambers away from the
sun-drenched swirl of life.

Across the Nile, temples and tomb
of Western Thebes awaited the dead.

Of the rising flood of tourists, he sputtered: "Some come for only four days, two at Cairo, two at Luxor. It is impossible to learn anything about Egypt in such a time." Nefertiti placed her hand on his. "Of course," he added, "even the briefest visitor may be stimulated to return."

They left the train near Tell el Amarna, home of the original Nefertiti and her heretic husband, Pharaoh Akhenaten, worshiper of a single deity, the sun disk Aten. Here, halfway between Memphis and Thebes, Akhenaten set about building a dream city of palaces and gardens. He called it "my testimony forever."

Today nothing remains. His city was abandoned, his name obliterated, his throne ascended by his son-in-law Tutankhamun. But he and Nefertiti, symbol of Egyptian beauty, still reign in rock-cut tombs nearby. Reliefs show them kissing on a chariot ride, dispensing gifts, romping with their

"Thebes shall be breached, and its walls broken down"

Ezekiel 30:16

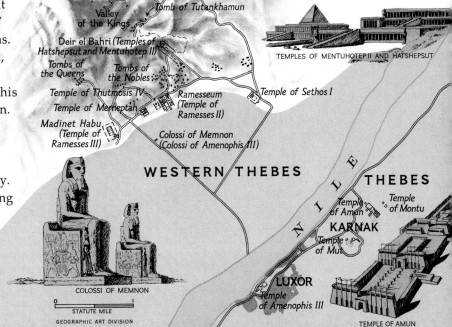

Tomb of Tutankhamun

Valley of the Kings

Deir el Bahri *(Temples of Hatshepsut and Mentuhotep II)*

Tombs of the Queens

Tombs of the Nobles

Temple of Thutmosis IV

Temple of Merneptah

Ramesseum (Temple of Ramesses II)

Temple of Sethos I

Madinet Habu (Temple of Ramesses III)

Colossi of Memnon (Colossi of Amenophis III)

TEMPLES OF MENTUHOTEP II AND HATSHEPSUT

WESTERN THEBES

NILE

THEBES

Temple of Amun

Temple of Montu

KARNAK

Temple of Mut

LUXOR

Temple of Amenophis III

COLOSSI OF MEMNON

0 STATUTE MILE 1

GEOGRAPHIC ART DIVISION

TEMPLE OF AMUN

daughters. No other pharaoh appears in such intimate portrayals. But Akhenaten's religious and artistic pursuits cost Egypt dearly; he had little time for affairs of state.

The cuneiform archives of Tell el Amarna, discovered by a peasant in 1887, reveal frantic pleas for Akhenaten's help from client kings in Asia. One missive from Jerusalem urges: "So let the king, the lord, care for his land. . . . The Habiru plunder all the lands of the king." The Habiru! Here on Egyptian records appears the name of these elusive people, identified by some scholars with the Hebrews.

Ramesses would have shunned the city of the heretic Akhenaten. He would have felt much happier at Abydos, sacred city of Osiris, where religious dramas recalled the legends of that all-important deity. Osiris was slain and dismembered by his jealous brother Seth, buried by his sister and wife Isis—whose tears swelled the Nile in an annual rebirth of the valley—and avenged by their son Horus. Resurrected, he offered eternal life to every man.

At Abydos Ramesses built two splendid temples that still stand, one dedicated to himself, another to his father Sethos I. Here as elsewhere, when he saw a chance to propagandize, Ramesses left no stone uncarved. One inscription has his father say of him, "Crown him as king, that I may see his beauty while I live with him."

On numerous other inscriptions Ramesses testifies to his own valor as a young warrior king. He captured Ashkelon "when it was wicked," and desolated Acre. In his greatest battle he met the Hittites at Kadesh on the Orontes in Syria. Surprised and cut off from his main force, he leaped into his chariot and charged the foe until "I found the twenty-five hundred spans of chariotry . . . becoming heaps of corpses before my horses."

Such claims gained him the title "Ramesses the Great" among moderns, but most scholars believe he blundered into a trap and narrowly escaped through personal bravery. Nearly 30 years later he signed a treaty of "good peace and brotherhood" with the Hittite king, who sent his daughter as a bride with a splendid dowry. The girl "was beautiful in the heart of his majesty."

T HE SUN STREAMED through dust-caked train windows, and we awoke to find our car aflame with orange light. Outside, fellahin headed for the fields pressed between bluff and river, while black-garbed women clustered like crows around morning fires. A whistle blast signaled our entry into Luxor, and we leaned from opened windows for a better view. Ancient Egyptians knew the town as Weset or "the city." Homer sang of it as Thebes, "city where rich are the houses in treasure, a hundred has she of gates. . . ." The modern name means "castles," and recalls the fabled ruins that draw tourists by plane, train, and boatload.

Here New Kingdom pharaohs launched Egypt's glorious Age of Empire. Each triumph called for new monuments and additions to old ones. A horse carriage whisked me north along the Nile, past shops and market stalls to the columned Temple of Amun at Karnak, largest ever raised by man, 2,000 years abuilding.

Ramesses' grand avenue of sphinxes led to the first pylon, a fortresslike gateway spreading 370 feet, rising 100, and formed by two sloping towers. In the forecourt, larger than a football field, I gazed on colossi, heroic reliefs, and minor temples. A second pylon opened onto a forest of stone—the famed hypostyle hall of Ramesses and his father. Here sandstone columns soar 69 feet; some still hold seven-ton beams of the clerestory that allowed light to penetrate the gloom. In this

STRUMMING HARP, *pulsing drum, and wailing pipe enlivened ancient festivals. Song soothed the gods, gladdened men, drove evil from mothers at birth. Its spell endures as a Luxor musician thumps a* tabla *(below); pipers at Beni Suef puff on the* mizmaar *(lower right); and a procession wends to Nag Hammadi's mosque to nasal notes. "Call no halt to music and dance, but bid all care begone," urges the ancient Song of the Harper.*

reception hall pilgrims and petitioners awaited the pleasure of priests and scribes.

I came at last to a small building, the innermost shrine of the god Amun, where only priests and kings could enter. Each morning a priest swung a censer to purify the area with the scent of terebinth resin. Breaking a clay seal on the sanctuary door, he prostrated himself before the god's gilt image, anointed it with unguents, and chanted hymns of adoration. He offered it a model of the eye of the falcon god

FIERY DAWN strikes ramparts of Western Thebes, city of the dead. Below spreads Deir el Bahri and the shrine of a queen who became king. Regent for her nephew, Thutmosis III, Hatshepsut seized the crown and proclaimed herself Pharaoh. Artists, depicting her as a male, clad her in kilt and beard. Court favorite Senmut·studded Egypt with her memorials. Her expedition to Punt (probably the Somali coast) fetched myrrh trees for these terraces. She drops abruptly from history; Thutmosis defaced her images, sought to obliterate her name and afterlife. Oblivion held a special dread for the ancients: "His remembrance shall perish from the earth, and he shall have no name" (Job 18:17).

DAVID S. BOYER, NATIONAL GEOGRAPHIC STAFF

"You will live again, you will live again forever!"

BAG and baggage, a wealthy Theban moves into his eternal dwelling while mummers dance and mourners wail in the New Kingdom funeral scene at right.

Oxen drew the mummy up from the river in a hearse shaped like a solar boat. Canopic chest, also on a sledge, contains stone jars preserving vital organs. Jackal-masked priest, impersonating Anubis, the divine embalmer, holds the carved, gilded coffin upright before the tomb chapel. In a final rite, priests "open the mouth" of the deceased, restoring the ability to move, to talk, and to eat.

Now mummy and furnishings will be borne down into a richly decorated multi-chambered tomb, tunneled perhaps a hundred feet into the living rock. Formulas in a papyrus Book of the Dead placed near the body will guide it past obstacles and dangers (such as agony in the Lake of Fire) on its journey in quest of reunion with the *ka,* or spirit.

Unless the body were preserved from decay, the spirit would fail to recognize it. There could be no rebirth, no eternal second life similar to the first, and the spirit would be condemned to search forever for a body that no longer existed. Thus the need for a mummy.

The 70-day ritual of mummification evoked the resurrection of Osiris. While a priest intoned, embalmers drew the brain out through the nostrils with hooks, then cut open the left flank to remove the viscera—save for the heart, seat of will and intelligence, which stayed with the body. They cleansed the abdomen with palm wine, filled it with crushed myrrh and cassia and dehydrated the shaven body in natron, a natural soda. After washing and anointing it, they wrapped it in hundreds of yards of resin-soaked linen (below), introducing amulets between the layers. Only the rich could afford this. Exit for the poor was a ritual cleansing and a hole in the sand.

During their sojourn in Egypt, the Hebrews apparently followed local custom. Genesis 50 relates that when Jacob died, Joseph ordered "the physicians to embalm his father." And when Joseph died, "they embalmed him, and he was put in a coffin in Egypt."

NATHAN BENN. ABOVE: PAINTING BY H. M. HERGET

COPY BY ROSELLINI OF WALL PAINTING, TOMB OF AMENEMOPET, 14TH CENTURY B.C.

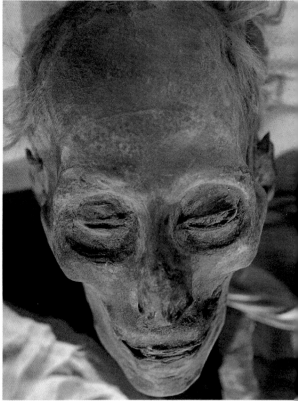

RAMESSES II *still seems to dream of glory after 32 centuries. Yet untold riches and life-and-death power over multitudes could not rid him of toothache. X-rays reveal that the god-king, who died at about 90, was a dental cripple.*

Horus and a statuette of Maat—truth and justice—the daughter of the sun god Re. Then he washed, dressed, and perfumed it, and burned food in front of it.

Only on great festivals like New Year's did the people share in sacred rites; Ramesses himself officiated. While a flotilla gathered on the Nile, the king in the temple sprinkled a libation. Priests lifted the small sacred boats containing the shrines of Amun and other gods and bore them to the barges. At a signal from Ramesses, sailors on the towpath hauled the fleet upstream toward the Temple of Luxor, where the gods would visit for a month. Pennants flew, musicians urged on the toilers while throngs applauded. One song survives: "There is a welcoming inn, its awning facing south. There is a welcoming inn, its awning facing north. Drink, sailors of the Pharaoh, beloved of Amun, praised of the gods."

Soon the barges tied up and priests carried the sacred barks between offering tables laden with food to the temple. Female acrobats performed to the rhythm of castanet, drum, and sistrum. As the procession vanished into the temple, the people gave themselves up to revelry, singing, "The gods of heaven shout for joy. . . . The inhabitants are drunk with wine, chaplets of flowers are on their heads. . . . All the children rejoice . . . from the rising to the setting of the sun."

I boarded a little skiff, popularly dubbed a felucca, at Luxor and crossed the Nile to Western Thebes. Here barren hills hold the famed necropolis, the Valley of the Kings. Thutmosis I started it, boring his tomb deep into the rock, "no one seeing, no one hearing." The quarrymen saw and heard but did not tell.

For generations mummified pharaohs had also made the river crossing in funeral processions. At the mortuary temple a son or trusted official touched the king's

mouth and eyes with a ceremonial adz to open them to eternal life. The following dawn, the procession moved on to the necropolis, where the king was laid to rest. Outside his sepulcher that night, torches lit an immense tent filled with banqueters. Mourning was over; now songs and dances evoked the act of creation.

Few held illusions as to the security of the tombs; grave robbing was too old a story. Of all the royal tombs, only Tutankhamun's preserved its mortuary treasures.

SENNEDJEM AND HIS WIFE (left) *have consorted with the gods since the reign of Ramesses II. Here the Theban official greets some of the 42 deities who will assess whether he led a righteous life on earth. They sit behind white-crowned Osiris (upper panel) and falcon-headed Horus, who wears the sun disk. Above a frieze of sacred cobras,*

twin jackals of Anubis face the eyes of Horus. On wall at right, Anubis in priestly form embalms Sennedjem, whose heart he will weigh against the feather of truth in final judgment before Osiris, ruler of the dead. Osiris stands to right in his usual mummy wrappings, grasping crook and scourge. Green skin symbolizes life's renewal in spring.

165

In the 12th century B.C., priests collected 33 desecrated mummies and hid them in a single tomb. Some 3,000 years later, a local family found them and began to sell items to dealers in Cairo and Alexandria. In the late 1800's agents of Gaston Maspero, French chief of the Egyptian Antiquities Service, pried the secret from the finders and penetrated the tomb. The grisly cache included Ramesses and his father.

I recalled other seekers of antiquities who roamed these hills of death: Giovanni Belzoni, Italian strongman turned archeologist, who used a battering ram to enter tombs where "Every step I took I crushed a mummy in some part or other"; and Edwin Smith, Connecticut Yankee and "Theban hermit," who entertained the Prince of Wales, later Edward VII, by going down a 90-foot shaft and bringing up 30 mummies and coffins. His activities scandalized many scholars, but none denied the greatness of his discovery of papyri detailing medical instructions like these:

"Examination: If thou examinest a man having a wound in the top of his eyebrow, penetrating to the bone, thou shouldst palpate the wound, and draw together for him his gash with stitching. . . . Now after thou hast stitched it, thou shouldst bind fresh meat upon it the first day. . . . and thou shouldst treat it with grease and honey every day until he recovers."

ONE MAY FLY south from Luxor to Aswan to reach the upriver monuments, but the proper way to approach Abu Simbel and the Biblical "Land of Cush" (Sudan) is to travel by boat, as the pharaohs did. When the steamer casts off and sets itself against the current, you ride the bloodstream of Egypt and share the sense of excitement known to countless generations of Egyptians.

At dusk your imagination may conjure ancient scenes: Graceful lotus-stemmed vessels glide upriver, squarish sails bellied by the constant north wind, rowers

FOUNDERING FOREST *of date palms proffers its last harvest as the Nile rises behind Aswan High Dam, Egypt's "wall against hunger." Storing water from fat years to nourish the lean, the 364-foot-tall barrier will make a million acres of desert bloom—a blessing to the 99 percent of Egypt's people who dwell on less than 4 percent of her land. Containing enough material for 17 Great Pyramids, the dam (completed since the author's visit) houses generators that feed electricity to the nation's industry. But to save the future meant to drown the past.*

As reservoir waters chewed into deserted villages as far as 300 miles upstream, engineers cursing Nubia's heat in a babel of tongues raced to salvage two dozen monuments, including El Dakka's temple (left).

GEORG GERSTER

166

TEMPLE OF DANDUR, *destined for a new home on the Hudson, rose beside the Nile in Nubia during the reign of Augustus. It honors the gods Isis and Osiris—also two heroes drowned in the Nile. Copts (early Egyptian Christians) used the temple as a chapel.*

Carvings adorn the sandstone shrine, which is 41 feet long, 21 wide, 21 high, with two chambers and an antechamber. Guardian cobras flank a solar disk above the gateway, floodlighted (below) as workmen take measurements prior to dismantling and eventual shipment to the United States.

Egypt presented the 2,000-year-old temple, threatened by Aswan waters, to the nation for its help in saving the Nubian monuments. New York's Metropolitan Museum of Art plans to reassemble the 660 pieces of its "most important acquisition in decades" in a glass-enclosed extension.

resting silently, two steersmen at the sweeps. At the bow a sailor probes the channel with a pole. Astern, a minstrel with a harp and a flutist serenade noble passengers. A passing vessel sweeps by, sail furled, rowers bent, its cargo of gold, ostrich feathers, ebony, panther skins, and ivory from central Africa lashed to the deck.

Like milestones, temples and sites glide by: Nekhen, ancient before the pyramids; Idfu, with its temple of Horus, built when the Ptolemies ruled Egypt; Kom Ombo, ancient Ombos, with its unique double temple. And then, Aswan.

Here dark granite reefs and white water signal the Nile's First Cataract, where Middle Kingdom pharaohs ordered a channel cut through the rocks. On Elephantine Island sat a viceroy, "Keeper of the Door of the South."

On the island a stone Nilometer still measures the river's annual rise. Anxiously the ancients sought to read on it the Nile's whim: "If he is sluggish the nostrils are stopped up, and all men are brought low; the offerings of the gods are diminished, and millions perish from among mankind."

Some 700 years after Moses, the Egyptian garrison here included a colony of Jews who fled their homeland in the face of Babylonian conquest. Their records, the famed Elephantine Papyri, reveal that they still observed Jewish marriage laws and festivals. How ironic that the descendants of the children of Israel who escaped Egypt's bondage should one day return seeking sanctuary.

Today the river's tyranny seems at an end; a few miles upstream thousands of workers toil on a project to rival the pyramids—Sadd el Aali, the new Aswan High Dam. Ramesses would have envied its size and enjoyed decorating its massive flanks with his endless inscriptions.

Impounded water will irrigate 1,000,000 previously barren acres, a dramatic gain for a nation which must feed an ever-growing population. But there is a price to pay. The backed-up waters will inundate all of Egyptian Nubia and part of Sudanese Nubia.

As I coursed the Nile, archeologists from a score of nations raced to complete the excavation of ancient sites. From the hydrofoils that speed south from Aswan to Abu Simbel, passengers glimpsed Nile-side temples being sliced up and packed off to higher ground. The ancient names rolled on the tongue: El Maharraqa, El Sibu, Amada, Qasr Ibrim. . . .

SANDSTONE SHINS *of Ramesses II front his Great Temple at Abu Simbel. The cliff-hewn colossi, inscribed by travelers for centuries, weathered 3,200 years before the rising Nile threatened to engulf them. One inscription reveals that Greek mercenaries passed here in 590* B.C.
GEORG GERSTER

169

HERCULEAN *face-lifting rescued Ramesses' most spectacular work from a watery grave. The god-king, whose monuments to his own glory extend from Lebanon to Nubia, built his Great Temple (right) and the neighboring Small Temple for Queen Nefertari on the southern fringe of the civilized world. The wilderness site challenged his architects; moving the temples challenged 20th-century engineers of many nations.*

Egypt and UNESCO, *the United Nations Educational, Scientific and Cultural Organization, chose to cut the shrines into giant jigsaw puzzles and reassemble the 1,060 keyed pieces 212 feet above the doomed site (below). To protect the 67-foot colossi (a head broke off centuries ago) during removal of the cliff top, sand was piled around them. Inside the Great Temple, steel beams braced halls, chambers, and the sanctuary where gods sat stonily awaiting the sun.*

In October, 1965, stonecutters with a surgeon's skill sawed off Ramesses' 19-ton face (opposite). A year later the temples stood rebuilt high above the Nile.

And the people of Nubia—proud descendants of the Wawat, Irthet, and Mazoi tribes that both plagued the pharaohs and served as their finest infantry—were already deserting their drowning land. Villages became ghost towns. But he who has passed this way will never forget how it was: Nubian women, attired for a festival in pink and white veils, golden necklaces and nose rings, and rainbow-hued bracelets. The pulse of drums and tambourines spurring a sword dancer to frenzy. White paintings of flowers, birds, steamboats, and scorpions brightening adobe houses.

The Nubians lived on a pitifully narrow rim of Nile-nourished green, and it was never enough. Men in their prime went to Cairo and Alexandria for work. Now in the great uprooting, 25,000 families—100,000 people—were

shifting north to Kom Ombo, to settle in neat and orderly government-built villages. Perhaps one day, when the great lake is stabilized, they will return to Nubia. But by then they may be Egyptians, not Nubians.

"HE MADE IT as his monument for . . . Nefertari, beloved of Mut—a house hewn in the pure mountain of Nubia, of fine, white and enduring sandstone, as an eternal work." Though the inscription adorns the temple of Ramesses' favorite wife at Abu Simbel, it also describes his own majestic temple, bored into the cliffside by "multitudes of workmen from the captivity of his sword."

With Abu Simbel, Ramesses capped his reign. Inscriptions do not record a visit, but I like to think of him celebrating a jubilee there. Amid pomp and ceremony he could look back on his considerable achievements—battles won, peoples subdued, treaties signed, some 110 children sired. And now he had a temple to match any in Egypt. The Old Kingdom might claim the pyramids; Thebes was wrought by many. But Abu Simbel was his alone.

Ramesses ruled a remarkable 67 years, a period that saw Egypt's glory peak once more, then decline. Studying his withered face in the museum in Cairo, seeing his famed Abu Simbel temples carved into neat blocks and transported atop bluffs they once dominated, inevitably invites us to meditate on the fate of mortal man. No one put it

Army of artisans creates a shrine worthy of a god-king

"As the sun comes up above the eastern hill-tops, one long, level beam strikes through the doorway, pierces the inner darkness like an arrow, penetrates to the sanctuary, and falls like fire from heaven upon the altar at the feet of the Gods." Thus did Amelia Edwards, novelist-Egyptologist who visited Abu Simbel in 1874, attest to the ancients' skill.

Putting their knowledge of astronomy to work, Pharaoh's engineers lined up the axis of the Great Temple so that twice yearly—in mid-February and mid-October—the sun would shine into the innermost chamber 180 feet from the entrance and bless the statues of Ramesses and of Amun, god of Thebes.

Guided by the painted red line established by the sun's rays, masons smoothed the face of a cliff into a pylon, traditional entrance to an Egyptian temple. Draftsmen, projecting the red line onto the rock, drew lines to help proportion the four colossi of Ramesses and the family figures between his legs.

Stonecutters chipped away the background, and monolithic blocks emerged. Stairsteps representing feet, lap, and double crown of Egypt evolved into robotlike forms. Sculptors with mallet and bronze chisel softened harsh lines into muscular legs, chests, and arms. Others molded lips more than three feet wide.

Clambering over scaffolding, painters with fiber brushes applied red ocher to the monarch's body, following a standardized color scheme. Sand and weather have long since erased the hues.

PAINTINGS BY ROBERT W. NICHOLSON,
NATIONAL GEOGRAPHIC STAFF ARTIST,
AND (OPPOSITE, LOWER) PIERRE MION

better than the poet Shelley, inspired by the great fallen colossus of Ramesses at Thebes:

> *. . . Two vast and trunkless legs of stone*   *". . . Look on my works, ye Mighty, and despair!"*
> *Stand in the desert. Near them, on the sand,*   *Nothing beside remains. Round the decay*
> *Half sunk, a shattered visage lies . . .*   *Of that colossal wreck, boundless and bare*
> *And on the pedestal these words appear:*   *The lone and level sands stretch far away.*

How much more enduring would be the spiritual achievement of Moses, whose exodus from bondage with the children of Israel I would now trace.

A LIVING GOD *walks the earth as Ramesses, Nefertari at his side, dedicates his own monument. The celebration, mid-October in 1274 B.C., marks his 30-year jubilee. History fails to tell if Ramesses ever visited the Great Temple; the artist followed a similar scene carved inside. To the blare of trumpets and beat of drums, priests shoulder the solar boat bearing images of the gods out to greet the sun. Draped linen hides the sacred figures from common eyes. The king wears the blue crown of the New Kingdom and carries royal crook and staff. The queen holds sistra, musical instruments sacred to Hathor; headdress of horns, disk, and feathers also honors the goddess. Falcons of Horus adorn bow and stern of the solar boat.*

175

TO SINAI AND

THE PROMISED LAND

Join modern pilgrims as they trace
the Exodus to the Mount of the Law,
and with John Putman follow Moses' trail
to the gateway of the Jordan Valley

BYZANTINE MOSAIC FROM ST. CATHERINE'S MONASTERY; FRED ANDEREGG, MOUNT SINAI EXPEDITIONS

TWO-THIRTY A.M. A knock at the door and a lusty shout, "Rise, pilgrims, we're on our way to Sinai!" I roll out of the sagging bed that characterizes my hotel room in Suez and slip into sweater and slacks. Doors slam and the murmur of voices builds as we gather in the dining room to gulp down bread and eggs. I am reminded of the Lord's instructions to Moses when the Hebrews prepared to leave Egypt: "with your loins girded, your shoes on your feet . . . ye shall eat . . . in haste" (Exodus 12:11).

We pile suitcases and food cartons atop Suez taxis— old American cars strengthened for desert work—already laden with spare wheels. We slide through dark, silent

"BEHOLD, THE BUSH BURNED *with fire, and the bush was not consumed" (Exodus 3:2). Here the Lord commands Moses: "put off thy shoes . . . for the place whereon thou standest is holy ground."*

Dwelling among the Midianites, Moses has herded a flock onto the "mountain of God"—called both Horeb and Sinai. Worshipers doffed sandals at such shrines. But God demands more of Moses: Return to Egypt "that thou mayest bring forth my people. . . ."

178

streets to the Suez Canal and cross, three cars at a time, on a rattling, wheezing ferry. Listening to the parting of ink-black waters at the bow, I think of those who have journeyed to Sinai before us: Stone Age hunters, prisoners bound for Pharaoh's mines, hermits and pilgrims, Byzantine bureaucrats and Arab conquerors, Crusaders and caravaneers, Bedouin freebooters, explorers, oil drillers. And Moses and the children of Israel.

In quest of Moses' footsteps, I had traveled like the Hebrews from Raamses to Succoth—modern Tell el Maskhuta, where lizards crawl amid crumbling brick walls built perhaps by Hebrew hands. I had gazed on rush-choked lakes near the ancient "Reed Sea," believed by scholars to be the "Red sea" of the Exodus. A gauntlet of police posts near Ismailiya helped me understand the Hebrews' decision to avoid the usual road to Canaan—the fortified "way of the land of the Philistines"—and to strike south. No man knows the precise Exodus route; the Hebrews left no mark on desert or mountain. But scholars have compared Bible narrative to geography, archeological discoveries, and tradition to determine the probable course.

The route took me alongside the Suez Canal, where great freighters seemed to steam through seas of sand, and around the Great Bitter Lake, where convoys meet and pass. At last I had come to Suez, its streets fragrant with the aroma of spiced meatballs sizzling on sidewalk grills, enlivened by the clang of horse cabs and the *hiss-s-s-s-s* of bicyclists as they scattered pedestrians. Arab dhows from the Indian Ocean and gossamer-winged local fishing craft rimmed its harbor.

Here I had met my fellow pilgrims: Dr. Otto Meinardus, our leader, an authority on Eastern Christian rites from the American University in Cairo; some of his colleagues and trustees; and American embassy people. We were a score, aged 16 to 60—a "mixed multitude."

The ferry bumped, and we stepped ashore on Sinai's fabled sands. The tricorn-shaped peninsula links Africa to Asia. Vast and desolate, it remains even today a frontier province. We rolled south along the coastal road, so rough that we often drove on the desert shoulder. We passed oil fields beside the Gulf of Suez, where tankers swung

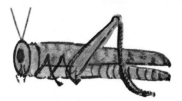

"And I will...smite Egypt with all my wonders"

Exodus 3:20

WHEN Pharaoh refuses to heed Moses' plea, "Let my people go," God sends plague after plague to scourge Egypt. The Nile turns to blood. Frogs, gnats, flies infest the land. Disease wipes out herds. Boils torture man and beast. Hail ruins young crops; locusts (above) devour what is left. A "darkness which may be felt" keeps men indoors three days. When Egypt's firstborn die—Pharaoh's son among them—the ruler relents.

Extraordinary as they seem, these plagues have natural counterparts today. Silt and microbes sometimes pollute and redden the Nile in flood. "The River," laments a text ancient in Moses' day, "is blood. If one drinks of it, one rejects it as human and thirsts for water."

Floodlands breed gnats and mosquitoes; even ancients took refuge under netting. Frogs breed when the river peaks; hordes hop ashore from freak floods. Heket, goddess of fertility and birth, often appears frog-headed. A frog (below) was her hieroglyph; a tadpole signified 100,000 or a multitude.

As frog swarms die, vermin breed on the carcasses. Pests such as the screwworm fly inflame skin of man and beast, sometimes killing animals.

Though hailstorms rarely hit Egypt, locusts menace it still. Some African swarms blanket 2,000 square miles, stripping the land, fouling the air with excrement, triggering epidemics as locust bodies rot. Modern Egypt has tried traps, poisons, even flamethrowers, but swarms still threaten devastation about once a decade.

And the khamsin still howls— the hot desert sandstorm that darkens spring days and clogs nostrils.

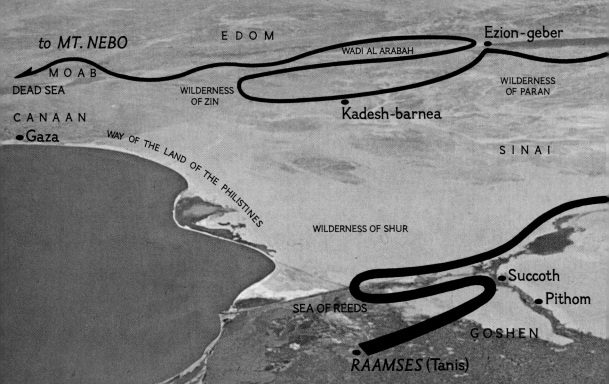

ARABIAN DESERT

MIDIAN

to MT. NEBO

EDOM

Ezion-geber

WADI AL ARABAH

MOAB

WILDERNESS
OF PARAN

DEAD SEA

WILDERNESS
OF ZIN

Kadesh-barnea

CANAAN

Gaza

WAY OF THE LAND OF THE PHILISTINES

SINAI

WILDERNESS OF SHUR

Succoth

Pithom

SEA OF REEDS

GOSHEN

RAAMSES (Tanis)

DAMIETTA MOUTH
OF THE NILE

Route of the Exodus led
to a land of "milk and honey"

*Footsteps to freedom track across an orbiting astronaut's photograph.
Probable path writhes from the Nile Delta's green webfoot
through barren Sinai to distant Dead Sea bluffs. Moses bypassed
Egyptian forts, sought waterholes, shunned patrolled trade routes
like the "way of the land of the Philistines." Forty years enroute,
the Hebrews trekked perhaps but two, sojourning the rest
in the region round Kadesh-barnea whence spies probed Canaan.
In the crucible of Sinai, the faith of Israel was forged.
Like panting pack mules, automobiles gape and cool (right)
as the author's Mount Sinai-bound caravan pauses in the
"wilderness of Sin," where the Israelites ate quail and manna.*

EGYPT

MEDITERRANEAN SEA

ROSETTA MOUTH
OF THE NILE

N

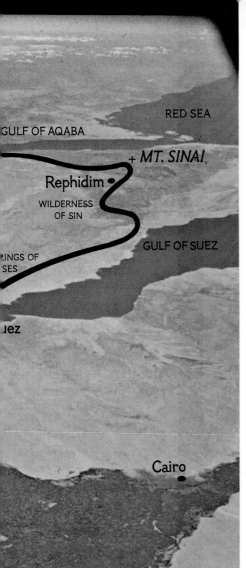

RED SEA

GULF OF AQABA

+ MT. SINAI

Rephidim

WILDERNESS
OF SIN

GULF OF SUEZ

INGS OF
SES

ıez

Cairo

at anchor, and the manganese port of Abu Zenima. Turning inland, our cars left the road and soon trailed plumes of desert dust. Here began the Biblical "wilderness of Sin."

On each side rose jagged peaks. Black seams snaked across the barren ridges and reached down for the desert like unearthly fingers. Millions of stones, worn smooth by winter's flash floods, littered the mile-wide wadi. Tumbleweed-like bushes clung to dust. Dr. Raymond McLain broke the awesome silence: "As a boy, I pictured the 'wilderness' as a dark forest, like those I knew in Kentucky. How different, and even more forceful, is this wilderness of rock."

Little wonder that here the children of Israel murmured against Moses, "for ye have brought us forth into this wilderness, to kill this whole assembly with hunger" (Exodus 16:3).

Semites knew this land before the Hebrews fled this way. In these mountains lay Pharaoh's turquoise mines. At Sarabit el Khadim rose a temple to the Egyptian goddess Hathor; dozens of stelae—stone slabs inscribed in hieroglyphs—still praise Egyptian deities. But the walls of one mine bear Canaanite characters carved by Semitic slaves. These famous proto-Sinaitic inscriptions, among the oldest writings in our alphabet, date from the 15th century B.C. From these crude pictographic symbols—altered by Phoenicians, Greeks, and Romans—developed the letters in which this story is written.

JOHN J. PUTMAN, NATIONAL GEOGRAPHIC STAFF. LEFT: GEMINI 4 SPACECRAFT
PHOTOGRAPHS AN EARLY HEARTLAND OF CIVILIZATION FROM 115 MILES UP; NASA

In my mind's eye I saw a forlorn group of Semites gather to bury a fallen comrade and then inscribe in their own language a memorial; "I am one who returned to be with the Serpent Lady, my mistress."

Now and then we saw the black-and-brown tents of Bedouin; like mirages, they faded against dun-colored wadi walls. Once three shepherdesses rose amid the boulders, black robes fluttering, veils aglitter with silver coins. They reminded me of Zipporah and her sisters, befriended by the young Moses as he fled Pharaoh's wrath in the land of Midian.

We came unexpectedly on date palms, tamarisks, and rushes beside a tiny stream—Feiran Oasis, largest in Sinai, and the traditional Rephidim of the Bible. Here "came Amalek, and fought with Israel." As we lunched on sandwiches in an arbor, Otto pointed across the wadi: "On that peak, tradition says, Moses stationed himself with Aaron and Hur, while Joshua

TOR EIGELAND, BLACK STAR. BELOW: "CROSSING THE RED SEA," FROM THE RAPHAEL LOGGIA (C. 1518) IN THE VATICAN; SCALA

battled the Amalekites here below. So long as Moses held high his hand, Exodus 17 tells us, Joshua prevailed; when it dropped, Amalek began to get the better of it. So Moses sat down on a stone while Aaron and Hur 'stayed up his hands . . . until the going down of the sun.' "

Hardy pilgrims climbed to the ruined Byzantine church atop the peak; others pulled out sketch pads and sat in the garden or walked the shard-littered remains of Pharan, a thriving town in the second century A.D. that fell under the sword of Islam 500 years later. Goats now graze its rubbled cathedral.

Seeking today's "Amalek," I visited a nearby village. A rock wall rimmed clusters of date palms and a few rock huts. Eyed by a donkey, circled by three curious children, I touched my forehead in greeting to a Bedouin. *"Salaam aleikum"* — "Peace be unto you." He opened the gate and led me to a clump of palms, his "living room." He spread a cloth on the sand, tossed straw onto a smoldering fire, and filled a teakettle. Blue smoke swirled through the palms, and the sweet odor of burning straw filled my nostrils. The children sat silently now, knees tucked under chins.

Their mother saw my camera and quickly covered her face each time I glanced her way. She pushed forward a boy, perhaps a year old, clad in Bedouin gown and bonnet. His name was Goma, and he too bore the fine features of the sons of Ishmael.

After tea — strong, sugary, wonderfully restoring — my host proudly showed me his grove of young lemon trees, the deep well with its battered gasoline pump, and the tiny ditches that irrigated his garden. As we parted, I wondered: Would this cruel land, this meager life be all these children could hope for? Perhaps not. The wadi now boasts a schoolhouse and a young teacher dedicated to leading them into the 20th century.

Our caravan moved on, past rock-cut cubicles where Christian hermits once lived and Bedouin now bury their dead. We stopped before a stand of willowy tamarisks. "Manna trees!" shouted Otto. "In spring insects

"AND MOSES STRETCHED FORTH HIS HAND . . . . *And the waters returned, and covered the chariots . . . and all the host of Pharaoh"* (Exodus 14:27, 28). *Egyptian records tell of a "Sea of Reeds" near Raamses, where the Exodus began; ancients thought this brackish Reed Sea part of the Red Sea. Modern scholars suggest that low tide and God's "strong east wind" bared a ford for the Hebrews through reed-choked shallows (upper), and that a storm caught marsh-mired chariots to complete the miracle.*

183

puncture their bark, drink the sap, and exude a clear liquid which solidifies as a sugary globule. This may well be the flaky substance, fine 'as the hoar frost on the ground,' which sustained the Hebrews when they faced starvation.''

Stark mountains rose before us, only to fall away as we twisted and turned onward. We rounded a final corner and there, looking like a toy fortress beneath the towering mass of Mount Sinai, huddled the 1,400-year-old monastery of St. Catherine. Medieval pilgrims went down on their knees at the sight. As we gazed on it, noses pressed to dust-caked windows, we could understand why.

BROTHER EUGENIOS, the *xenodochos* (receiver of foreigners), led us through the iron-studded doors of the sally port and up to our quarters in the pilgrim wing. From our balcony we looked down on a labyrinth of passageways and whitewashed buildings pierced by doors and windows in all shapes and sizes. It seemed as if a corner of medieval Constantinople or Athens had been lifted by a giant hand and compressed within these massive Byzantine walls.

We quickly established our routine. KP duties were assigned, for pilgrims must prepare their own food. In the evening we gathered in a dormitory for our first

IN MOSES' FOOTSTEPS, *a camel caravan threads a Sinai wadi (left). Pilgrims inspect a tamarisk tree (above) whose sap converts into the sweet substance that, some scholars believe, Hebrews called manna; the name asks "What is it?" Bedouin tossed stones for luck into a cleft (lower left), traditional spot where Moses smote the rock and brought "water out of it, that the people may drink" (Exodus 17:6).*

"They encamped there by the waters"

Springs dot the Sinai wasteland, sustaining nomads and their flocks today as they did the wandering children of Israel. Tradition links brackish, palm-fringed Uyun Musa, Springs of Moses (below), with the waters thirsting Hebrews called Marah (bitter). "What shall we drink?" they complained. Exodus 15 says God then showed Moses a tree; when he cast it in the spring, "the waters were made sweet."

Bashful Bedouin (left) billows her shawl for a fleeting portrait. Hornlike hairdo, seldom untied, proclaims she is married. Daughters of the desert hide faces but flaunt wealth on veils ajingle with coins and trinkets. Islamic law forbids interest on loans. Bedouin shun banks and invest, often heavily, in jewelry.

"story time," a Bible reading and discussion. Pilgrims sprawled on bunks and pulled up blankets; the desert night was cool. Otto sketched the monastery's history: "Christian hermits came to Sinai in the third century. They sought to escape Roman persecution and to follow the example of the prophet Elijah and John the Baptist by dwelling in the wilderness. They lived in scattered caves, drank from springs, ate dates from palms, and came together only to worship. But continued attacks by Bedouin led them to appeal, in the sixth century, to the Emperor Justinian for 'a monastery in which we shall be safe.' Justinian ordered it built."

The next morning we awoke to the clatter of a stick beaten against wooden bars. Soon the clang of bells summoned us to the ancient Church of the Transfiguration, dimly aglow with the red and gold of icons. Oil lamps flickered. Incense rose in clouds. Rich brocades covered altars, splendid robes adorned the priests. We stood in stalls and listened to ancient litanies: *"Kyrie eleison, Kyrie eleison"* . . . "Lord have mercy, Lord have mercy."

How reminiscent of the passages in Exodus 25 and 28 in which God gives Moses instructions for the erection of a holy tabernacle and for the making of priestly raiment: "And this is the offering which ye shall take of them; gold, and silver, and brass . . . and fine linen . . . Oil for the

JOHN J. PUTMAN AND (OPPOSITE) ROBERT F. SISSON, BOTH NATIONAL GEOGRAPHIC STAFF

ROBERT F. SISSON, NATIONAL GEOGRAPHIC PHOTOGRAPHER

FOR 1,400 YEARS, *men of God have dwelt at the foot of Mount Sinai in St. Catherine's, oldest existing Greek Orthodox monastery. Granite walls and iron roof belie the splendor inside their church. Here American scholars measure the whitewashed dome of a chapel.*

light, spices for anointing oil, and for sweet incense. . . . And thou shalt make holy garments for Aaron thy brother for glory and for beauty."

After the service, Brother Anastasius led us behind the iconostasis to see the great Transfiguration mosaic (foldout, page 31) above the altar. A marble chest holds the relics of St. Catherine, a fourth-century martyr whose remains were miraculously transported from Alexandria to a mountaintop near here. Found by monks centuries later, they were brought down and the monastery was renamed for her.

Two Greek pilgrims had obtained permission to view the relics. We watched as a monk unlocked the chest and removed two bejeweled reliquaries. The Greeks reverently bent and kissed the blackened skull and skeleton hand.

"And it came to pass on the third day in the morning, that there were thunders and lightnings, and a thick cloud upon the mount. . . . And Moses brought forth the people out of

the camp to meet with God" (Exodus 19:16, 17). We breakfasted quickly, filed outside to the waiting camels, and mounted Bedouin saddles of wood and cloth. Lacking stirrups, we hooked a leg around a saddle horn and started up a trail to the top of Mount Sinai.

Halfway up we dismounted and climbed rough steps, resting often. Bare mountains seemed to surge around us like storm-tossed waves. I pictured Moses climbing alone "unto the thick darkness where God was," while His frightened people "stood afar off." At last, we gathered at the small chapel that marks the top and listened to a reading of the covenant struck here by God and His Chosen People:

I am the Lord thy God, which have brought thee out of the land of Egypt, out of the house of bondage.
Thou shalt have no other gods before me....

In this awesome setting the words of each commandment in Exodus 20 rang like hammer strokes on an anvil.

Several of the older men found the descent difficult. Each placed his hands on the shoulders of a younger man before him, just as Moses drew on the strength of Joshua and the younger Hebrews. We came to the "Well of Elijah," marked by a single cypress. Here, tradition says, the prophet Elijah of a later era was fed by ravens and heard God speak, not with thunder and lightning but in "a still small voice."

That evening we gathered on the broad rampart overlooking the Plain of El Raha, the traditional site where Moses assembled his people to meet with the Lord. A pale moon spilled milky luminescence over cliff and desert.

We wondered about the monks who had come here through the centuries, spurning this world

BENEATH BURNISHED BYZANTINE CHANDELIERS *of the sixth-century Church of the Transfiguration, a deacon holds aloft the sacred elements. To celebrate the Liturgy, he steps behind the iconostasis, the gilded screen of icons that separates from the congregation the altar and relics of martyred St. Catherine of Alexandria. Beyond lies the chapel honoring the site of the burning bush.*

ROBERT F. SISSON, NATIONAL GEOGRAPHIC PHOTOGRAPHER

191

"Monks whose life is but a careful rehearsal of death"

Holy men of St. Catherine's live separate lives, recalling hermits described by a historian of Emperor Justinian's day. A monk (opposite) cooks in his private quarters. He wears the usual black, high-crowned hat and fastens his unshorn hair into a neat bun. Monks eat a single meal at noon, spend most of the day at prayer preparing for the next world. Duties may include stamping the images of St. Catherine and Mary, mother of Jesus, on holy bread (below). Once some 400 monks crowded the monastery; now only a few greet pilgrims. Most are Greek.

to concentrate on the next. The Byzantine historian Procopius found their lives "but a careful rehearsal of death. . . . superior to all human desires." But the appeal of this quiet life seems to have declined. Today the monastery has trouble gaining recruits. Housekeeping chores fall to servants called Gebeliyah—Men of the Mountain. They are believed to be descendants of Wallachians from the Danube, settled here in Byzantine times to protect the monastery.

Deacon Porphyrios told us his seminary at Athens required him to serve at St. Catherine's for a time. His good humor and command of English enhanced our tour of other monastery sights: the mosque, built in the 11th century for Moslem neighbors; the ancient winch which lifted pilgrims up the walls in days when ground-level entrances were considered too risky; a tree labeled "Burning Bush" to appease questioning pilgrims; the great library with its matchless icons and manuscript treasures in Greek, Arabic, Syriac, Georgian, Ethiopic, and other languages.

The monastery no longer holds its most precious manuscript, the fourth-century Codex Sinaiticus, one of the three oldest Greek manuscripts of the Bible. The German

Vestments cloak the skeleton of the monk Stephen (right), who guarded the way up Mount Sinai and expressed the wish that he might always do so. But when he died, about 580, his comrades placed him in the charnel house, where he still keeps vigil. The cemetery holds only six graves; when space runs short, monks dig up bones and neatly stack them.

193

scholar Konstantin von Tischendorf found it at the monastery in 1844 and took it to Russia, where it remained until purchased by the British Museum in 1933.

On our last morning the monks gathered to bid us goodbye. Our cars raced downhill, dropping 7,000 feet in a few hours. Five times we stopped to change rock-gashed tires. We reached Cairo at dusk. After Sinai's serenity, how strange the great city seemed: shrill, frantic, jarring to the eye and ear. Soon I took leave of my pilgrim friends, stepped onto a jetliner, and flew off for the Hashemite Kingdom of Jordan. There I would again pick up Moses' trail.

ROM MOUNT SINAI the Hebrews marched north to Kadesh-barnea, an area of springs near the Negev border, murmuring the while of their plight. "Who shall give us flesh to eat?" they ask in Numbers 11. ". . . there is nothing at all, beside this manna, before our eyes." Spies sent to Canaan brought mixed news: "It floweth with milk and honey. . . . Nevertheless the people be strong that dwell in the land" (Numbers 13:27, 28). When Moses' people lost heart at this report, the Lord condemned them to wander in the wilderness until a stronger generation arose. Moses turned south toward the Gulf of Aqaba. He would try another route into Canaan, along the King's Highway.

I dived into the cool waters of the gulf. Before me spread the fine white beach of Jordan's saltwater port and spa, Aqaba. I waterskied and boarded a glass-bottomed boat to view brilliantly colored fish and rare black coral. And I peered across barbed wire at the twinkling lights of Elat in Israel. I could only look, for I could not cross those strands without risking machine-gun fire.

Moses found his way barred too, despite a pledge of good conduct. The King of Edom refused him entry on the King's Highway. His people were forced to trek up the Wadi al Arabah, a great canyon stretching from the gulf to the Dead Sea.

But the 4,000-year-old highway lay open to me. I climbed into the highlands near Ras an Naqb, where ruins of an Edomite fort still stand. Below, granite outcrops like schooling whales marked the desert. Once these humps had concealed the raiders of Lawrence of Arabia. On donkeyback I explored the rock-hewn city of Petra, whence Nabataeans ruled the King's Highway before the Romans came.

196

"And the Lord called Moses up to the top of the mount" Exodus 19:20

Three thousand stone steps lead pilgrims to the summit of Mount Sinai, past tiny chapels and gates once guarded by monks. There the Lord "gave unto Moses . . . tables of stone, written with the finger of God" (page 106).

Moses returned to find his people worshiping "a molten calf" (opposite), fashioned by Aaron from golden earrings. Exodus 32 relates that "Moses' anger waxed hot, and he cast the tables . . . and brake them." He took the calf, burnt it, ground it to powder, strewed this upon the water, "and made the children of Israel drink of it."

Their God forbade graven images; instead He prescribed "a sanctuary; that I may dwell among them," and told how to erect the Tabernacle, or tent shrine, and the Ark of the Covenant for the sacred tables.

Again ascending the mountain, Moses "was there with the Lord forty days and forty nights" while scribing new tables to replace those broken in anger. On his return, the Israelites built the Ark and Tabernacle as God had commanded.

THIS MOSES SAW *when he climbed Mount Sinai: saw-toothed peaks, eroded slopes, desolate valleys. Gebel Musa (Mount of Moses), as the 7,497-foot summit is named today, overlooks a zigzag track to the tiny white chapel at right.*

St. Catherine's lies hidden in the mountain fold behind the monk. "And when we departed . . . we went through all that great and terrible wilderness . . . and we came to Kadesh-barnea" (Deuteronomy 1:19).

There, for failing to trust in God, a generation was condemned to perish in the wilderness before the Israelites would reach the Promised Land.

A wrong turn led to a magnificent view of the Wadi al Arabah. In the setting sun it seemed a Palestinian Grand Canyon—pink, purple, orange, its eroded walls spilling some 4,000 feet to its floor. I could picture Moses' band down there, tiny specks toiling northward. Perhaps it was around here that "fiery serpents" afflicted them. Moses made a serpent of bronze; those who beheld it survived the snakebites. The wadi holds copper deposits, and the earth of Canaan has yielded bronze serpent images.

Reaching the border of Moab, the Hebrews climbed into the highlands. But Moab refused them passage too, so they turned into "the wilderness which is before Moab, toward the sunrising." I headed east from At Tafilah on a twisting mountain road, then north on the Aqaba-Amman highway. It remains a lonely way. Eastward, sterile desert and steppe stretch 1,500 miles across the Arabian Peninsula.

Turning back toward the mountains near Wadi al Mawjib, the Hebrews determined now to fight. They smote Sihon, King of the Amorites, "with the edge of the sword, and possessed his land" (Numbers 21:24). I passed the cities cited in the Hebrew bards' victory song: Heshbon, where Sihon reigned; Dibon, where archeologists unearthed city walls more ancient than Moses; Madaba, with its Roman ruins and sixth-century mosaic map of Palestine (page 296).

"And Moses went up from the plains of Moab unto the mountain of Nebo. . . . And the Lord shewed him all the land" (Deuteronomy 34:1). Over blue-green hills the road wound to the hallowed mount crowned by the ruins of a Byzantine

LUIS MARDEN AND (OPPOSITE) HELEN AND FRANK SCHREIDER, ALL NATIONAL GEOGRAPHIC STAFF

WARLIKE CHIEFTAINS, *encamped near Madaba, recall Amorites and Moabites who fought Moses. Jordan's Beni Sakhr, like tribes of ancient Israel, claim a common ancestor, are led by family heads, and range a recognized territory.*

The King of Jordan, honored at a desert feast, heard petitions— like Moses, who "sat to judge the people . . . from the morning unto the evening" (Exodus 18:13). Two white camels were sacrificed and 250 roasted sheep served on metal platters amid rice and pine nuts basted in yogurt and butter. Food is rolled into a ball with right hand and popped into mouth.

Khaki robes, red kaffiyehs (left) mark Jordan's famed Desert Police.

church, the sheds of archeologists, and picnic tables for tourists. On a nearby slope spread a Bedouin encampment with its tents, animals, and campfires. Surely Moses' band looked something like this as it reached the threshold of the Promised Land.

I scrambled down the mountain and a grizzled old Bedouin beckoned me to his fire of twigs and goat dung. Others joined us. In Arabic I could only ask their names and make small talk about the weather and the animals. With a metal tent peg one man ground coffee beans in an old artillery shell case, then brewed them in a long-beaked brass pot. The patriarch produced a tiny cup. Each of us drank from it, signaled our satisfaction, and passed it on.

One tribesman wanted his watch fixed. I shook it. No movement. From his robes the Bedouin drew out a foot-long curved dagger, a tool to pry off the back. No use; it would take a special wrench. He understood. I breathed

201

RACING HORSEMEN *on splendid mounts and long lines of cameleers greet Jordan's king with "joy shots" and cheers in the highlands of Moab. A royal feast warms Bedouin hearts, for these tribesmen lead a life as stark as the uplands they rove. They once prized the razzia, or raid, as great sport— seeking camels and booty, not bloodshed.*

Though horse-drawn chariots thundered in patriarchal days, cavalry is first recorded in Assyrian art of the ninth century B.C. *The Bedouin had camels before horses. Camel-borne Midianites, from near the Gulf of Aqaba, raided Palestine around 1100* B.C. *Crossed girths held early boxlike saddle (left).*

The true Bedouin (desert dweller) became a camel breeder, drinking dromedary milk, using the hair for tent curtains and carpets, the skin for leather, the dung for fuel. Camels extended his grazing, trading, raiding range; a laden "ship of the desert" can do 25 miles a day, go three days without water.

On war marches the tribe's most beautiful girl rode in a litter atop a camel to spur on the fighters. Even today Syria's Ruwalla migrate with a she-camel bearing a feathered standard, the Markab or Ark of Ishmael— recalling the Ark of the Covenant which led the Israelites in war and migration.

Hardy camels and fleet steeds gave speed and range to desert raiders

LUIS MARDEN, NATIONAL GEOGRAPHIC STAFF. OPPOSITE: LIMESTONE RELIEF FROM TALL HALAF, SYRIA, 9TH CENTURY B.C.; WALTERS ART GALLERY, BALTIMORE

a sigh of relief — and accepted from an old woman a bowl of *laban*, fermented goat's milk. I rose, thanked my host, clasped each man's hand, and walked back up the mountain.

ATOP MOUNT NEBO AT SUNSET I stood on the traditional ground where Moses glimpsed the Promised Land. Before me lay the Jordan Valley, hidden in swirling mists of sand and dust raised by afternoon storms. The Dead Sea glinted like dull copper through the haze. Beyond, the blue Judaean hills marched in tossed rows to the horizon. On the farthest ridge I could make out a tower. Could it be Jerusalem, 30 miles away? The old guard beside me nodded. He disappeared and returned with a huge telescope sheathed in brass and leather.

As he focused it, his wrinkled hawk face reminded me of the passage in Deuteronomy 34 that describes Moses at this spot: "an hundred and twenty years old . . . his eye was not dim, nor his natural force abated." I squinted through the dim lenses. Sure enough — there stood the tower of the Russian Church on the Mount of Olives above Jerusalem. I clapped my hands in appreciation. The old man glowed.

I drove through the darkness past Bedouin campfires, no longer in the footsteps of Moses. His great mission completed, "the servant of the Lord died there in the land of Moab. . . . but no man knoweth of his sepulchre unto this day." As I hairpinned down into the valley of Jericho, the closing verses of Deuteronomy ran through my mind: "And there arose not a prophet since in Israel like unto Moses, whom the Lord knew face to face, In all the signs and the wonders, which the Lord sent him to do in the land of Egypt to Pharaoh. . . ."

A few weeks later, chatting on a hotel terrace by the Sea of Galilee, I mentioned my trek to an Israeli acquaintance. His eyes lit up. He had been there too, briefly, in 1956 when Israeli paratroopers fluttered down on Sinai. "I'm not a religious man," he mused. "But there were archeologists with us. We watched them work, and we read the Torah, and we studied the land. And you know, *it fit . . . it all fit.*"

This man had made his own Exodus, from the concentration camps of Europe. He had entered Palestine by stealth, and fought to make it his. As we talked, hostile artillery stood on the hills across the sea; and in the bluffs behind us Israelis manned mortars. Within a few months, in 1967, he and his people once again would be at war with their neighbors. So it was when Joshua, taking the mantle laid down by Moses, led his people against the Canaanites to claim the Promised Land.

"And the Lord shewed him all the land of Gilead, unto Dan"

Deuteronomy 34

Serpentine coils of the Jordan near Damiya twist through its green valley, "well watered . . . as the garden of the Lord." Moses, looking upon such a sight, pleaded with God to let him cross the Jordan, but the divine command held: "thou shalt not go over." Upon Moses' death the Israelites, with Joshua leading, passed over near here — miraculously "on dry ground" — and invaded Canaan to the west (at left in picture).

Walled cities dotted the valley; their tells beckon archeologists. Wild beasts lurked in the dense growth of the lower valley, well-named Zor (thicket) in Arabic. Jeremiah 49:19 describes the Lord as coming up "like a lion . . . from the jungle of the Jordan."

Fed by the snows of 9,232-foot Mount Hermon, the river courses valley formed millions of years ago when earth's crust shifted and a crack opened from southern Turkey to southeast Africa — the Great Rift. From the Sea of Galilee in the north the Jordan loops and swirls some 200 miles, only 3 to 10 feet deep, to empty and die in the Dead Sea — earth's lowest spot. Here rapid evaporation leaves a landlocked sea seven times as salty as the oceans.

Both Jordan and Israel divert the river water for irrigation. A natural hothouse, the valley sends fruits and vegetables to grace Europe's winter tables.

THOMAS NEBBIA

By G. Ernest Wright

The World of David and Solomon

FASTER AND FASTER the sling whirls, its singing strings the only sound
in a valley ringed by silent warriors. One slope bristles with
Philistine javelins; on the other glint the swords of Israel.

On the floor of the Valley of Elah the lithe young shepherd uncrooks
a finger and a string flies loose, speeding a smooth, fist-size stone at the giant
who lumbers forward, armored in bronze from helmet to greaves.

The stone smashes his forehead. Goliath falls.

With hands that can draw sweet notes from a lyre, David severs the giant's head.
As the blood of their champion soddens the dust, the Philistines flee from this
shepherd who slays in the name of Israel's fearsome God.

You can still find water-smoothed stones like those David plucked from the brook
in the valley southwest of Jerusalem. They bridge the 3,000 years between us
and this unforgettable leader whose history unfolds in the Books of Samuel and Kings
amid some of the most beautiful passages in the Bible. Heroic yet all too human,
legendary yet historical, the "sweet psalmist of Israel" is as captivating today
as he was when his exploits brought him before Saul, Israel's first king.

David both enthralled and enraged that mercurial monarch. When "the evil spirit . . .
was upon Saul," David played his soothing lyre. In battle he killed so many Philistines
that adoring women sang, "Saul hath slain his thousands, and David his ten thousands."
As his star rose, David won the hand of the king's daughter Michal and the devotion
of the king's son—"the soul of Jonathan was knit with the soul of David."
And Saul brooded: "What more can he have but the kingdom?" (I Samuel 18:8).

Though the real threat to the kingdom came from the Philistines,
Saul's hatred focused on David. Quick-witted and daring, the young leader
evaded every royal attempt on his life. First he fled to the wilderness of Judah,

TRIUMPHANT DAVID, *Goliath's head at his feet, wields a weapon*
that "could sling stones at an hair breadth and not miss" (Judges 20:16).
Shepherds still use the formidable sling to drive off predators.

"THE YOUTHFUL DAVID" BY ANDREA DEL CASTAGNO, C. 1450; WIDENER COLLECTION, NATIONAL GALLERY OF ART, WASHINGTON

whose cave-pocked canyons west of the Dead Sea long had harbored hunted men. Later, in despair, David turned to Philistine territory. With his guerrilla band of exiles, debtors, and resistance fighters, he lived as a Robin Hood, raiding rich seminomads. The end of his exile would bring the dawn of the Hebrews' golden age—less than 80 years in the tenth century B.C. when David and then Solomon ruled a united, powerful people.

*T*HE LONG NIGHT of war and peril had started some two centuries earlier, when Joshua crossed the Jordan in quest of the Promised Land. Mammoth tides of history were surging across the ancient world: the fall of Troy, immortalized in Homer's *Iliad;* the flowering and dying of the Mycenaean empire in Greece; the crumbling of Hittite and Egyptian power in western Asia.

Armed with religious zeal and crude weapons, the Hebrew tribes stormed the city-states of Canaan, a rich but vulnerable land, its name synonymous with that of the purple-dyed wool it produced. In business records inscribed on clay we find merchants trading wool for copper from Cyprus and carved ivory from Egypt. And from the rubbled layers of Palestinian tells we sift stark evidence of conquest between 1250 and 1200 B.C. that evokes the Bible's account of the Hebrew sweep.

I first tasted Biblical archeology more than 30 years ago with an expedition directed by Dr. William F. Albright. For ten weeks we lived in tents pitched in a fig orchard, slept on beds as humped as a herd of dromedaries, went on breakfast-food diets to avoid the concoctions of our native cook, and drank boiled water. But our iron self-discipline failed to save us from dysentery.

"AND SAUL CAST THE JAVELIN," *aiming to "smite David even to the wall" at Gibeah (I Samuel 18:11). The lyrist in warrior's kilt dodges the spear. Mind clouded by jealousy at David's popularity, the king drives the youth into exile.*

Saul's queen plaits her hair in Canaanite fashion. Guards game with dice on the dirt floor of the thick-walled, turreted stronghold commanding a hill four miles north of Jerusalem. Sling stones, bronze arrowheads, and weapons found there indicate Israel's first royal residence was a place of war, not splendor.

Dr. Wright, whose teacher Dr. Albright probed those ruins at Gibeah, sifts shards at Shechem (opposite). There he unearthed earrings and silver used as money 200 years before David, when Joshua led Hebrews to victory in the Promised Land. He also found a limestone slab recalling the "great stone" that marked where Hebrew tribes assembled to pledge fidelity to God. Around 1020 B.C. the tribes united under Saul to repel Philistine invaders.

PAINTING BY HENRY J. SOULEN (ALSO OVERLEAF). OPPOSITE: JOHN S. HOLLADAY

We probed layer upon layer of rubble, each a jumble of ruin pathetically like the other. Yet, oddly, this monotonous succession of devastation, rebuilding, and more devastation gave me a stirring insight into how our religious heritage was born: in violence, pillage, and sudden death.

"Joshua burnt Ai, and made it an heap for ever" (Joshua 8:28). How could this be? Ai had been abandoned long before Joshua's time; its very name, in fact, means ruin in Hebrew. Our dig at Bethel, only two miles away, yielded a vital clue. Stripping away the swaths of rubble, we worked our way past 1200 B.C. Suddenly, we encountered signs of a raging fire—piles of charcoal debris, some five feet deep, in the remains of well-built homes. Undoubtedly, Hebrew scribes had accurately recorded the burning, but tradition shifted the incident to the "ruin" nearby.

The Hebrew invaders smote Lachish "with the edge of the sword, and all the souls that were therein" (Joshua 10:32). In 1965, while exploring the commanding site of Lachish in the Shephelah, the foothill country southwest of Jerusalem, I found

"BLOW YE THE TRUMPETS!" *Gideon commands, raising his javelin on Mount Gilboa. Ram's horn blasts rend the air and Israelites smash jars hiding torches. The sudden flares in the night create the impression of a huge force in the hills. With this ruse Gideon's 300 men panic the encamped Midianite horde, Arabian nomads who plundered Israelite land in the time of the Judges with the first large-scale use of camels.*

great piles of smashed pottery that we could readily date to the time of Joshua. From the side of one trench my son Daniel extracted not a shard but a whole bowl that had somehow survived the destruction of a Canaanite temple.

Other tells fill out a picture of a series of city-state capitals destroyed, strongly supporting the account of the campaigns in Joshua 10. On the other hand, precisely according to Biblical tradition, we find no evidence of destruction from this time at Gezer, along the old road from Jerusalem to the coast.

At Jericho, we read in Joshua 6, seven priests marched round the city seven days, blowing rams' horns; on the seventh, "when the priests blew with the trumpets . . . the wall fell down flat, so that the people went up into the city. . . . And they utterly destroyed all that was in the city, both man and woman, young and old. . . ." Archeologists have found little evidence of this storied conquest, though the ancient mound has yielded phenomenal finds, including the oldest known city fortifications. Perhaps the centuries have eroded all signs of Joshua's victory.

In sturdily walled Canaanite cities of this time we find substantial homes graced by fine native pottery and imported objects of art. (Egyptian tomb robbers had a ready market for loot in Canaan.) Israelite homes, in the straggly new towns that dotted the hill country, were jerry-built, their pottery crude and poorly kilned.

The new settlers farmed and worshiped in a land where agriculture and polytheism intertwined. Alluring goddesses (page 90) personified fertility in crops, herds, and man. Enticed by erotic rites, many Israelites "forsook the Lord God of their fathers." Ultimately, however, the Hebrews came to strip nature of pagan myth. For they saw nature's bounty stemming not from the mating of the deities of rain

PIT OF TIME *yawns at the feet of tourists treading Jericho, man's oldest known walled town. They walk atop a 30-foot-high stone tower whose roots plunge to 7000* B.C. *The Stone Age bastion defended a spring that still waters Jordan Valley gardens.*
Even deeper in time and ruin lie the flint and bone tools of Jericho's first families, hunters whose huts evolved into dome-roofed, mud-brick homes.
During war-filled centuries the primitive town walls rose and fell. From 3100 to 2100 B.C. *inhabitants repaired or rebuilt them 16 times. But in Joshua's era, the rubble record shows only "a tantalizing gap," reports archeologist Kathleen Kenyon. Here she examines shell-eyed, plaster-covered skulls of Jericho men who lived 8,000 years ago.*

213

and fertility but from the blessings of a righteous God.

As the Chosen People, they fought a "holy war," massacring, devastating, taking their Promised Land— but, by divine injunction, sparing the fruit trees and keeping no booty. In battle they relied on faith, not numbers. Gideon, with 300 men, their blaring trumpets, and "The sword of the Lord," routed the Midianite host that lay in the Valley of Jezreel "like grasshoppers for multitude" (Judges 7:12).

Gideon's trumpets sounded when "there was no king in Israel"—the time of the Judges. Charismatic leaders called forth by God, the Judges served only in crises. The day-to-day power lay with tribal leaders and community elders. They settled boundary disputes, conscripted troops, and supervised "cities of refuge" founded by divine command to protect the "manslayer" until he stood "before the congregation for judgment."

Leaders of the tribal league met in the northern hill country at Shiloh, sanctuary of the Ark of the Covenant and gathering place for three great annual festivals: the spring Passover, commemorating the deliverance from Egypt; the harvest fete, 50 days later; and the Feast of Booths—eight joyous days during which "they went out into the fields ... and trode the grapes, and made merry" (Judges 9:27). They lived in tents or huts, recalling the days in the Sinai wilderness.

ABOUT 1175 B.C. invaders—"Philistines" in the Bible, "Sea Peoples" to the Egyptians—seized the coastal plain of Canaan. Judging from the Mycenaean grace of the pottery found in their distinctive rock-hewn tombs, they originally came from Aegean lands.

To trace their thrust into Canaan, I followed the trail of their marvelous pottery. Preening swans and spiraling designs adorned vessels from which they ate and drank, scenes on the pots reminding them of their homeland. Two-handled craters held food; strainer-spouts on beer jugs trapped barley husks.

By 1050, Philistine charioteers had swept into the northern hills. Near present-day Tel Aviv 30,000 Israelites fell, tradition says, in futile defense of the Ark. Hebrews began defecting; Israel faced extinction.

Desperate, the tribal elders turned to Samuel, last of the Judges: "Now make us a king." He hesitated;

PAINTING BY HENRY J. SOULEN

PHILISTINES STORM *the coast of Canaan. Swarming from Greek isles in goose-billed ships, feather-helmed invaders with a monopoly on iron weapons defeat bearded Canaanites and burn Ashkelon.*

Settling here, in nearby Gaza, and three other city-states, Philistines will harry the Hebrews nearly two centuries—until David subdues them. Yet between hostilities, both peoples cross frontiers, even intermarry— as in Samson's story in Judges 13-16.

From Ashkelon's export of small-bulbed onions sprouted the term scallion. Palestine takes its name from the Philistines.

a king would mean conscription into a royal army and heavy taxation.
But the people prevailed, and Samuel planned a monarchy befitting Hebrew traditions—
the king would rule like a permanent Judge, only by God's will, conveyed to him
by a prophet. Samuel chose Saul of Gibeah, tall and goodly, as Israel's first king.

Saul swiftly mobilized the best fighting men and rescued Israel, though
the Philistine peril remained. When the king violated the rules of holy war
by taking prisoners and booty, Samuel proclaimed that the Lord had spurned Saul.
At God's command Samuel secretly anointed the next king: David.

Despite this sign of divine favor, David would not seize the throne of the man
who murderously pursued him. Once David stole up on Saul, flourished a torn piece
of cloth, and cried: "See . . . I cut off the skirt of thy robe, and killed thee not"
(I Samuel 24:11). Not by David's hand would Saul die.

Instead, Saul's tragic end came by his own hand. Pierced by Philistine arrows
at Mount Gilboa, three of his sons slain before his eyes, Saul fell upon his sword.

"AND HIS WORD *was on my tongue,"*
this worshiper may say with David
(II Samuel 23:2) while reading a psalm
at the site in Jerusalem revered as
David's tomb. Scholars believe that
"the sweet psalmist of Israel" inspired
rather than penned the psalms.

His cry of grief—"O my son Absalom,
my son, my son Absalom!"—echoes in
the Valley of Kidron, flanking the city.
There lies the rebellious prince,
tradition says of a spired tomb (below),
despite its Greek decor. In nearby
Silwan (Siloam), archeologists found
a tomb whose epitaph ("... Cursed be
the man who will open this!"), dating
to 700 B.C., suggests it belongs to King
Hezekiah's aide Shebna, who lost favor
when he presumptuously "heweth him
out a sepulchre on high" (Isaiah 22:16).

Apprised of the news in his outlaw lair, David rent his clothes and wept, and lamented the death of Saul and Jonathan in an immortal elegy (II Samuel 1:19-27):

> *The beauty of Israel is slain upon thy high places:*
> *how are the mighty fallen!*
> *... Ye daughters of Israel, weep over Saul. ...*
> *O Jonathan, thou wast slain. ... my brother Jonathan.*

For seven years, by sword and by intrigue, David struggled with the survivors of the House of Saul. Finally, unrivaled king of his people, he captured Jerusalem for his throne. The city stood on neutral ground between the northern tribes, who called their land Israel, and Judah, David's southern homeland. To the newly proclaimed City of David the king brought his people's symbol of God and nationhood: the Ark of the Covenant. Still housed in a tent, it rested at last in the capital of a united Israel. God, said David, "hath made with me an everlasting covenant."

The promise of this covenant—that God would support David's dynasty in Jerusalem forever—would ring down the ages. Isaiah hailed the city as the fountainhead of

"the word of the Lord," and even when Solomon's Temple toppled in Jerusalem's ashes, the hope of the covenant endured. For some day a new "Anointed One"— *Messiah* in Hebrew, *Christos* in Greek—would again triumph in the City of David.

*I*N JERUSALEM, David honored an elite force of "mighty men"—The Thirty. During the Philistine wars he once expressed longing for a drink from the best well in his hometown of Bethlehem. Three of The Thirty slipped through enemy lines to fulfill his casual wish. He poured the water on the ground as a libation to God because he could not drink what men had brought at such great risk.

Leading such fiercely loyal troops, he swept the Philistines out of the lowlands that fringed the Judaean hills, bottling the Sea Peoples in three coastal towns—Gaza, Ashkelon, and Ashdod—and recaptured nearly all Canaanite territory within the Promised Land. He forged an empire that ranged from Sinai and the Gulf of Aqaba to southern Syria. For one generation within the reigns of David and Solomon Israel stood as the strongest power between the Nile and the Euphrates.

Triumphant as king and warrior, David the man was defeated by sin and sorrow. The "Court History of David" (II Samuel 9-20 and I Kings 1-2), written by a witness to dramatic scenes in his life, re-creates the temptation that launched tragedy: "And it came to pass in an eveningtide, that David arose from off his bed, and walked upon the roof of the king's house: and from the roof he saw a woman washing herself; and the woman was very beautiful to look upon."

Soon the beautiful Bathsheba conceives David's child, and soon David sends her husband Uriah to certain death in battle. The child born to Bathsheba dies. Absalom, David's son by another wife, kills a half-brother and later leads a revolt. "Deal gently for my sake with the young man," David commands his general Joab. But Joab, torn by duty to king and country, slays Absalom—and saves the realm.

Tragedy upon tragedy in the royal family convinced the people and the prophet Nathan that divine wrath stalked David. Psalm 51 bears David's name and the memory of his despair before God: "Cast me not away from thy presence; and take not thy holy spirit from me."

Now David, 40 years a king, is senile and soon to die. His eldest surviving son Adonijah, backed by the older military and religious factions, stages a ceremony to proclaim himself king. Nathan, a leader in the younger group, hurries to Bathsheba and pleads with her to convince David that he should immediately name their second son Solomon his heir. Protected by the faithful guard of mighty men, Solomon is anointed king. Trumpets and pipes resound in rejoicing Jerusalem.

"God save King Solomon!" his subjects shout. And some, foreseeing the glory to come, say to David: "God make the name of Solomon better than thy name, and make his throne greater than thy throne" (I Kings 1:47).

HERE ON THE HEIGHTS OF AMMAN, *Uriah the Hittite fell. Coveting Uriah's wife Bathsheba, David sent him into "the forefront of the hottest battle . . . that he may be smitten, and die" (II Samuel 11:15). Royal city of the Ammonites when conquered by David's army, Amman today serves as Jordan's capital.*

HELEN AND FRANK SCHREIDER, NATIONAL GEOGRAPHIC STAFF

IN THE DAYS OF

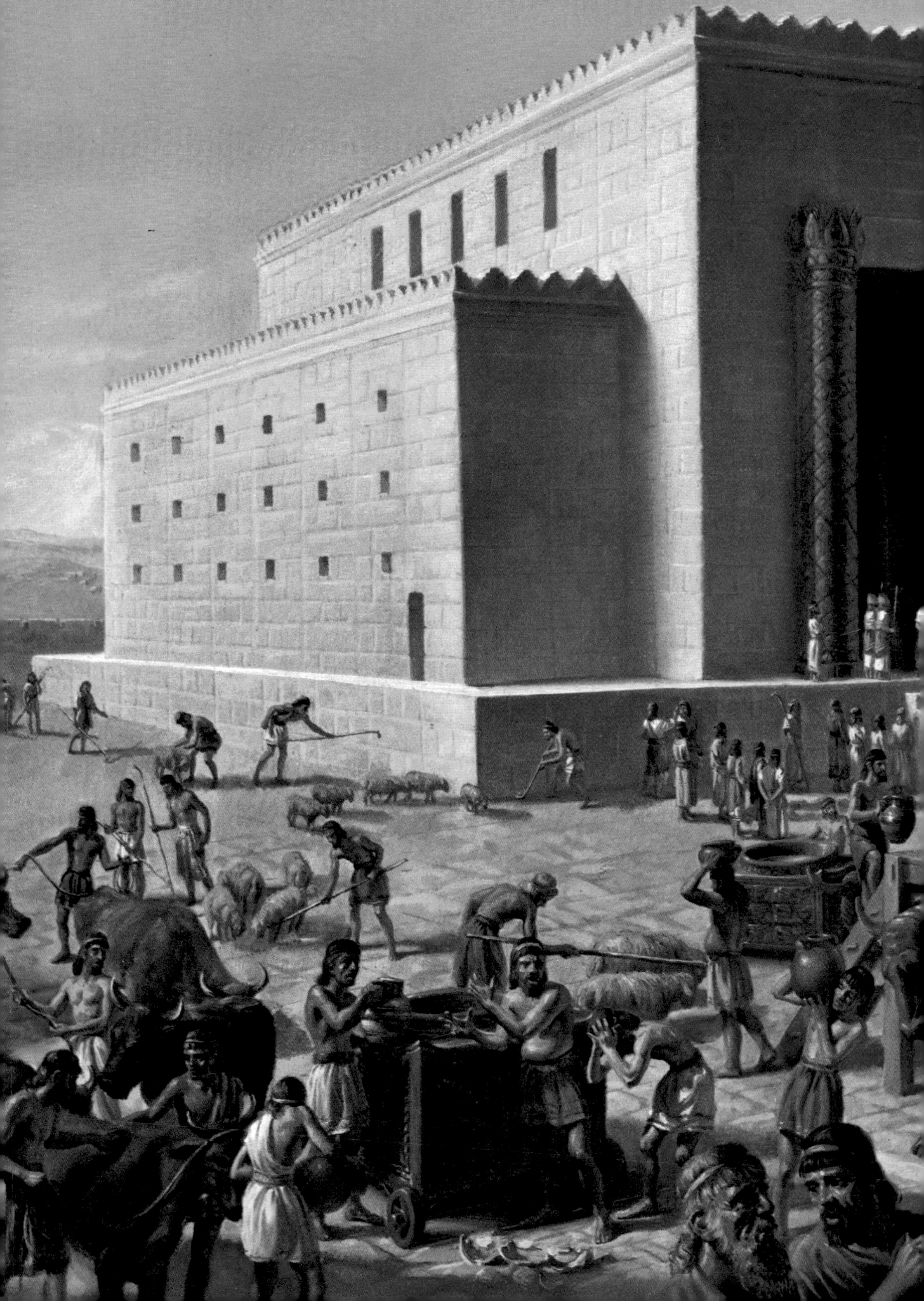

FOR SEVEN YEARS all Israel has toiled to see this day. Solomon's Temple, the House of the Lord, awaits God and king atop the holy mount in the City of David. The autumnal sun of the new year bathes its splendid limestone and burnishes the bronze columns that frame its massive doors. Flame and smoke, wafting the savor of roasting meat, rise over Jerusalem from the altar of burnt offerings. Drovers herd sheep and oxen into the courtyard. From a great bowl, burden of 12 bronze bulls, men draw water and pour it into lavers, wheeled to speed the washing of beasts and instruments of sacrifice. So many animals will be offered on these eight joyous days that they can "not be told nor numbered for multitude."

Now over the tumult sounds the clarion of trumpet and pipe, the crash of cymbals, the beckoning song of the lyre. The Ark comes! White-robed priests and musicians trained by Canaanites bear the gleaming palanquin from the older quarter, a Zion fit for David but too small for mighty Solomon.

"Lift up your heads, O ye gates; and be ye lift up, ye everlasting doors; and the King of glory shall come in," the Psalms shall sing of this day.

Solomon's Temple; painting by Peter V. Bianchi, National Geographic staff artist **222**

VALLEY OF HINNOM
(Gehenna)

IMMORTAL JERUSALEM *spans history's horizons: City of David, showplace of Solomon, crucible of Christ, citadel of Islam, sacred goal of Crusaders and pilgrims from all the world, symbol of a sundered Holy Land.*

Solomon's Temple rose where the Dome of the Rock stands at right in this view looking northwest. The temple fell, but his wisdom endured. To him came two women, each with a baby boy, one dead. Both claimed the live one. When the king moved to cut him in half, one woman yielded rather than see him slain. "She is the mother," Solomon ruled (I Kings 3:27).

"THE JUDGMENT OF SOLOMON" BY RAPHAEL, C. 1510; THE VATICAN. ABOVE: THOMAS NEBBIA

"For the Lord hath chosen Zion; he hath desired it for his habitation" (24:7, 132:13). The temple's wooden, gold-inlaid doors swing open, metal-tipped pivots turning smoothly in their sockets. The Ark vanishes into "the thick darkness," pierced only by the light that shafts downward from clerestory windows. Tiny birds flutter through them, into the holy place—and into a Psalm (84:3): "Yea, the sparrow found an house, and the swallow a nest for herself. . . ."

NO TRACE of Solomon's Temple, built about 950 B.C., has been found; archeologists have not been permitted to dig in the Haram Esh Sharif, the sacred area crowned by the Dome of the Rock. Little could remain in any event, after the devastations by Nebuchadnezzar in 587 B.C. and the Romans A.D. 70. Besides, later builders of the Roman era would have swept away all to reach bedrock.

How then can we so confidently describe the temple? From the Bible itself and archeological information from elsewhere. In I Kings 6 and Ezekiel 40 we get our first clues: detailed descriptions and dimensions in cubits (17½ inches) or again in

ISRAEL'S GLORY

A wise king builds a great temple,
chariot cities, and a trade-rich realm.
Archeologist Wright re-creates Solomon's era

ANCIENT CITY OF DAVID | WALLED CITY OF JERUSALEM

VALLEY OF THE
TYROPOEON

CHURCH OF
THE HOLY SEPULCHER

SPRING OF GIHON

DOME OF THE ROCK
(Site of Solomon's Temple)

DUNG GATE   MOUNT OPHEL   VALLEY OF KIDRON

"sacred" cubits a handbreadth wider (about 21 inches). Our painting shows the
temple built to sacred-cubit specifications.

Now let us join with Solomon and the elders and heads of all the tribes of Israel
in the dedication of the temple. In procession behind the Ark, we pass between
the pillars, known as Jachin ("he will establish") and Boaz ("in strength"), probably from the first words of inscriptions on them. They may have stood as towering
cressets, incense-burning fire-altars.

We stand now in the Ulam, or vestibule, a room about 17½ by 35 feet. Before us
opens a double door glittering with gold-inlaid carvings of palm trees, flowers, and
strange figures that look like sphinxes—winged lions with human heads. We pass
through the Ulam to the Hekal, or holy place, a high-ceilinged chamber of pungent
cedar, 70 feet long, 35 feet wide. From three-story storehouses built along the
temple's sides priests have brought to the Hekal the furnishings of ritual. Golden
candlesticks gleam on a table bearing 12 loaves of "shewbread," cakes of pure
wheaten flour set forth each Sabbath in ancient nomadic rite. A small cedar altar,

adorned with gold leaf, stands before steps leading up to a carved and gold-flecked door that opens as we ascend the steps.

We enter the hush of the Debir, the holy of holies, the special abode of God. Dark except for the dim light in the doorway, the Debir is a 25-foot, cedar-lined cube. We can faintly discern the outline of two 15-foot figures carved in olivewood and garbed in gold leaf. Their outstretched wings span the chamber, and the Ark rests beneath them. God has at last found a place "to abide in for ever."

Since "neither hammer nor axe nor any tool of iron" was heard while the temple "was in building" (I Kings 6:7), wooden sections of it may have been prefabricated and brought to the site, along with the dressed limestone blocks, some 12 to 15 feet long. Such limestone still lies in Jerusalem caverns known as Solomon's Quarries.

The Bible also tells us that Solomon called upon Hiram the Great of Tyre, who had been an ally of David, to help build the temple. We know that Israel had no experience in designing or erecting the lavish structures Solomon envisioned. So Hiram supplied not only his cedars of Lebanon but also architects and artisans.

The hiring of outsiders to build Israel's first temple helps to explain the use of ornate decor and religious symbolism foreign to the Hebrews' long practice of

DEAN CONGER AND (LEFT) JOHN J. PUTMAN, BOTH NATIONAL GEOGRAPHIC STAFF

rustic ritual. In the prayer Solomon offered at the dedication (I Kings 8) we see that he recognized the new concepts implied by the replacement of the "tent" of tradition with a permanent temple.

"But will God indeed dwell on the earth?" he asks. Polytheists believed this, and built temples as palaces for divine tenants who needed human servants to supply their needs. But though the Israelites called their temple the House of the Lord, they thought of it as a place where God's *name* dwelt. The mystic presence of the name hallowed the temple as a house of prayer where God, Who lived in heaven, could still "tent" among His people.

Thanks to archeological discoveries in recent years, we know that Solomon's Temple essentially followed the plan of a Phoenician temple. Hiram's men conceived the Hebrews' God as a sovereign in his palace. They placed on guard over the Ark the winged sphinxes of Phoenician iconography: *kerubim*, genies who served the gods. These, not chubby angels, were the cherubim mentioned in Biblical descriptions of the temple.

We have found Phoenician ivory carvings portraying cherubim-and-tree tableaux probably similar to those carved on the temple's doors and walls. Others show Canaanite kings sitting on cherub-thrones. From knowledge

227

"And when the queen of Sheba heard of the fame of Solomon... she came to Jerusalem"

I Kings 10:1, 2

Drums and trumpets resound in Solomon's Hall of Judgment. Leading a train of gift-bearing slaves, the royal visitor from far Arabia enters. Her eyes sweep the room, sweet-scented by sandalwood, muraled by Phoenician artists. On a throne flanked by winged lions of ivory and gold sits the king. A slave boy brings him drink in a golden goblet; silver "was nothing accounted of in the days of Solomon."

"I believed not the words, until I came," Sheba's queen says, astounded by the splendor; "and, behold, the half was not told me."

Solomon's scribe records her gifts on wooden tablets. In return the king will give her "of his royal bounty."

"To prove him with hard questions," the queen may have tested his wisdom with a riddle. In such a duel of wits, one might ask for four things both wondrous and unfathomable. Proverbs 30:19 provides the reply: "The way of an eagle in the air; the way of a serpent upon a rock; the way of a ship in the midst of the sea; and the way of a man with a maid."

More likely the "hard questions" concerned trade. The queen told him "all that was in her heart." Solomon answered all her questions; there was nothing "which he told her not." Negotiations must have gone smoothly, for it is written in the 10th chapter of I Kings that "Solomon gave unto the queen of Sheba all her desire, whatsoever she asked."

PAINTING BY HENRY J. SOULEN

of Phoenician art of Solomon's day we can assume that the imported artisans would have delicately blended Egyptian and Asian motifs. The Egyptians would have given them the idea of lighting a room from windows under the roof—the ancient origin of the cathedral's clerestory. Babylon's reverence for the life-giving sea may have inspired the Bible's name for the great bowl—"the molten sea." Cast in the clay beds of the Jordan Valley, it weighed 25 to 30 tons and held some 10,000 gallons of water.

Solomon enlarged Jerusalem in his royal urban renewal of the City of David. Year after year his palace rose in stone, wood, and gold: the House of the Forest of Lebanon, an aptly named chamber of cedar pillared like a grove; the Hall of Judgment, where he sat on a throne of ivory and gold to receive the Queen of

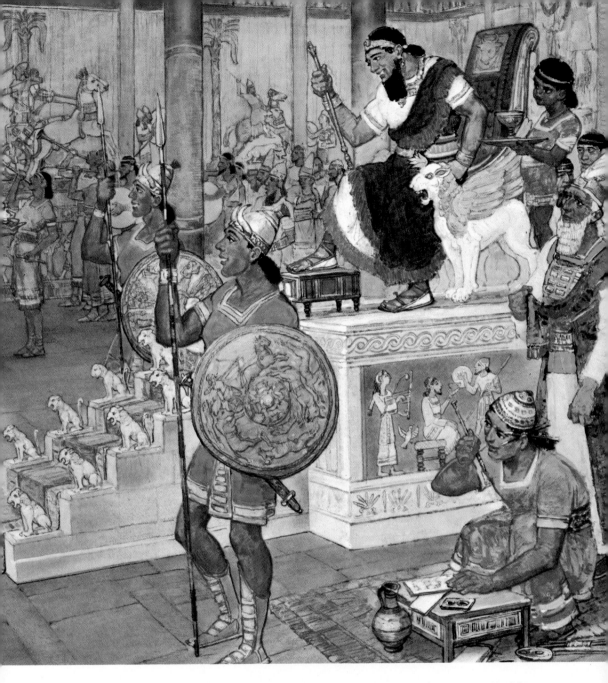

Sheba. For his many wives he built magnificent homes and shrines. The buildings stood as monuments to Solomon's grandeur—and to Israel's eventual bankruptcy. In his reign Israel became a center of trade and culture. He drained the treasury to sustain a lavish royal court, which Israel could not afford. And, on the profits of selling the trappings of glory, the Phoenicians prospered.

MERCHANT-SAILORS had long controlled the ports of Palestine. Egyptian trade with Byblos, a Phoenician city-state, went back to 3000 B.C. "Byblos-ships" the Egyptians called the vessels that bore cedars of Lebanon to their untimbered realm. Solomon probably did not call these traders of Tyre Phoenicians. That name came later from the Greeks, who adopted Phoenician

"A PLACE...CALLED ARMAGEDDON." *Etched by diggers, strategic Megiddo looms on Israel's Plain of Esdraelon. University of Chicago archeologists, in a major expedition, uncovered 20 cities, one atop the other. Bronze Age javelins began the bloody saga about 3500 B.C. Thutmosis III of Egypt boasted of victory about 1468 B.C. when defenders "fled headlong to Megiddo with faces of fear." By the time the 13-acre mound was abandoned after 3,000 years of siege and war, so many decisive battles had been fought here that the Book of Revelation prophesied the final cataclysmic battle between good and evil would take place at Armageddon—har (Mount) Megiddo.*

WOMAN'S TASK: *the daily bread. Grandmother grinds barley on a quern, a stone hand mill. Mother kneads the dough, flavored with olive oil or honey. Daughter puts loaves on a clay pan to bake in a pit oven.*

Woman's treasure: From a cloth purse found at Megiddo came these nine ivory spindle whorls, two bronze pendants shaped like pomegranates, iron bracelets, numerous beads and semi-precious stones. Tiny bronze weights at center depict a goat and, enlarged below, left, a monkey eating an apple.

sailors into their navies and Phoenician letters into their writing. Today's Roman letters and Arabic script bear traces of the original consonants of the Phoenician alphabet. All modern alphabetical systems stem from it.

Long before Greek and Roman armadas ventured into the Mediterranean, high-decked Phoenician galleys would pass the Pillars of Hercules into the Atlantic. Descendants of Hiram's traders would sail the known world with their cargoes of purple cloth and exquisite glass.

Solomon paid on the installment plan for the skills of Hiram's artisans and for the cedars rafted to Joppa. Each year Hiram received "twenty thousand cors of wheat ... and twenty thousand cors of beaten oil" (I Kings 5:11).

Continued on page 238

FROM "HAZOR: THE REDISCOVERY OF A GREAT CITADEL OF THE BIBLE," BY YIGAEL YADIN; OPPOSITE: PAINTING BY HENRY J. SOULEN

"Live joyfully…in thy labour"

Ecclesiastes 9:9

Tribesmen turned townsmen thrive at crafts.
Wheels hum in a shop where "the potter treadeth
clay" (Isaiah 41:25). An aged artisan finishes
a bowl on a hand-turned wheel. Boy spins a
wheel bearing a cone of clay for small jugs.
At a foot-turned wheel a man burnishes a bowl
by holding a spatula to the rotating clay.
Firing creates a shine; glazing is yet unknown.

At the dye house men transmute drab wool
and flax into "blue, and purple, and crimson."
They dip threads into vats, rinsing with water
drawn from a cistern. Tugging on a weighted
lever squeezes out the precious excess dye.

Excavations at Tell Beit Mirsim revealed the
textile town of Debir: Weavers kept guildsmen
in 20 to 30 dye plants busy. Crushed kermes
insects yielded a red dye. Costliest was the
kingly Tyrian purple extracted from murex
shellfish by craftsmen of Phoenicia and Canaan;
both names may mean Land of the Purple.

The finest oil was extracted by beating the olives with a stone or pestle. These payments equaled 125,000 bushels of wheat and 1,162,000 gallons of oil. After 20 years Solomon still owed Hiram. Desperate, but shrewd, he ceded to Hiram a score of coastal towns in western Galilee. In his bitter name for the district — Cabul — Hiram punned on a word meaning "good for nothing."

Solomon's people ultimately paid for his extravagance. But he gave them what his name meant: peace and prosperity. "And Judah and Israel dwelt safely, every man under his vine and under his fig tree, from Dan even to Beersheba, all the days of Solomon" (I Kings 4:25). Fortified cities guarded his borders. His well-equipped army — "he had a thousand and four hundred chariots" — never had to fight a major battle.

The typical Israelite's everyday life reflected not the glory of Solomon but the stability of a new nation built on old ways. Farmers went home to towns after

GALILEE FARMERS *carry tools of peace and war near the border with Syria where armies clashed in 1967. Their ancestors took to arms after spring planting, "when kings go forth to battle" (II Samuel 11:1). Gezer calendar of 10th century* B.C., *oldest known Hebrew inscription, divides year by chores, from olive picking to "month of summer fruit." Hebrews of old knew citrons but not Jaffa oranges (right), Israel's major export. Water lifeline from Sea of Galilee makes desolate Negev "become like the garden of Eden" (Ezekiel 36:35).*

HUB OF FERTILE FIELDS, Nahalal embraces in a defensive circle the homes of 75 families on the Plain of Esdraelon. Unlike members of the more rigidly controlled communal kibbutzim, the independent shareholders of this cooperative town own and decide the use of their 25-acre spokes of land, reclaimed by Jewish settlers from a swamp six miles west of Nazareth in 1921. Moderns and ancients posted sentinels, but the Psalmist (127:1) warns, "except the Lord keep the city, the watchman waketh but in vain."

KENNETH MACLEISH, NATIONAL GEOGRAPHIC STAFF

Solomon "spake also of beasts, and of fowl, and of creeping things" I Kings 4:33

"THE KING'S WRATH is as the roaring of a lion," says Proverbs 19:12. Solomon's subjects knew the sound, for lions prowled Palestine until the 12th century A.D. Samson slew one bare-handed "as he would have rent a kid" (Judges 14:6). He also sent 300 foxes with torches on their tails to scorch Philistine grainfields. Many scholars would translate them into "jackals"—here and in the Song of Solomon (2:15), where "little foxes . . . spoil the vines."

For his part in man's fall, the "subtil" serpent must crawl. The dog appears some 40 times in the Bible, mainly as a scavenger; the cat but once. In contrast we find much praise for the sheep that fed and clothed man, the ox that tilled his fields, the donkey and camel (page 202) that bore his burdens. But archeology has yet to confirm the camel's domestication as early as Patriarchal days.

Job 39 portrays the war horse: "the glory of his nostrils is terrible . . . he smelleth the battle afar off, the thunder of the captains, and the shouting." Isaiah (11:6) foresaw peace when "The wolf also shall dwell with the lamb, and the leopard shall lie down with the kid . . . and a little child shall lead them."

Scriptural birds fly in rich variety— from eagles to tiny songsters. The dove brought Noah tidings of dry land; the raven never returned. But it redeemed itself by bringing food to Elijah in the wilderness.

Mosaic law decreed that an animal with cloven hoofs who "cheweth the cud" was clean to eat: sheep, goat, and ox, for example, or the antelope browsing below. Swine, hare, and cony were prohibited.

On the Day of Atonement, the high priest symbolically heaped the people's sins on a goat and let it escape. From this ritual in Leviticus 16 came our word "scapegoat."

IVORY PLAQUE, 8TH CENTURY B.C., FROM "NIMRUD AND ITS REMAINS," VOL. II, BY M. E. L. MALLOWAN

tending their fields. Each town lay within the orbit of a fortified city. In the chronically overcrowded cities, houses—sometimes two-storied—were jammed into every cubit of space. As a result, bizarre architectural angles abound in the ruins.

The Israelites' nomadic past showed in the lack of furniture in their homes, and in their garb, little changed since Patriarchal days. A man wore a kind of T-shirt and a short wrap-around skirt girded by a sashlike belt that held weapons and valuables. In brisk weather he donned a sleeved cloak that also served as a blanket. A woman wore a long skirt, tunic, and cloak, with a narrow scarf that framed her face and draped back to the tunic's hem.

The Sabbath had evolved since the days of Joshua . Though related to the Babylonian *sabattu* ("day of quieting of the heart"), the Hebrew Sabbath that created a six-day workweek had no parallel in the ancient world until Roman times. The Israelites enhanced the Sabbath by making it a gladsome day of worship.

Like many Arabs today, the Hebrews ate meat only on festive occasions. To vary the monotonous daily diet of parched or cooked wheat and barley, the Hebrew housewife would grind the grain into a coarse flour, mix it with olive oil, and bake it into flat cakes of bread. She garnished the cakes with lentils, broad beans, and other vegetables, including cucumbers. Onions, leeks, and garlic perked up bland dishes. Fresh and dried fruit and wild honey sweetened the meals. In a water-short land, the Hebrews heartily quaffed wine and prized the milk of goat and sheep.

Solomon and his sumptuous court demanded richer fare for their golden table. His "provision for one day was thirty cors of fine flour [about 335 bushels] and sixty cors of meal, ten fat oxen and twenty pasture-fed cattle, a hundred sheep, besides harts, gazelles, roebucks, and fatted fowl" (I Kings 4:22-23).

Each of the 12 administrative districts of Israel provided him and his court with a month's supplies, including barley and straw for the royal horses. Centralized government replaced the tribal league. Officials appointed by the king roamed the realm, ignoring ancient tribal boundaries and rights. Royal tax collectors, agents of a vast new

"And Ruth said...whither thou goest, I will go" *Ruth 1:16*

The Book of Ruth relates a cherished story of ancient Israel. In time of famine a woman called Naomi emigrated with her husband from Bethlehem to Moab. There the husband died; later her two sons married Moabite women. When both sons died, Naomi decided to return to Bethlehem. Ruth, one of her Moabite daughters-in-law, insisted on accompanying her, saying: "Whither thou goest, I will go; and where thou lodgest, I will lodge: thy people shall be my people, and thy God my God."

They arrive during harvest, when Hebrew law says the poor may glean. Now, holding sheaves of barley, Ruth kneels before the wealthy Boaz, who allows her to gather what the reapers have left. When she reminds him that he is a relative of her dead husband, he marries her in accord with the tradition that made kinsmen responsible for a widow's care. In this "levirate marriage," their first-born shall be deemed son and heir of her first husband—so that his "name be not put out of Israel" (Deuteronomy 25:6). And the son of Ruth and Boaz was grandfather of David the King.

bureaucracy, levied taxes in kind—much of it grain. They channeled Israel's wealth into store cities in each district. Archeologists have found thick-walled, high-floored warehouses apparently designed to keep the king's capital-grains taxes from spoiling.

Freedom-loving Israelites also paid for Solomon's glory with their own toil: "King Solomon raised a levy of forced labor out of all Israel" (I Kings 5:13). He sent 30,000 men to Lebanon to cut down cedars; another 150,000 to hew and haul stone in the hill country. Other corvées helped erect his buildings and likely the temple itself. Solomon, highly receptive to foreign ideas, may have followed the Egyptian practice of impressing men during slack farming seasons.

FOR CENTURIES Israelite farmers had reaped with flint sickles. Now grain fell under iron blades. No longer could it be said "there was no smith found throughout all the land of Israel" (I Samuel 13:19). For David had vanquished the Philistines, who guarded Palestine's ore and the secret of smelting it. Solomon exploited the lodes of the Promised Land, "whose stones are iron, and out of whose hills you can dig copper" (Deuteronomy 8:9).

The oldest rock formations in Palestine and Transjordan

"No razor shall come on his head"

Judges 13:5

A pious Jew gathers "the fruit of the land" for the harvest Feast of Booths. Onions and corn will adorn his sukkah, *a temporary shelter evoking the Exodus sojourn. Celebrants of old entwined their booths or tents with "boughs of goodly trees . . . and willows of the brook" (Leviticus 23:40). Solomon dedicated his temple during this joyous week.*

Skull-capped lads play in Jerusalem's intensely orthodox Mea Shearim quarter. Here echoes Leviticus 19:27: "Ye shall not round the corners of your heads, neither shalt thou mar the corners of thy beard." Long hair, secret of Samson's strength, was torn out or cut in mourning, sacrificed on fulfillment of a vow. Baldness brought derision.

B. ANTHONY STEWART, NATIONAL GEOGRAPHIC PHOTOGRAPHER. OPPOSITE: BRIAN BRAKE, MAGNUM

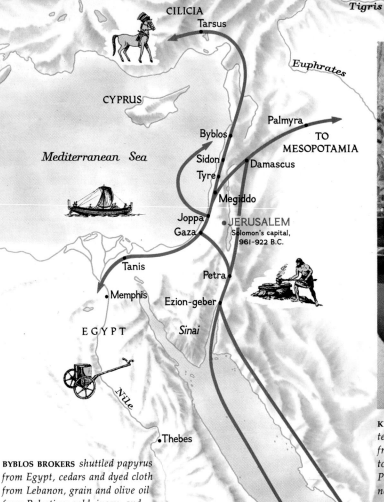

CILICIA
Tarsus

Tigris

Euphrates

CYPRUS

Byblos
Palmyra
TO
MESOPOTAMIA
Sidon
Damascus
Tyre

Mediterranean Sea

Megiddo

Joppa
JERUSALEM
Gaza
Solomon's capital,
961–922 B.C.

Tanis

Petra

Memphis
Ezion-geber

EGYPT
Sinai

Nile

Thebes

Red Sea

TO
OPHIR
LAND OF
SHEBA

0   100   200
STATUTE MILES

KING OF THE CROSSROADS, *Solomon spread tentacles of trade over sand and sea, from Egypt to Mesopotamia, from Cilicia to the land of Sheba. Galleys of his Phoenician allies sailed from Tyre, now tranquil Sur (above), and Sidon, modern Sayda, where a Lebanese fisherman mends his nets (opposite).*

BYBLOS BROKERS *shuttled papyrus from Egypt, cedars and dyed cloth from Lebanon, grain and olive oil from Palestine; gold, ivory, and slaves from Africa; copper from Cyprus, island for which the metal is named. Byblos, Greek name for the seaport, is synonymous with the scrolls of papyrus (biblos) traded here— whence our word "Bible." Gebal, the Biblical name for the 6,000-year-old Phoenician town, lives on in its Lebanese name, Jubayl. Roman and Crusader ruins gird this silted relic of Byblos' old harbor.*

crop out along the eastern wall of the Wadi al Arabah, the parched trough that runs from the Dead Sea to the Gulf of Aqaba. Copper ores vein these sandstone outcrops. Modern Israelis work copper at what they call King Solomon's Mines in Timna, where an estimated 20 million tons of commercial-grade ore remain untapped. Along the wadi, archeologists have found other ancient mining sites, marked by slag heaps and the ruins of walled encampments. The walls may have kept enslaved miners from running away. Few places on earth could be less desirable for heavy work. Cisterns caught what little rain fell; water often had to be carried for miles. Miners would not have worked in the fierce heat of summer.

Following a trail of slag heaps, miners' huts, and crude furnaces, Dr. Nelson Glueck explored the wadi until he reached the tip of the gulf. There where "Solomon made a navy of ships in Ezion-geber . . . on the shore of the Red sea, in the land of Edom" (I Kings 9:26), he found a remarkable fortress of the king.

From the sands of Ezion-geber emerged what Dr. Glueck saw as relics of ancient shipbuilding and fishing: "nails and timbers and resin and ropes . . . fishhooks and net-weights." Other remains indicated that sturdy buildings stood at Solomon's port. Well-guarded warehouses undoubtedly held exports destined for other lands and imports awaiting transport on caravans out of Ezion-geber.

Solomon's Red Sea fleet, built and manned by Phoenicians, sailed once every three years on voyages lasting more than a year. The ships plied the coasts of Africa and Arabia, presumably touching many ports, though the Bible mentions only one, Ophir, probably in southern Arabia. From Ophir came gold, precious stones, and "almug wood," probably sandalwood, that gave timbre to harp and

lyre. The fleet also brought back spices, ivory, and, to amuse the court, apes and baboons.

On land and on sea Solomon fostered trade. Through Israel passed caravans linking Mesopotamia, Syria, and Egypt. By regulating them, he made his kingdom a key crossroads.

He operated as a middleman in chariots, buying them in Egypt and selling them "to all the kings of the Hittites and Aramaeans"—the area around Damascus and northward. His agents also bought and sold fine horses from the stud farms of Cilicia, in what is now southern Turkey. A standard rate of exchange evolved— four Cilician horses for one Egyptian chariot. Solomon undoubtedly held an exclusive franchise on virtually all exports and imports. Private traders could scarcely compete with the monarch who controlled the frontiers.

CEDARS OF LEBANON, *monarchs of the mountains, still reign; some have seen a thousand snows. Name of the lofty Lebanon range comes from a Semitic word for "white." Treasured survivors of antiquity's great forests, 400 "cedars of the Lord" enjoy government protection. The aromatic timber built fleets for trade, solar boats to carry pharaohs' souls, and graced Solomon's Temple and palaces as far as Assyria. Phoenician oarsmen (below) toiled to supply the demand.*

WOMAN OF THE DESERT, *hauntingly hidden by tent drapery and veil, stirs memories of days when Arabian queens ruled caravan-tracked realms, and evokes the woman in the Song of Songs, "dark, but comely . . . like the tents of Kedar, like the curtains of Solomon" (1:5).*

Romance and pageantry dramatized the Queen of Sheba's visit with Solomon. Surely, though, they met in a summit conference called to discuss their competing royal monopolies.

We can see the glitter and whiff the fragrance: "And she gave the king an hundred and twenty talents of gold, and of spices very great store, and precious stones" (I Kings 10:10). In gold alone her gift amounted to several million dollars. Only as a trade mission can we truly comprehend the queen's 1,200-mile trek from Sheba to Jerusalem.

Her journey began in today's Yemen, on the southwest coast of the Arabian peninsula. There, some 3,000 years ago, caravan raiders grown rich on plunder banded to found a powerful state—the kingdom of Saba, the Biblical Sheba. Their realm straddled the vulnerable incense roads that coursed from the Hadramaut, on Arabia's south coast, to the ports of the Mediterranean.

"The multitude of camels...from Sheba" (Isaiah 60:6) paced these roads, after the caravaneers paid tolls to Sheba's menacing collectors. The camel, able to bear heavier loads farther over desert than the ass, had revolutionized the transport of spices, silk, and incense from India and southern Arabia. But Solomon's fleet cut into this lucrative trade.

SOLOMON SHONE in Israel's memory as a man "wiser than all men." Tradition credits him with the Proverbs, Ecclesiastes, and the Song of Songs. Just as David inspired song and psalmody, so did his cosmopolitan son enrich Israel with the proverbial wisdom of the Near East.

"Go to the ant, thou sluggard," the Proverbs (6:6) advised; "consider her ways, and be wise." Like the ant, Israel toiled. She gained in wisdom too. In scribal schools, schoolboys learned: "The fear of the Lord is the beginning of knowledge: but fools despise wisdom and instruction" (1:7). The schools spurred writing. And, stirred by the glory of their times, men began to set down the epic story of their nation and her God.

As Solomon grew old, his hold on Israel weakened. The head of a forced-labor battalion in the north brewed a revolt. Rebellion erupted in Edom, the province that guarded the port of Ezion-geber. An Aramaean guerrilla leader, wrenching the great Syrian empire away from Solomon, crowned himself king in Damascus.

CAMEL CARAVAN *treads an ancient incense road in Yemen. Classical writers dubbed this terraced, rain-blessed land Arabia Felix—Happy Arabia. Along such storied routes Sheba's traders carried spices, myrrh, and frankincense.*

THOMAS J. ABERCROMBIE, NATIONAL GEOGRAPHIC STAFF (ALSO OPPOSITE)

251

PILLARS *of a moon-god temple spike the sands near Marib. Here centered the kingdom of Saba, Biblical Sheba. Sabaeans, who sculptured in alabaster (above) and made gardens bloom with a giant dam and irrigation system, built the temple about 650 B.C. Ethiopia's kings claim descent from a son of Solomon and the Queen of Sheba who meet once more in a ballet (left) danced by Yemenite Jews in Israel.*

B. ANTHONY STEWART AND (RIGHT) THOMAS J. ABERCROMBIE, BOTH NATIONAL GEOGRAPHIC STAFF

What caused the downfall of a king so blessed for most of his life? The Bible traces it to the fact that he "loved many strange women." They and their retinues continued their own forms of worship, defiling the holy City of David with their foreign rituals. And the aging Solomon not only tolerated this paganism but alienated many of his people by indulging in it himself.

Solomon's subjects, yoked by harsh taxes and forced labor, saw only evil in Solomon's harem, traditionally 700 wives and 300 concubines. But the exotic women were living treaties. He had kept Egypt out of Israel by marrying an Egyptian princess, and thus became the only Asian king known to have wed a daughter of a pharaoh. And he maintained other alliances by taking a wife from the family of almost every potentate willing to sign a treaty.

But the Lord said, "Forasmuch as ... thou hast not kept my covenant ... I will surely rend the kingdom" (I Kings 11:11). And rent it was, for after Solomon died, about 922 B.C., the northern tribes formed a new kingdom of Israel with a capital at Shechem. In the south, Judah arose, faithful to Jerusalem and the dynasty of David. The empire died, sundered into two rival and doomed states.

But the glory of Solomon—and his realm—would live on, in the chronicles of his temple, in the sagas the Bible would immortalize. Most of all the glory would endure in the memory of a king of whom it was written: "there was none like thee before thee, neither after thee shall any arise like unto thee" (I Kings 3:12).

The March of Empires

VILLAGERS in western Judah see a distant dust cloud raised by the invaders. Runners carry the news from town to town. The Assyrians are coming! Jerusalem, capital of Judah, hears that the foe has already besieged Lachish, only 25 miles to the southwest. Along Jerusalem's walls guards eye the horizon. Suddenly they raise a shout, for a column of smoke rises from a beacon fire. The signal is clear: An Assyrian force is on the march toward the City of David.

Horns blare. Peasants leave the fields and hurry inside the city. The great bronze-clad gates swing together ponderously and are bolted. Grain stores are commandeered. At least there will be ample water. Judah's King Hezekiah has tunneled to the spring of Gihon so it will remain accessible. Now men draw javelins and shields from the well-stocked armory and mount the walls to reinforce the guards.

Among these Judaean troops let us imagine one Tobiel, armed and ready, but

By H.W. F. Saggs

KING ASHURBANIPAL *hunts at full cry across a stone relief
from his palace at Nineveh, Assyrian capital on the Tigris.
Assyrians scourge the Fertile Crescent, and princelings quail before them.
Babylonians follow; their tide of conquest levels Jerusalem.
Persians restore Hebrew exiles, build a vast empire. Greeks shatter it;
Romans engulf it. The prophets saw most new invasions as punishment
upon sinning Hebrews. But through the darkest days the prophets also
held forth a beacon of hope for Zion—and for all mankind.*

7TH CENTURY B.C. CARVING IN THE BRITISH MUSEUM, LONDON

filled with doubt. As evening falls he sees Assyrian cavalry dotting the skyline.

Since boyhood, Tobiel has heard tales of these fierce warriors. Their land astride the Tigris and Euphrates had been the seat of a great kingdom when the Hebrew Patriarchs were still wanderers tending flocks. In the two centuries since Solomon's death and the division of Palestine into two squabbling kingdoms—Israel in the north, Judah in the south—Assyrians have seized control over most of the Fertile Crescent. Only 20 years ago they overwhelmed Israel and its capital, Samaria, fulfilling the warnings of the prophets: "Samaria shall become desolate . . . they shall fall by the sword: their infants shall be dashed to pieces" (Hosea 13:16).

In 724 B.C. Assyrian troops "went up to Samaria, and besieged it three years. . . . and carried Israel away into Assyria" (II Kings 17:5-6). Assyrian cuneiform inscriptions also mention the campaign, but as scarcely more than a listing in a catalog of conquests. To the victors it was no more than the logical solution to the problem of a troublesome vassal.

For Israel's people the deportation marked the end of all they had known. Those exiles who had carts or pack animals were allowed to bring them, to carry their few possessions and to spare their women and children the worst rigors of the trek. Assyrian troops guarded them from molestation. At halts, men would light fires and women cook rations issued by the convoy commander or local administrator. Across the Euphrates they went, and shuffled into oblivion, the so-called "lost" tribes of Israel.

The Assyrians repopulated Samaria with deportees from elsewhere. Their descendants, intermarrying with Israelites who had escaped exile, became known as Samaritans. But the old kingdom of Israel was finished. "There was none left but the tribe of Judah only" (II Kings 17:18).

A score of years after Israel's fall Judah faced the same fate, for it had become entangled in the ambitions of a rebellious Babylonian chieftain, Merodach-baladan. This intriguer stirred revolts against Assyria's new ruler Sennacherib in the west while he himself planned to seize Babylon. Some years ago I was delighted to discover his name on cuneiform tablets. Both the Bible and the ancient tablets testify to his skill as a diplomatist.

His mission to Judah was enthusiastically received by King Hezekiah, who joined a coalition backed by Egyptian troops. But the prophet Isaiah thundered dire predictions: "Woe to the rebellious children. . . . For the Egyptians shall help in vain" (30:1, 7).

As JERUSALEM GIRDS for the Assyrian onslaught, Tobiel reflects that Isaiah has thus far been proved right. Already nearly 50 Judaean towns have fallen to Sennacherib, and even now he sits outside the walls of Lachish awaiting its collapse. How much of his army has he dispatched to Jerusalem?

The next day provides the answer: The main enemy force draws near. The van bears wooden or metal standards of Assyrian gods. On the flanks light infantry deploy as scouts. Tribal levies comprise the main column—slingers, archers, cavalrymen, distinguished by varied dress for they come from every corner of the empire. The transport brings up the rear, along with the engineers. They bridge streams, cut roads, and build ramps for wheeled battering rams, armored to protect the men who trundle them into position. Metal-clad rams swing on chains, striking powerful blows against the gates of any city foolish enough to resist Assyria.

"Sennacherib king of Assyria...himself laid siege against Lachish"

II Chronicles 32:9

The king hurls Assyria's might against the Judaean city southwest of Jerusalem in 701 B.C. Even as defenders rain boiling oil and firebrands on siege engines, attackers pour through a breach in

the wall. Forlorn Hebrews shuffle out a gateway to make obeisance to enthroned Sennacherib. Soon his troops will march on Jerusalem 25 miles away to confront King Hezekiah of Judah, who has withheld tribute.

Captives face impalement or flaying alive; exile awaits many. Scholars probing the war-scarred ruins of Lachish found the bones of 1,500 bodies in a pit— probably the siege's grim toll.

By evening, Tobiel can see the enemy settled into camp, dark tents lit by flickering fires. At daybreak a stir of excitement grips the watchers on the city wall, for a pair of chariots, their horses decked in blue, red, and gold, roll out from the Assyrian lines. A strong cavalry escort trots beside the vehicles. They halt at extreme bow-shot range and a herald summons the defenders to a parley.

Hezekiah's ministers give the Assyrian party, led by a general known as the Rabshakeh, safe conduct to the gate. The Hebrews want to negotiate in Aramaic, a language the watchers on the city wall will not understand. A Semitic tongue which originated in the Syrian desert, Aramaic is becoming the language of diplomacy; future centuries will find it in general use among Jews.

But the Rabshakeh calls out in Hebrew for all to hear, and offers terms direct to the people of the city over the heads of their rulers: "Let not . . . Hezekiah make you trust in the Lord. . . . Make an agreement with me . . . then eat ye every man of his own vine" (II Kings 18:29-31).

(It was an old trick. Fifteen years ago I was present at the discovery of hundreds of Assyrian letters on clay, and it was my privilege to be the first to read them since the days of Assyria's greatness. In one I found a remarkable parallel—the same bit of psychological warfare had been tried in an earlier campaign!)

The citizens stand silent. Despairing, Hezekiah turns again to his prophet. Isaiah's unhesitating reply rings from the Bible: "Thus saith the Lord, Be not afraid of the words that thou hast heard, wherewith the servants of the king of Assyria have blasphemed me. Behold, I will send a blast upon him" (37:6-7).

The decision is made. Resist! Grimly, Tobiel watches the Assyrians lay their siege. Working behind leather shields, they cart earth for a ramp and stack brushwood beneath the walls to crack the stones with fire. They set up towers for the archers and position the battering rams. Within

"Nineveh is laid waste: who will bemoan her?" Nahum 3:7

The prophet's paean echoes over the bleak tells of Nineveh (below), razed by Babylonians and Medes in 612 B.C. "O king of Assyria," exulted Nahum, "your nobles slumber." So did the city, lost for 24 centuries. Then diggers at its site across the Tigris from modern Mosul found reliefs of Ashurbanipal at war and hunting.

The mosque in background, Moslem tradition says, holds the tomb of Jonah and a tooth of the "great fish" (called a whale by Jesus) that swallowed him. Sent by God to preach at wicked Nineveh, Jonah fled to sea instead. After three days in the fish's belly, Jonah agreed to preach.

Kurdish madonna (opposite) descends from mountain tribesmen who ceaselessly fought Assyrians and helped bring down Nineveh.

the tense and crowded city the people can only watch and hope. Isaiah continues to encourage them.

As dawn breaks one morning a shout rises from the sentries on the walls. The Assyrians are withdrawing—not with their usual precision but in disorder, leaving equipment strewn behind. A Hebrew patrol, scouting the camp, finds that an epidemic has struck. Corpses lie in the tents. Isaiah's faith and encouragement were justified.

"SO SENNACHERIB king of Assyria departed . . . and dwelt at Nineveh" (II Kings 19:36). To him the failure to take Jerusalem was a minor setback. Hezekiah had acknowledged himself Assyria's vassal by paying tribute.

Nineveh was Sennacherib's pride and proved him a creator as well as a destroyer. With the sweat of his war captives he raised this great Assyrian capital soon after he gained the throne in 705 B.C. Many of its splendors remain, hidden in the tells across the Tigris from the city of Mosul in northern Iraq. Devoted Iraqi archeologists are attempting to restore parts of the vast encircling stone

261

Scholar-adventurers of the 1800's braved cutthroats and cholera

THREE HUNDRED Arabs strain at towropes. Drums thump, fifes wail. Lancers gallop about. The cart, with iron-bound tree sections for wheels, groans forward under its ten-ton burden—a colossal human-headed winged bull from the palace of Ashurnasirpal II, entombed some 25 centuries in the mound of Nimrud on the upper Tigris. Ahead of the procession rides a young Englishman, Austen Henry Layard (opposite upper), who has unearthed for the British Museum this touchstone to the Assyrian capital mentioned as Calah in Genesis 10.

"Wonderful!" exclaims a sheik riding with Layard. "He shows us what has been all our lives beneath our feet, without our having known any thing about it. Wonderful!"

Layard's finds sometimes terrified his Arab workmen. Giant statues conjured "fearful beings which are pictured . . . as appearing to mortals, slowly ascending from the regions below." One emerging colossus (lower) to them was Nimrod himself, "a mighty hunter before the Lord," for whom this tell was named; an official halted the dig until assured that Layard was not exhuming the legendary hero.

Arabian Nights had fired young Layard with the romance of the East. Leaving England in 1839

for a job in Ceylon, he went adventuring in Bible lands instead. Robbed naked by cutthroats, beset by hunger, thirst, and fever, bled with leeches by a "doctor," treated for toothache by a "dentist" who pried and pounded at his tooth with an iron awl, he survived— only to be infected by the infant science of archeology. In the Tigris-Euphrates region he unearthed battle reliefs, studied ancient texts, wrote of his exploits: "A deep mystery hangs over Assyria, Babylonia, and Chaldea. With these names are linked great nations and great cities dimly shadowed forth in history; mighty ruins, in the midst of deserts. . . ."

An earlier English adventurer shared his zeal: Claudius James Rich, a prodigious linguist. As Baghdad agent of the East India Company, Rich surveyed the mound of Nineveh, made the first scientific study of the site he confirmed as Babylon, and collected inscribed bricks, cuneiform tablets, and cylinder seals as proof. During a visit to Persia in 1821, Rich found cholera raging. He stayed to help the sick. Stricken himself, he died within hours.

But his finds stirred others. Paul Émile Botta, French consul at Mosul ("a scientific man but a damned bad consul," quipped a friend),

to find Assyria's royal cities

sought to dig at Khorsabad to the north.
From a conniving one-eyed pasha (notorious
for feigning death, then seizing the property
of all who rejoiced!) he wheedled a permit.
There in 1843 he found the 209-room palace
of Sargon II. For years the site yielded
stunning Assyrian treasures.

Woes plagued the dig. Wood was scarce,
so thieves stole the props, letting reliefs
fall and shatter. A finely preserved
winged bull bogged down on the road
to Mosul; locals burned it to make gypsum.
Rafts capsized in the flood-swollen Tigris,
dumping a hoard of antiquities to the bottom.
Excavators were unready for Khorsabad's trove.

Even so, Rich, Layard, and Botta cast light
on realms and rulers glimpsed in the Bible.
Still the wedge-shaped writing defied scholars.
When Layard unearthed Calah's Black Obelisk,
he could only call its salaaming figure (center)
"a prisoner"—never guessing that the stone
names "Jehu, son of Omri," King of Israel
in the 9th century B.C.! No other contemporary
portrait of a Hebrew king has ever been found.

Experts labored to decipher cuneiform.
Finally another scholar-adventurer found the
key—high on a Persian cliff (page 284).

walls. With them I have roamed Nineveh's ruins and seen in imagination the city of Sennacherib standing almost impregnable within its defenses.

Here his builders diverted a stream, filled in its bed, and protected it from flooding with a limestone retaining wall. On this terrace the king raised a fine new palace decorated with ornamental hardwoods and ivory. Alongside the palace he set out a great park planted with herbs and fruit trees.

Other splendid buildings rose beside broad streets and wide squares. Sennacherib dispatched prospectors to find new sources of decorative stone such as alabaster. He worked out ways to move huge cedar logs from the mountains and to ferry 20-ton carved stone bulls across the Tigris. He claimed to have invented a process that would help mass-produce big bronze statues.

An ardent warrior, Sennacherib mounted campaigns against Babylonia and the irrepressible tribesmen of the mountains north and east of Mesopotamia—today's Kurdistan. His annals record that "where the terrain was difficult I rode a horse and had my chariot carried. Where it became very steep I scrambled up on foot like a wild ox." Age was creeping up. He admits that "where my knees became weary, I sat down on a mountain rock and drank cold water from a water-skin. . . ."

Assyrian troops suffered in such campaigns, but when they met their enemies in open action, they struck fast and hard. The king would then ride a light chariot amid his guard of young noblemen, charging on foot, and his personal squadron of mounted archers and lancers. They would cut straight into the enemy center and try to panic the foe and shatter his formations. To protect his men from guerrilla action after a battle, the king would use terrorism as a psychological weapon. Word would spread of rebel chieftains staked out and flayed alive, of severed heads paraded through the streets of Nineveh. As one account put it, rebel sympathizers on hearing such tales "became like dead men."

I NSCRIPTIONS about Assyrian kings dwell lovingly upon their prowess in war: "the great king, the powerful king, the king of hosts, king of Assyria, who slew all who were hostile to him. . . ." They were also good administrators. In reading their letters I have again and again been struck by the efficiency of the men at the head of the empire. Everything—from details of ambassadorial negotiations down to the provision of shoes for deportees—had to be reported to the king.

Tiglath-pileser III, who took the throne 40 years before Sennacherib, reorganized the provinces and sent inspectors to check up on their administrators. To

Continued on page 273

■ Assyrian Empire c. 650 B.C.
---- Babylonian Empire c. 570 B.C.

*"A sound of battle
is in the land, and of
great destruction"*

Jeremiah 50:22

■ Persian Empire c. 500 B.C.
---- Alexander's Empire 326 B.C.

TIDES OF EMPIRE *flowed and ebbed over Biblical lands. Assyria,
Babylonia, Persia loom in the Old Testament, Rome in the New.
From Mesopotamia Assyria strode west to the "Great Sea,"
then lost all to Babylonia and Media. Cyrus of Persia
seized the Median capital of Ecbatana, made it his own;
Darius pressed into Europe. Rome girdled* mare nostrum — *our sea.
Some conquerors spread culture, others merely looted.
Yet all kept order and snuffed out petty wars, averting chaos
that could have threatened civilization's early gains.*

BRONZE RELIEF FROM "GATES OF SHALMANESER," 9TH CENTURY B.C., AND (OPPOSITE) ALABASTER RELIEF FROM NINEVEH,
7TH CENTURY B.C.; BOTH IN BRITISH MUSEUM. MAPS BY ISKANDAR BADAY, GEOGRAPHIC ART DIVISION

ASSYRIAN TROOPS *level the walls of an enemy city, stone by stone. Carving from Ashurbanipal's palace at Nineveh shows flames bursting from towers. Victors force vanquished to haul booty away.*

Assyrian chronicles resound with such scenes: "I destroyed them," records one king, "tore down the walls and burned the towns with fire; I caught the survivors and impaled them on stakes in front of their towns."

A reputation for savagery proved an effective weapon when Assyrian kings campaigned for tribute. Princelings paid up. If not, they faced an army which had perfected the art of the siege.

Bronze relief (left) shows a battering ram with a boar's head rolling toward a city gate while archers in coats of mail pour in covering fire. A besieged town could fall in a few months.

Roman Empire 14 A.D.

thens
•Ephesus
•Tarsus
•Antioch
ea •Baalbek
•Jerusalem
lexandria•

Not so Samaria, capital of the northern kingdom of Israel. Facing oblivion, the plucky Hebrews held out three years. But the outcome was inevitable. In his palace at Khorsabad Assyria's king ticked off the triumph, completed in 721 B.C.: "I besieged and conquered Samaria, led away as booty 27,290 inhabitants of it.... I installed over them an officer of mine...."

his capital at Calah, on the Tigris about 20 miles south of Nineveh, messengers came from all parts of the realm, sped by fresh mounts at way stations along the routes.

News of unrest or rebellion brought swift retribution; accounts of many such actions appear in the king's annals. They substantiate the Biblical narratives, which call him Pul. In II Kings 15 we read, "And Pul the king of Assyria came against the land: and Menahem gave Pul a thousand talents of silver. . . ." The Assyrian's annals, engraved on slabs found in the ruins of Calah, have been translated thus: "As for Menahem I overwhelmed him like a snowstorm and he . . . bowed to my feet. I returned him to his place and imposed tribute upon him, to wit: gold, silver, linen garments with multicolored trimmings. . . ."

The Bible also notes that Tiglath-pileser took Hazor in Galilee. In that huge tell archeologists in the 1950's found, at a level corresponding to the Assyrian's invasion, a devastated palace choked with charcoal debris. Above the ruin stood a small fort built by the Assyrian army.

Over the years the Assyrian empire expanded. Under King Ashurbanipal it reached deep into Egypt. He even captured Thebes, the Egyptian capital, but could not hold it. Through the last half of the seventh century B.C. Assyrian power dwindled as the influence of Babylonia increased. Revolts shook the empire. In 614 B.C. the Babylonians and their allies, the Medes, whose kingdom in the mountains of Iran adjoined Assyria on the east, sacked some cities in the Assyrian heartland. Among them was the sacred city of Ashur, whence came the name Assyria. The attackers now turned on Nineveh itself, and from Palestine the voice of the Judaean prophet Nahum rang out: "Woe to the bloody city!" In 612 B.C. Nineveh fell. Assyrian power was on the wane. Babylonia was in the ascendant.

CROWN PRINCE NEBUCHADNEZZAR of Babylonia claimed his country's throne soon after the fall of Nineveh. His position was shaky. Egypt was fomenting rebellion in Syria and Palestine. Among the rebels stood the King of Judah, though some prophets saw the folly of revolt. "Therefore thus saith the Lord of hosts," warned Jeremiah in chapter 25: "I will send . . . Nebuchadrezzar the king of Babylon. . . . And this whole land shall be a desolation. . . ."

But Judah's king scorned the prophet's words. He ordered a scroll of Jeremiah's oracles read, and as each few columns were intoned the monarch slashed them away with a knife and tossed them into the fire.

In 597 B.C. Nebuchadnezzar laid siege to Jerusalem, and no pestilence saved it. The Babylonians captured it, and though the Judaean king died before the disaster, his successor was herded off to Babylon on the distant Euphrates as a captive along with leading citizens and much booty.

Yet irrepressible Judah failed to learn its lesson. Still courting Egyptian aid, the Judaeans rebelled again, ten years after their first failure. This time Nebuchadnezzar besieged Jerusalem for a year and a half. When famine forced its surrender, the Babylonians leveled the city, including Solomon's Temple. They blinded the king, slew the leading citizens, and deported king and commoners. The epic of the Hebrew nation had begun in bondage in Egypt. And now it seemed to be ending the same way—on the long road to Babylon.

Tablets found in the ruins of Babylon note rations issued to Judaeans who had arrived from Jerusalem in the deportation of 597 B.C. The lists mention a certain

Shelemiah, obviously a nobleman, who may well have enjoyed considerable freedom in exile. We may imagine him as a young man walking Babylon's streets.

Dust fills the air from the rubble of old buildings, for Nebuchadnezzar is engaged in his most enduring work—the rebuilding of his capital. Thousands of men, some of them Judaean captives, toil in the sun to repair and strengthen the double wall of the city, to dig a moat, and raise defensive towers.

Shelemiah is struck by the multitude of shrines to the many Babylonian gods; there seems to be an altar at every street corner. He watches a Babylonian carry a lamb to one of the small temples that abound throughout the city. The worshiper apparently owes this offering, for a scribe draws up a receipt for the lamb on a clay tablet and hands it over. The Judaean notes that the form of sacrifice is not markedly different from that he had known in Jerusalem.

He sees men mount to the flat roofs of their thick-walled houses to start the day by prostrating themselves before the rising sun. He hears grace said to certain gods at mealtime and glimpses evening festivals in temples lit by reed torches dipped in tar. Here a bull or a sheep is slaughtered, and priests enact symbolic battles and dances and intone ritual texts in the long-dead Sumerian language.

Over the years Shelemiah finds that the great temples take on new splendor as craftsmen beautify their interiors with fine woods, gold and silver overlay, precious stones, and statuary. He is shocked to see Judaean exiles working on these pagan places. But they have no choice. At the great festivals, when Babylonians lead out their god Marduk, gorgeously arrayed, and treat the figure with solemn awe, Shelemiah and most other Judaeans turn aside with contempt at the ways of the pagan. Isaiah 44 scorns the man who "maketh a god, even his graven image: he falleth down unto it, and worshippeth it, and prayeth unto it, and saith, Deliver me; for thou art my god."

As the years of exile creep by, Shelemiah sees many of his own people attaching themselves to the pagan cults and joining in their rites. He remains firm to his faith. And this tends to exclude him from the social life of Babylon as well as from its religious community.

Yet the Judaean can appreciate the city's growing magnificence. The old ziggurat, the great stepped structure perhaps underlying the tradition of the Tower of Babel, is rebuilt. Now it dominates the city from a height of nearly 300 feet. But to Shelemiah, from the hills of Judah, the most pleasing feature of the city is the Hanging Gardens, a tree-clad

"Then shall this city be given [to] the Chaldeans and they shall burn it"

Jeremiah 38:18

274

PAINTING BY HENRY J. SOULEN. OPPOSITE: BABYLONIAN CHRONICLE IN THE BRITISH MUSEUM

NEBUCHADNEZZAR'S GENERAL *offers white-bearded Jeremiah glory in Babylon as "Chaldeans," or Babylonians, destroy Jerusalem in 587* B.C. *and herd Hebrews into exile. Restless under the yoke imposed by Nebuchadnezzar ten years earlier, Judah's King Zedekiah had revolted and jailed the seer—then sought his cell for prophecies that never varied: doom. Now freed, the prophet chooses to stay, without honor, in his own land.*

Babylonian account, in cuneiform (opposite), of the earlier chastisement of Jerusalem bears a date corresponding to March 16, 597 B.C.

Seers served most ancient faiths. They formed guilds, taught apprentices, sought the will of the gods in trances, dreams, miracles, even the flight of birds. Hebrew prophets—whose title connotes "declarer," not "predicter"—came to rely less on wonders, more on inspired eloquence as they chided sinning Israelites.

In hallowed passages the prophets still speak to men and nations. "Come now, and let us reason together," declares the first chapter of Isaiah. Micah 6:8 distills the prophets' message: "what doth the Lord require of thee, but to do justly, and to love mercy, and to walk humbly with thy God?"

275

DAUGHTERS OF BABYLON *thread a palm grove shading their
mud-walled hamlet beside the great city's ruins in central Iraq.
They carry donkey and camel dung to dry and stack—
fuel for fires in the Fertile Crescent since antiquity.*

artificial hill created by Nebuchadnezzar to simulate mountain scenery and — according to one report — please a princess homesick for the mountains of her native Media. Centuries later, awed Greek travelers will label it one of the Seven Wonders of the World.

Shelemiah grows accustomed to the life of Babylon's streets — the crier calling news of a runaway slave, the litigants arguing over lawsuits. Passing a temple courtyard, he hears a moan of pain and sees a man bathing with oil a raw weal on his forehead. He learns that the sufferer has forged a clay tablet. For punishment, his handiwork was heated and used to brand him on the brow.

He watches a foreign ship that has come up the Euphrates from the Persian Gulf unloading copper ingots. A smaller vessel waits her turn at the quay, her hold filled with alum from Carchemish, far up the river. But though commerce thrives, extravagant building projects and the cost of keeping an army in the field are crippling the economy. Taxes weigh ever more heavily. Prices soar. Parents are sometimes forced to sell their children into slavery.

With the death of Nebuchadnezzar in 562 B.C., the discontent could no longer be repressed. The next seven years produced three kings; only one died a natural death. Finally Nabonidus, son of a priestess, came to the throne and rode out the trouble. We have reason to believe some of the Judaean exiles supported him. In an effort to secure trade routes he captured a string of Arabian oases and colonized them. A thousand years later five of them were found to be inhabited by Jews. Apparently Nabonidus had settled trusted Judaeans in the vital desert outposts.

While he was in Arabia, his son Belshazzar governed Babylon. The Bible's Book of Daniel tells how Belshazzar "made a great feast. . . . In the same hour came forth fingers of a man's hand, and wrote . . . upon the plaister of the wall. . . . Then the king's countenance was changed . . . and his knees smote one against another" (5:1-6). Only the young Hebrew Daniel could read the handwriting on the wall: MENE, MENE, TEKEL, UPHARSIN. The words represent weights. Daniel interpreted them to mean that Belshazzar was "weighed in the balances and found wanting" and his kingdom would be given to the Medes and Persians.

T HE MEDES AND PERSIANS came from a land east of the Tigris, where snow-tipped mountains gleam against the sky. The Persians — named for Parsua, a district north of the Zagros Mountains — rose from obscurity to world dominance within the lifetime of one man, Cyrus

"Is not this great Babylon, that I have built?"

Daniel 4:30

Nebuchadnezzar's query yet haunt visitors to the remains of his city. They enter by this half-size replica of the towering Ishtar Gate that opened on the Babylonian capital. In bright relief against glazed blue brick, some 575 bulls and serpent-headed dragons glowered, reminders that one did not lightly enter Babylon, "glory of kingdoms.

Ishtar, goddess of love and war, was symbolized by an eight-pointe star. One adorns a kudurru, *or boundary stone (above). Sun and moon stand for gods Shamash and Sin. As these and the five planets then known moved in the skies, stargazers saw portents for their people. From temple towers — ideal as observatories — they fancied constellations as beast and humans. Babylonians' ideas persist in the signs of the Zodiac, as does their name Chaldean, a synonym for astrologer. Hebrews damned the art. "Let now the astrologers, the stargazers . . . stand up, and save thee," Isaiah 47 taunts doomed Babylon.*

the Great. In 550 B.C. this Persian ruler rebelled against the Medes, whose empire stretched across much of today's western Iran. Cyrus captured the Median capital Ecbatana (site of modern Hamadan) and won control over the whole empire.

Next he invaded Asia Minor and in 547 B.C. seized Sardis, capital of fabulously wealthy King Croesus of Lydia. This won him the trade marts of Ionia, on the Aegean's eastern shore. Eastward, Cyrus drove into what is now Afghanistan —homeland of the religious teacher Zoroaster. In 539 B.C., 11 years after he emerged from vassalage, Cyrus moved on Babylonia, richest and most advanced area of western Asia. Its capital surrendered with scarcely a struggle.

Many Babylonians welcomed the Persians, for Cyrus spread smooth words about his own goodness, tolerance, and piety. The Hebrews welcomed him too: "Thus saith the Lord to his anointed, to Cyrus, whose right hand I have holden, to subdue nations before him...I will go before thee, and make the crooked places straight" (Isaiah 45:1-2).

Perhaps Shelemiah, grown old in exile, stood and watched as the thousands of Persian soldiers, on foot and horseback, marched through the Ishtar Gate. Certainly we can imagine the aged Hebrew's joy at one of the new ruler's first

"And they brought Daniel, and cast him into the den of lions"
Daniel 6:16

Though captives, Hebrews in Babylon might rise to high status. Beloved Bible chapters tell of one who did: Daniel, palace page grown to royal adviser. When he, alone of court seers, recounted Nebuchadnezzar's dream and its meaning, the king set him "over all the wise men of Babylon." When Prince Belshazzar, ruling as regent, feasted with vessels from Solomon's Temple, only Daniel could read the words blazoned on a wall by a disembodied hand: "Thy kingdom is...given to the Medes and Persians."

Next morning Belshazzar lay dead; the Persians ruled Babylon.

Daniel still held office, but jealous rivals plotted his downfall. When they found him flouting a royal edict by praying to his God, they forced the king to invoke the "law of the Medes and Persians, which altereth not."

Daniel was cast to the lions. The next morn found him unhurt. "My God...hath shut the lions' mouths," cried Daniel (6:22). His accusers died in the den instead.

Such tales cheered Hebrews in the turbulent centuries before Christ.

PAINTING BY PIERRE MION AFTER HERBERT ANGER, FROM "BABYLON" BY ECKHARD UNGER © WALTER DE GRUYTER

BABYLON'S PARAPETS *once ringed
a city of palaces, broad boulevards,
and scores of temples — which
Judaean exiles helped build. From a
suburb added by Nebuchadnezzar,
a bridge spanned the Euphrates
to the temple of the god Marduk
and the blue-browed, seven-story
ziggurat (painting, opposite).
Ancients described the famed tower;
modern explorers found only its
foundation plan. Flooding and
irrigation channels shifted the
river's course. Today it passes to
the west, and Babylon's broken
walls (left) slumber in the dust.*

281

decrees—that captives would be liberated, their shrines restored. As Cyrus chronicled of some of his conquered cities, "I returned to these...the images which used to live therein and established for them permanent sanctuaries. All their people I assembled and returned to their habitations."

Many Judaeans, comfortably settled in Babylonia and more prosperous than their forefathers ever had been in Palestine, remained. Shelemiah, though loyal to his faith for 58 years of exile, would now, ironically, have been too far advanced in age to make the long trek home to Jerusalem. We read of the resettling of the city and the rebuilding of its temple in the first chapter of the Bible's Book of Ezra: "Thus saith Cyrus king of Persia, the Lord God of heaven...hath charged me to build him an house at Jerusalem, which is in Judah. Who is there among you of all his people? his God be with him, and let him go up to Jerusalem...."

FROM ZAGROS MOUNTAIN *villages like Heshmatabad in western Iran (below) Cyrus the Great drew strength to found the Persian empire in the sixth century* B.C. *He toppled the Medes, overlords of the Iranian plateau, then swept into the Fertile Crescent, freeing the Hebrews from Babylon's yoke. Among his conquering hordes were ancestors of proud Kurdish patriarch (right), dagger in belt. Yard-long cuffs like his served to bind wounds in more violent days.*

THOMAS J. ABERCROMBIE, NATIONAL GEOGRAPHIC STAFF

Persia's kings carved history in ageless rock

Fresh from far-reaching conquests that
toppled Persia, Alexander the Great stoc
before a tomb (above) at Pasargadae, Iran.
The young Macedonian read words there
that gnawed his soul: "O man, whosoever
thou art and whencesoever thou comest,
for I know that thou wilt come, I am Cyrus
son of Cambyses, and I won for the Persia
their empire. Do not, therefore, begrudge
me this little earth that covers my body."

The story comes to us from Plutarch.
From another Greek chronicler, Herodotus,
we know the "Ten Thousand Immortals,"
Persian guardsmen who still parade (left)
in glazed brick from the royal city of Susa.
But the centuries had erased all memory of
the cuneiform script of Assyria, Babylonia,
and Persia. Pioneer archeologists early in
the 1800's found the wedge-shaped writing
etched on walls, statues, bits of clay.
They sent home examples, and museum
visitors scoffed at "bird tracks on wet sand
Scholars lacked a Rosetta Stone (page 22)
to match the forgotten with the familiar.

Were the symbols vowels, consonants,
words, or syllables? Did lines read to the
left, right, or boustrophedon—as the ox
plows—once to the right, then to the left?

By deduction, a young German, Grotefen
amazingly deciphered a third of the Persia
cuneiform alphabet in 1802. An obscure
teacher, he attracted little attention.
Everyone noticed the towering Behistun
rock on a road near Kermanshah, Iran.
Above a 340-foot cliff a bold relief with
cuneiform texts had puzzled generations.
Here, in 1835, came an English army office
adept at "pigeon-shooting, pig-sticking,

steeple-chasing." Henry C. Rawlinson (below) should have added cliff-hanging. Inching up to a tiny ledge, then to a ladder's top rung, he came eye-to-eye with carved figures and columns of symbols (right).

Rawlinson felt that the one life-size figure was a Persian king. To learn more, he had a native helper dangle from ropes. Often he himself clung to the smooth rock with little more than his fingernails (the sculptors had hacked away their own steps), copying inscriptions. "The interest of the occupation," he wrote, "entirely did away with any sense of danger."

Unaided by Grotefend's work, Rawlinson toiled for years over 200 lines, deduced that the symbols formed an alphabet, and found a pattern ancient Persians used in naming their kings: "So-and-so, Great King, King of Kings, son of So-and-so."

By 1846 he could read the Behistun text. It tells how "Darius, Great King, King of Kings," won the throne after slaying a pretender who "lied to the people." The figures depict the king, backed by guards, glaring at nine tethered rivals and grinding a tenth underfoot while his god, Ahura Mazda, floats overhead.

Told in three languages, the tale gave scholars their key to cuneiform. Now they could read the long-collected writings, including Ashurbanipal's "library" found at Nineveh, a trove of texts still treasured by Assyriologists today.

SIR HENRY C. RAWLINSON BY H. W. PHILLIPS, 1850; BRITISH MUSEUM. RIGHT: GEORGES BOURDELON-NOËL BALLIF. OPPOSITE: DETAIL OF A FRIEZE FROM SUSA, 5TH CENTURY B.C., IN THE LOUVRE. UPPER: MERLE SEVERY, NATIONAL GEOGRAPHIC STAFF

For a century following Cyrus' decree groups of exiles journeyed back. Between 520 and 515 B.C. they erected a modest temple. Jerusalem became the capital of a small province of some 50,000 people within the Persian empire.

CYRUS DIVIDED his realm into 20 administrative regions, each ruled by a satrap, or governor. After his death in 529 B.C., his son and successor, Cambyses II, took the obvious step of stretching the empire into Egypt and captured Memphis. Trying to win acceptance as Pharaoh, Cambyses visited the temples and wore Egyptian royal robes. His expeditions up the Nile toward Ethiopia failed. But Hebrews under Persian protection garrisoned Elephantine Island, just north of the Nile's first cataract. The records they left in the next century—the Elephantine Papyri—have helped reconstruct life under the benign rule of Persia.

Darius took the throne in 522 B.C. To consolidate the empire, he built a canal between the Nile and the Red Sea. "After this canal had been dug as I commanded," says a stela set up along its course, "ships went from Egypt through this canal to Persia according to my wish." Eastward across

"THE KING LOVED ESTHER *above all the women . . . so that he set the royal crown upon her head"* (Esther 2:17). *The Hebrew heroine dines with her Ahasuerus on a colonnaded terrace (right); scholars identify him as Xerxes, son and successor of Darius the Great. Esther and a kinsman foiled a plot to kill the king, then thwarted a pogrom against her people in Susa, one of many cities where exiled Hebrews had taken root. Jews still hail her in the Festival of Purim. Persia's rulers wintered at Susa.*

Gaunt columns mourn the ruins of Persepolis (below), ceremonial capital created by proud Darius: "I built it secure and beautiful."

PAINTING BY PETER V. BIANCHI, NATIONAL GEOGRAPHIC STAFF ARTIST. BELOW: HELEN AND FRANK SCHREIDER, NATIONAL GEOGRAPHIC STAFF

the deserts, Darius expanded his domain to include the Indus Valley—the very edge of the Indian Peninsula. He then sent an expedition down the Indus and along the southern coast of western Asia to the Gulf of Suez to show how ships could link the flanks of his empire. A Greek navigator, Scylax, led the exploration. Darius had the genius to find and use the talents of the various peoples in his realm.

Artisans from all corners of imperial Persia raised two splendid cities. The ancient town of Susa on a tributary of the lower Tigris was sumptuously rebuilt. Darius recorded the places that supplied precious stones, timber, ivory, and the men who fashioned them—Medes, Babylonians, Ionians,

ALEXANDER THE GREAT *pierces a Persian and clears a path to empire at Issus in Asia Minor in 333 B.C. Outnumbered 20 to 1, the Macedonian routed Darius III, who fled, leaving even his harem. Alexander "fought among the foremost," recorded Plutarch, "and was wounded in the thigh." At Persepolis—where stone lancers still stand guard (opposite)—he rifle the royal treasury, departing with 4,500 tons of gold and silver. In his wake Greek culture spread.*

Egyptians, and men from Sardis. The Ionians were probably Greek sculptors from the coast of Asia Minor who produced the bas-reliefs for which Susa is famous.

Darius' second city rose at Persepolis on a plain beyond the Zagros Mountains, far to the east of Susa. Here artists and masons fashioned new wonders. This high country was Darius' native land—a pleasant change from the breathless summer heat of Susa, where, according to Greek records, lizards were grilled if they tried to scuttle across the street in the noonday sun. The old capital at Ecbatana, however, remained the summer residence of the Persian kings.

Darius utilized not only the skills of his diverse subjects, but also their inventions. The Lydians, for example, had developed a medium of exchange in the seventh century—metal disks officially stamped to guarantee weight and quality. Darius adopted the idea and introduced a coinage system into the empire. It was to revolutionize commerce.

The religion of Darius differed from that of earlier Persian kings. His inscriptions often proclaim his faith in Ahura Mazda, an old Persian deity, as the sole god. In his monotheism Darius followed the teaching of Zoroaster, who had lived a century earlier. Like the Hebrew prophets, Zoroaster faced a theological problem: If there is but one good and all-powerful god, why is there evil? The Hebrews answered that God's purposes are too vast for man's understanding. As Elihu, debating afflicted Job, put it: "Behold, God is great, and we know him not" (Job 36:26).

Zoroaster offered a different solution. For him two spirits emanated from Ahura Mazda. Each was associated with one of the eternal principles, Truth and Falsehood. A man had to choose which he supported, and his choice strengthened the side he picked.

In 513 B.C. Darius crossed the Bosporus on a bridge of boats and invaded Europe, threatening Greek trade routes.

DETAIL FROM A FRIEZE AT PERSEPOLIS, 6TH–5TH CENTURIES B.C. UPPER: PAINTING BY H. M. HERGET

AS OLD TESTAMENT PAGES CLOSE, *Rome's legions "spare the submissive and war down the proud." Pompey adds Judaea to the province of Syria; thus the New Testament begins on a Roman stage: "there went out a decree from Caesar Augustus. . . . when Cyrenius was governor of Syria" (Luke 2:1-2). Roman temples and sculptures dotted the empire from Britain to the Euphrates. At Baalbek in Lebanon, where Phoenicians enshrined their god Baal and Greeks built Heliopolis (City of the Sun), Romans erected temples with 750-ton wall stones set 20 feet above ground; no one knows how.*

Amid the ruins the Royal Ballet of London (below) performs at a festival where modern pilgrims pay homage to art.

ROMAN FRIEZE, 2ND CENTURY A.D., IN THE LOUVRE. BELOW: AIR FRANCE

When mercantile city-states struck back, he sought to crush the leading one, Athens. But he suffered a surprise defeat at Marathon in 490 B.C., and before he could try again he died. He left the greatest empire the world had ever known.

CHRONIC REVOLTS and military disasters in Greece plagued Darius' successors. In Judah the population grew until all available land was taken up. This pressure on the land led to economic troubles. When crops failed, the wealthy foreclosed on mortgages and reduced the dispossessed to slavery. The Persian authorities sent two officials, both Hebrews, to Jerusalem to improve conditions.

The Bible's Book of Nehemiah tells how the priest Ezra recalled the people to the law of Moses: "And he read therein . . . before the men and the women, and those that could understand" (8:3). Nehemiah arrived as governor and proclaimed that all able-bodied men would rebuild the walls of Jerusalem. Raids by Nehemiah's opponents threatened the city, so "every one with one of his hands wrought in the work, and with the other hand held a weapon." Nehemiah called for a cancellation of debt, and the economic climate improved.

But the empire had seen its best days. Egypt broke away. Philip of Macedon ended the rivalry of Greek city-states by conquering them all. And the Persian army proved no match for the Greeks led by Philip's son, soon to be called Alexander the Great.

Alexander moved on Asia in 334 B.C. He took Persepolis and soon stood at the Indus, weeping for more worlds to conquer. A century or so later many in Jerusalem wore Greek garb and watched Greek sports. Even the sacred writings were translated into Greek.

Rebellious Jews, calling themselves Maccabees (from the Hebrew for "hammer") won short-lived freedom. Then the strong arm of Rome reached round the Mediterranean. In 63 B.C. Pompey conquered Judah. On the Day of Atonement he entered Jerusalem's temple and broke into the holy of holies itself.

But the ancient faith endured. And a new power, more lasting than Rome's, was at hand, heralded, perhaps, in Isaiah 52: "How beautiful upon the mountains are the feet of him that bringeth good tidings, that publisheth peace . . . that saith unto Zion, Thy God reigneth."

"CHRIST ENTERING JERUSALEM" BY GIOTTO, 1305–6, IN ARENA CHAPEL, PADUA; SCALA

ACCLAIMING JESUS as the King, the Son of David, and the Messiah, "a very great
multitude spread their garments in the way; others cut down branches from the trees,
and strawed them in the way" (Matthew 21:8). Entering Jerusalem on an ass,
the humble Nazarene carpenter moved toward the greatest drama in the memory of Christian man.
Later, history's events would be counted, not from the foundation of Rome, or according
to the years of a King Herod or an Emperor Tiberius, but before or after Christ.

By Roland de Vaux

The World of Jesus

"IN THE FIFTEENTH YEAR of the reign of Tiberius Caesar, Pontius Pilate being governor of Judaea, and Herod being tetrarch of Galilee . . . the word of God came unto John . . . in the wilderness." Thus does Luke (3:1, 2) describe the year when John the Baptist began preaching by the Jordan, and Jesus came to be baptized and began His public ministry.

The message Jesus taught rings through the centuries for all men. Yet He lived and preached in a small country during a troubled time. To know that land, to understand that time gives us deeper insight into His words. For more than half my life I have worked in the Holy Land, digging in its soil, studying the peoples, customs, beliefs which prepared the way for Christianity.

To re-create the world of Jesus I have imagined a journey through this land by a stranger, a Greek trader like many I have encountered in records of those days. Our story unfolds in the same year that Jesus set forth on His mission, A.D. 28, but before the impact of His teachings was felt. In later chapters we will return to many of these sites, in the footsteps of the Master.

A Syrian trading vessel, plying regularly between Alexandria and Tyre, puts in at Joppa. The small harbor, shallow and exposed to the north winds, has been little frequented since Herod the Great built Caesarea farther north. But Joppa is the closest port to Jerusalem. Our traveler, one Apollonios of Alexandria, son of Ariston, strides down the gangplank and counts the bundles of Egyptian linen being stacked on the landing. He bargains with donkey drivers, gets his merchandise loaded, selects a good beast for himself, and sets out on the centuries-old track toward Jerusalem.

A day's journey takes him across the fertile coastal plain into the Judaean hills, marked by olive trees, vines, goats, and sheep. On the second day he catches his first glimpse of Jerusalem: It sits atop two hills, rimmed by a great wall with towers. At the Joppa Gate his company's agent takes charge of the linen and shows him to his lodgings. Afterward, Apollonios is free to roam the twisting streets.

He rubs shoulders with Roman soldiers, tax collectors, merchants, peasants driving in flocks of bleating sheep. The common language is Aramaic, but he also hears Hebrew, Greek, and Latin. He finds two main streets of shops,

the Upper Market and Lower Market. Behind the shops, craftsmen make what they sell. Each trade has a special location: Dried-fish dealers congregate at the Fish Gate, fullers process cloth outside the city wall near the Pool of Siloam. The valley separating the city's two hills is called Tyropoeon, a name Apollonios understands, for in Greek it means "cheesemakers." Here indeed one may buy all the products of the Roman empire: dried figs from Cyprus, slaves from Phoenicia, fabrics from Babylon, and all the spices of Arabia. Apollonios hears the jingle of silver coins of Tyre and Rome and the bronze small change of Judaea.

Why all this prosperity in a town off the great caravan routes, no longer even the capital of a province?

Jerusalem is the center of the Jewish world. Heart of a religious community with its own laws, worship, and customs, the city stands unique in the empire.

ROME recognizes this special status, exempts the Jews from military service, and allows them to govern themselves—within limits. For two years the emperor's direct representative, the procurator, has been Pontius Pilate, headquartered at Caesarea. He makes the four-day journey to Jerusalem but rarely, coming with a strong military escort to maintain order during feast days.

The high priest, chosen by the procurator, is recognized as the head of the Jewish nation. He presides over the Sanhedrin, a senate of 70 members whose decisions apply to Jews in Damascus, Alexandria, and Rome as well as Palestine. Three groups constitute it: the high clergy, the elders, and the scribes, or doctors of the law. The Sanhedrin meets near the temple and decides civil and criminal as well as religious cases. In two or three years this august body will hear the charge of blasphemy against Jesus. But when the Sanhedrin decrees death, the sentence must be ratified by the procurator and executed by his officers.

The Jews are split into two major religious parties. The Sadducees, attracting the more aristocratic priests, landowners, and merchants, accept only the Torah, the written law of Moses, as authoritative. They pay court to Roman power and are indulgent toward Hellenistic culture. The Pharisees, mainly middle class and led by the doctors of the law, add to the Torah the edicts of oral tradition.

HELEN AND FRANK SCHREIDER, NATIONAL GEOGRAPHIC STAFF
OPPOSITE: BRIAN BRAKE, MAGNUM

"IF I FORGET THEE, O Jerusalem, let my right hand forget her cunning," sang the Psalmist (137:5) of the Holy City, where ancient ways persevere. Farmwife (left) balances a load of pomegranates on Inn of the Olive Oil Street. Villager (above) draws water from a storied pool in the Valley of Kidron. "Go, wash in the pool of Siloam," Jesus said to a blind man. He went, and "came seeing" (John 9:7).

295

They believe in angels, resurrection of the dead, and immortality of the soul.
The Pharisees will denounce Jesus for fraternizing with sinners and for laxity
in observing the Sabbath. He in turn will speak of them as hypocrites who
"strain at a gnat, and swallow a camel," and who neglect "judgment, mercy, and faith."

Differences between Sadducees and Pharisees do not weaken the vital Jewish
religion. Even Jews seduced by Greek or Roman custom cling to strict monotheism.
Hear, O Israel: the Lord our God, the Lord is one, begins the *shema*, in the daily prayer.
The law also teaches: *Thou shalt love thy neighbor as thyself.* "Neighbor" generally
is interpreted as a fellow Israelite, a member of God's chosen people whose males carry
the sign of God's covenant on their bodies by being circumcised. Judaism is a closed
community, protecting the treasure of its faith by keeping away from *goyim*, the pagans.

How galling, then, for God's people to be dominated by pagans, having to offer sacrifice
and render taxes unto Caesar. Not long ago, Jerusalem basked in royal glory—Herod's glory

WHAT A REMARKABLE CREATURE, that last king of the Jews! Herod was not even
of Jewish blood but an Idumaean—an Edomite descendant of Esau. Scarcely a century
ago the Judaeans had converted the Idumaeans to the Jewish faith by conquest.
Apollonios had heard how Herod, with cunning and violence, had eliminated rivals
for the throne. He had charmed not only Cleopatra, but
successive rulers of Rome. Recognized as an ally of the
Roman patrons he flattered, he used terror to control
his subjects. An able general, shrewd politician,
excellent administrator, he managed to enlarge his realm

SEEKING NEW CLUES *to life in ancient Palestine, Father de Vaux examines shards excavated by Dr. Pritchard—consultant for this book—at Tell es Saidiyeh. Green fields beyond them flank the Jordan.*

Razed by the Romans, Jerusalem flourished again in 4th century under Constantine. Its oldest map dates two centuries later—mosaic (below) in a Byzantine church at Madaba. Towers stud the walls. Great gate at left stands on site of today's Damascus Gate. From nearby pillar all distances in Palestine were measured. Columned main street leads to old Zion Gate; midway, like a pendant, appears the gilt-domed Church of the Holy Sepulcher.

Middle line of Roman inscription found at Caesarea (far left) reads [PON]TIVS PILATVS—*Pontius Pilate!*

THOMAS NEBBIA. FAR LEFT: COURTESY ISRAEL DEPARTMENT OF ANTIQUITIES AND MUSEUMS

until it almost matched Solomon's. His hospitality was magnificent, his works lavish. All over Palestine, and even beyond, rose his temples, amphitheaters, and palaces. Herod thirsted for power. Having achieved it, he grew increasingly unstable and suspicious. His own household became a nest of intrigue. In a fit of jealousy he ordered his beautiful wife Mariamme executed. Her brother, the high priest, he had drowned. Sinking deeper into madness, he had three of his sons killed, two by strangulation. And, Matthew would record in his Gospel, when Herod learned of a babe born in Bethlehem whom men called "King of the Jews," he ordered the death of "all the male children in Bethlehem and in all that region . . . two years old or under."

Having clung to the throne for more than three decades, Herod himself died of natural causes. That was some 30 years ago. Three other sons divided the kingdom; they proved less strong. When rioting broke out in Jerusalem, Roman troops occupied Judaea and Samaria. Now people remember Herod's glory, even regret his passing. They refer to him as "Herod the Great." Weeds grow in the Greek theater where troupes performed, the amphitheater where chariots raced, the hippodrome where beasts tore the life from men—an outrage to pious Jews. But you cannot forget Herod. His landmarks stand everywhere: the fine gardens and ponds; the Antonia fortress, where troops are quartered; the palace, where the procurator stays on visits. Above all, Herod's glorious temple on the eastern ridge between the Kidron and Tyropoeon Valleys, set precisely on the foundations of Solomon's Temple. Here 10,000 men labored for years raising columned buildings and courts. Now the temple is girded by an esplanade 550 paces long, 400 wide, rimmed by a massive portico.

297

Through one of its gates Apollonios enters. Beyond the esplanade he is stopped by a railing. Slabs of stone on it proclaim in Greek and Latin that foreigners may go no farther, under penalty of death. Through a bronze gate—gleaming with gold panels and so large that it takes 20 men to open it—lies the women's court, which all Israelites may use. Then comes the court of Israel, reserved for men, and finally the priest's court, with its great sacrificial altar. This stands before the temple itself, which rises a hundred cubits (about 150 feet), topped by golden spikes to prevent birds resting on the roof and fouling it. Over the entrance, facing east, hangs a richly decorated curtain of Babylonian fabric.

Apollonios cannot see beyond this. Even his Jewish friends have not gone beyond the court of Israel. But they know that the interior of the temple is divided into three rooms: a vestibule; the holy place, where stands the altar of incense and the big golden candlestick with seven branches; and the holy of holies, inhabited by the mysterious, awesome presence of the God of Israel.

Besides the high clergy, the temple is staffed by ordinary priests who come from throughout Palestine. Divided into 24 groups, they perform a week's service in rotation, 300 each week. There are also the Levites, the lowest order, who serve as cantors, doorkeepers, and servants. In all, the clergy numbers about 18,000. With their families, they represent perhaps a tenth of Palestine's Jews.

Each morning as the sun rises over the Mount of Olives, priests sacrifice a lamb, offer flour, wine, and incense, and recite the shema. Levites intone hymns, trumpets sound, and the faithful prostrate themselves.

Because of the many private sacrifices, sellers of oxen, sheep, kids, and doves throng the esplanade. Here too are the money changers whom Jesus will scourge, sitting behind little tables with scales,

"THEY FOUND HIM IN THE TEMPLE...
*in the midst of the doctors . . .
asking them questions. And all
that heard him were astonished"*
(Luke 2:46-47). *When 12,
Jesus came with His family
to Jerusalem for Passover.
On the homeward journey
they discovered Him missing—
and found Him in Herod's temple,
here commemorated on a silver shekel.*
"I must be about my Father's business," Jesus explained.
    *Doctors of the law, or scribes, served as judges and teachers.
They had their origin during the Babylonian exile, when the
Jews were deprived of temple and priests. To interpret the law
they used two aids: the* halakah, *a legal commentary,
and the* haggadah, *a compilation of traditional narratives.
Doctors and scribes were also called* rabbi—"*my master.*"

"CHRIST AMONG THE DOCTORS" BY JUSEPE DE RIBERA, C. 1625; KUNSTHISTORISCHES MUSEUM, VIENNA.
COIN STRUCK BY BAR KOCHBA A.D. 135; BIBLIOTHÈQUE NATIONALE, PARIS

exchanging foreign money into the half-shekel of silver which every male Jew over 20 must give annually to the temple, in addition to a tenth of his crops.

Annual feasts highlight the temple ritual: the Day of Atonement when the high priest enters the holy of holies alone; the Feast of Dedication, when voices rise in the Hallel—the Psalms of Alleluia—and for eight days lamps flicker in all the windows of Jerusalem. Greatest of all are the pilgrimage feasts of the Passover, Feast of Weeks, and Feast of Booths, when the law calls for every Jew to come and pray in Jerusalem.

Now, as Passover approaches, the city throbs with life. Apollonios hears all languages, sees all kinds of dress. Merchants, beggars, cutpurses prosper. Pilgrims fill all inns and the hostels attached to synagogues. Apollonios' host takes in his cousins from Galilee. So that those who cannot find lodging in the city may still fulfill the decree that feast days must be spent in Jerusalem, the city extends its boundaries as far as the village of Bethphage on the Mount of Olives.

By the evening of 13 Nisan, in the Roman month of April, each house has been cleaned and any leavened bread eaten or burned before the feast—for Passover signals a complete rejuvenation. The following afternoon, sacrifices begin. Families or friends in groups of 10 to 20 join to buy a lamb or kid.

Their representatives carry the victim to the temple courtyard and slaughter it.
Priests gather the blood in cups, pour it at the foot of the altar, and burn
the entrails on the perpetual fire. The sacrificial animal, carried back to the house
where the family waits, will be roasted on a rod of pomegranate wood.

At the temple the slaughter goes on amid fervor and joy, punctuated by the blast
of trumpets, the chanting of the Hallel, the bleating of victims. The east wind
carries over the city the smell of blood and spilt entrails, burnt fat and incense.

When the sun has set, families partake of the paschal meal. Apollonios, despite
his host's courtesy, finds himself excluded as a non-Jew. In olden days one ate
the meal standing, with loins girded and staff in hand, as the Hebrews had done
in the Exodus. Nowadays one reclines on a couch in the Greek and Roman manner.

The father says a blessing, and the family drinks
the first glass of watered wine. Then come vegetables,
which are dipped in sauce. The father explains the meaning
of the feast, the marvelous deliverance from Egypt,
which betokens future deliverance through the mercy of God.
The family drinks a second cup, eating the lamb with
unleavened bread and bitter herbs—remindful of the
wandering in the wilderness. A third and fourth cup follow,
during which the Hallel is recited. The feast continues
long into the night. The full moon lights a town
alive with song and laughter.

Next morning begins the feast of matzoth, or unleavened
cakes. The family makes an offering of the first harvest
sheaf of barley, and eats bread made from the new grain.
At the end of the week of unleavened bread, the pilgrims
depart and Jerusalem settles back to await the next festival.

APOLLONIOS is eager to visit Galilee. He arranges to join
his host's cousins on their return north. It is unwise
to travel alone, with brigands abroad. The party leaves early.
In the clear light of morn he sees peasants bringing fruit
and vegetables on donkeys, lepers beseeching alms outside
city gates they are forbidden to enter, women gossiping
as they fetch water at the Pool of Siloam. The path crosses
the Kidron and climbs the Mount of Olives, then winds
down through rocky wilderness; Jericho lies 3,000 feet lower
than Jerusalem. With rhythmic strides, a string of camels
swings by, laden with grain from across the Jordan.

The track traverses an aqueduct built by Herod, and skirts
the deep and wild Wadi Qelt. Suddenly, as they round a bend,
the Jordan Valley stretches before them—wide, fawn-colored,
cut by a green and winding ribbon where the Jordan flows
between reeds and oleanders. On its banks a lone prophet,
John, has recently begun to preach and baptize.
Beyond, purple in the waning sun, rise the mountains
of Peraea. To the right extends a sheet of deep-blue water,
the Dead Sea. And on its northwest shore, cloaked in the
shadows of cave-riddled cliffs, can be seen the plateau
where a pious sect called the Essenes have their settlement.

At Apollonios' feet spreads the green oasis of Jericho
with its gardens, sycamores, and palms. Descending into
the town, the party passes the palace where Herod died
and the customs post farmed out by the Romans to Jewish
profiteers, who extract what the traffic will bear from

"AND WHEN THEY *had performed
all things according to the law
of the Lord, they returned
into Galilee" (Luke 2:39).
Two routes led from the Holy
City to Nazareth; one by way of
Jericho, up the Jordan Valley.
The other, winding through the
hills of Samaria (above), passed
Jacob's Well and Samaria's old
capital, grandiosely rebuilt
and renamed Sebaste by Herod.
Either way, some 70 miles,
took four or five days on foot.*

301

caravans crossing the Jordan from Peraea. Before resting the night, Apollonios eats of Jericho's dates, the best to be found. Next morning the party heads north up the hot valley. In three days' hard going they reach the Sea of Galilee, around which Jesus will soon spend the brief years of His public teaching.

*H*ow DIFFERENT from stark Judaea this land of Galilee, so fertile and rich in cultivation! Flowers carpet the gentle hills, golden wheat sways in the breeze, and farmers already are bending to the sickle, harvesting the barley.
The lake too yields a rich bounty. Salted fish from Magdala is sold in Jerusalem, even exported to Rome. Apollonios and his friends go along this Sea of Galilee as far as Capernaum, another fishing port. Here two brothers, Simon and Andrew, cast off in their boat and throw their nets, while their fellow fishermen John and James, with their father Zebedee, repair tackle. Simple people but honest. Yet Jerusalem citizens scorn Galileans as coarse and ignorant, laughing at their rustic pronunciation of Aramaic. They tell of one who ordered sheep's feet for dinner and got lentils instead—he had mispronounced a syllable!

Galilee is governed by a son of Herod the Great, the tetrarch Herod Antipas. By the lake, Antipas has built a capital of Hellenistic grandeur, complete with Roman baths, and named it Tiberias in honor of the emperor. Jews avoid it: Thermal resorts are notoriously immoral, and part of the town surmounts an old cemetery—contact with the dead makes everything unclean. Scandalously, Antipas has left his wife, a Nabataean princess, and married his niece Herodias, already the wife of one of his brothers.

Judaism has been reborn in Galilee. The region's full name, *Gelil ha-goyim,* means "district of the pagans." Only 150 years ago a Jewish king reunited it with Judaea, giving its people a choice: circumcision or banishment. Jewish families were transported here and given large tracts of land. The faith took root. Now each town or village—whether Nazareth, Cana, or Chorazin in the hills, Magdala or Capernaum on the lake—has at least one synagogue. Here the faithful come three times a day to recite the shema, facing Jerusalem. On the Sabbath all join for prayers, Scripture reading, preaching, and benediction.

The synagogue serves also as a center of village life. Its leaders administer the community's financial affairs and settle differences between members. It provides links with Jerusalem: local priests and Levites travel there regularly to perform temple services, and Pharisaic missionaries come to recruit novices. The landowners make common cause with the Sadducees, and the small people grow as impatient with subtle interpretations of the law as they are reluctant to part with a tenth of their crops. One Pharisee was asked if, on a Sabbath, one might turn a pot over on a scorpion to prevent a sting. No, he replied; that seemed too much like a hunt, and hunting was forbidden on the Sabbath!

"EXCEPT YE...BECOME AS LITTLE CHILDREN, *ye shall not enter into the kingdom of heaven"* *(Matthew 18:3). City of shrines in the Galilee hills, Nazareth crowds churches and chapels into nature's amphitheater that sheltered a hamlet, Jesus' childhood home.*

THOMAS NEBBIA

302

APOLLONIOS comes at last to Nain, a humble village of mud-built houses near Nazareth. He finds his hosts rejoicing: A young wife has just given birth to a boy, her firstborn. How much better than a girl, who will leave home and is therefore a "false treasure"! (But at least she is not disposed of, as often happens in Egypt, Greece, and Rome.) The mother had an easy birth, resting on a special seat and helped by a midwife.

The baby, bathed, rubbed with oil and salt (said to harden the muscles), and wrapped in swaddling clothes, is presented to the father. Taking the child on his knee, he proudly affirms the boy's birthright; one day he will head the family. For a week family and friends celebrate. On the eighth day, the village *mohel*, a specialist, circumcises the child. Becoming a Jew, the boy receives a name, usually his grandfather's.

A second ceremony attends birth, Apollonios learns. The mother is considered impure. Forty days afterward (80 days for a girl) she must journey to Jerusalem's temple to be purified and to sacrifice a lamb and a pigeon. Because her first-born son belongs to the Lord, he must be "bought back" by paying the priest six silver shekels. It is a large sum to most, so the priest may return it as a present.

Nursed until two or three, the lad will frolic in the village square, dancing, singing, playing with spinning tops or balls, pushing little clay animals set on wheels.

When the boy is six or seven, the father takes over. He recounts the Hebrew traditions and takes the lad to the synagogue to learn the law's precepts. On the Sabbath, for example, one may not exceed the "Sabbath walk," 2,000 cubits (about half a mile). On this day of rest and prayer one may not do business, cook, write, build a fire— 39 activities are forbidden. The boy is not strictly bound by the precepts until his 13th birthday, when he passes the threshold of puberty. If the synagogue has a school, he learns to read and write—using the Torah as a text.

The father must be firm as well as just. The wise men of the Bible said: "He who spares the rod hates his son" (Proverbs 13:24). But affection is what really binds child to parent. A sedate doctor of the law may go down on all fours like a puppy to make his boy laugh. In such moments a boy may call him *Abba*, "Papa." Usually a lad addresses his father as *Mari*, "Sir," and speaks in his presence only with permission.

A rabbi has said: "He who does not teach his son a trade brings him up to be a robber." And in the field, marketplace, or family

"THERE WAS A MARRIAGE in Cana of Galilee; and the mother of Jesus was there: And both Jesus was called, and his disciples, to the marriage" (John 2:1-2). At the feast wine ran short and Mary instructed the steward to follow Jesus' command. He ordered six pots filled and transformed water into wine. Afterward the toastmaster complimented the bridegroom: "Thou hast kept the good wine until now." The miracle spared the young man embarrassment, for custom decreed he entertain for a full week. In return, guests brought gifts—perhaps a fine amber pitcher like this at left, bearing the signature of Ennion, famous Phoenician glassmaker of Jesus' day.

workshop, the son learns at his father's side. When the father grows old, he will depend on the son to clothe him and take him by the hand when he goes out. Even so, "Youth is a crown of roses, old age is a crown of rushes."

A rabbi says: "A young man is like a young horse, neighing; he is looking for a wife. But married, he resembles a donkey, charged with heavy loads." Boys marry at 18; girls when they reach puberty, officially at twelve and a half. Usually they marry within the clan. Once the bride's father and the suitor's best man have agreed on how much shall be brought in money and goods, the betrothal is celebrated.

The groom declares: "She is my wife and I her husband, from today and forever." Attested by witnesses, these words bind the couple. During the year's betrothal that follows, the girl cannot be dismissed except by letter of divorce. If the boy dies, she will be regarded as a widow.

305

At last the great day arrives. The bride, in crown and showy dress, waits at her father's house, surrounded by friends. The groom arrives with his friends and best man, who serves as master of ceremonies. The girl takes her place in a litter and men jostle to carry it. Women sing of the bride's beauty; men chant the groom's bravery. To the music of flute, harp, zither, castanets, and tambourines, everyone steps off, singing and clapping hands. Celebrants pour oil, wine, and perfume, and scatter nuts and roasted grain—omens of happiness and fecundity.

At the groom's house, his parents pronounce a blessing and everyone enters. The groom presides, blushing bride at his side, while all eat and drink to the full. The feasting resumes the next day and lasts for a week until all friends and relatives are entertained. They bring gifts. We may forgive the groom if he calculates his expenses against returns.

But the village sees more burials than marriages. When the sick or aged breathes his last, the head of the family—the eldest son if it is a father or mother— closes the eyes. A drumbeat announces the death to the village. Interment follows swiftly—the same day or the next morning. All work stops. Men and women walk in separate groups. Even the poor must hire at least two flutists and one mourner. Men take turns shouldering the bier. The next-of-kin make a rent in their clothes, the women uttering cries and clapping in rhythm, the men beating their breasts and recalling the virtues of the deceased: "Alas, my father...."

*I*N GALILEE, as elsewhere in the Jewish world, a great hope sustains many Jews, especially the poor. Each Sabbath in the synagogue they listen to the prophets of old foretelling that the Jews scattered over the earth will return, that the Holy Land will become wonderfully fertile, and that the people of God will triumph. There will come a Kingdom of God on earth under a king anointed as were the kings of ancient Israel. Isaiah predicted that this anointed one, *messiah* in Hebrew, will be of the race of David. Micah has said he will come from Bethlehem. Jeremiah, Ezekiel, Zechariah—all describe his reign as a time of peace, justice, and joy.

At times the waiting becomes a fever. Adventurers rise and claim they are the Messiah, stirring popular movements which the Romans repress harshly. But hope does not die. Jesus of Nazareth will fan that hope, though the synagogues of Palestine will scorn Him.

Apollonios re-embarks at Caesarea, the harbor nearest to Galilee. As the coast slips away, he wonders if this restless land will ever know contentment. He thinks of the Zealots, preparing for a holy war. Of wealthy men, come to terms with Roman rule. And of the strange holy men who dwell in a desert-girt monastery by the Dead Sea, copying sacred writings on scrolls.

What did they call themselves? Ah yes; Essenes, was it not....

FROM THE SOIL OF PALESTINE, *still cultivated by wooden plows drawn by yokes of oxen, sprang the great faiths of Judaism and Christianity. Jesus likened His words to sown seed. Some "fell on stony ground" and "among thorns." But some "fell on good ground, and did yield fruit that sprang up and increased" (Mark 4:5-8).*

THE MEN WHO HID

UR VINTAGE STATION WAGON careened up a steep, twisting path more readily navigable by donkeys. Below us stretched the sun-scourged plain that skirts the northwest shore of the Dead Sea. Above, on a rocky terrace, brooded the skeletal remains of an ancient monastic settlement, aloof and starkly ascetic even in decay.

As he drove with careless ease, Père Roland de Vaux of Jerusalem's Ecole Biblique et Archéologique Française briefed me. This was Khirbat (Ruins of) Qumran, home of an apocalyptic Jewish sect, the Essenes, which flourished near the Dead Sea before the birth of Christ. Here lived the men who copied, studied, cherished, and at last hid the famous Dead Sea Scrolls. Discovery of their library, in thousands of fragments and several entire scrolls, has had a tremendous impact upon Biblical scholarship. The old manuscripts are providing profound new insights into the history of Judaism and early Christianity.

Sheer accident brought the scrolls to light. In 1947 Muhammad Adh-Dhib, a Bedouin boy of the Taamirah tribe, was searching for a strayed goat among the stark cliffs near the ruins. Idly he cast a stone into a small opening. He heard the sound of shattering pottery and ran away. But later he returned with a companion. They clambered into the cave and found several large earthen jars containing aged leather scrolls wrapped in foul-smelling linen rags.

Several scrolls, including the complete Book of Isaiah, eventually reached Jerusalem, where experts at first pronounced them worthless. But since then, every test of modern science, including carbon-14 dating, has indicated that they are at least 1,900 years old—antedating the oldest known Hebrew manuscripts of the Old Testament by 1,000 years.

Early in 1949 an expedition led by Père de Vaux and Gerald Harding, then head of the Jordan Department of Antiquities and acting curator of the Palestine Archaeological Museum, probed the cave. They found the interior well rifled, but from the debris they sifted fragments of some 70 scrolls. Nearby stood the desolate ruins of Qumran. Harding and De Vaux made a preliminary sounding, but found no answers to the questions: Who had concealed the scrolls so long ago? For what reason? Muhammad's discovery stood as a freakish, inexplicable windfall.

And so it might have remained, save for the impoverished Taamirah Bedouin. Spying a new source of income, they began to explore the thousands of fissures which honeycomb the Wilderness of Judah. In 1952 they again struck fragments near Qumran. A task force from the American School of Oriental Research, the Ecole Biblique, and the Palestine Museum hastened to the area. A combing of the cliffs located still another

THE DEAD SEA SCROLLS

A tossed stone leads to a startling find!
Archeologist A. Douglas Tushingham
brings to life the lost colony
whose writings throw new light
on the time of Jesus

cache, which included, along with scraps of leather, two rolls of copper so oxidized that scientists could not open them. Six months later the tireless Bedouin uncovered Cave 4 and the remains of the sect's main library, tens of thousands of fragments belonging to almost 400 scrolls. Subsequently, more caches were discovered. Cave 11, found in 1956, contained the best preserved scrolls recovered since Muhammad threw his fateful stone.

By that time Père de Vaux had unlocked the mystery of who had hidden the scrolls. In 1951 he had begun a major excavation at Qumran. In the ruins he found clay jars identical with those from the nearby caves. Archeology and the testimony of early writers revealed that the men who lived here were Essenes, or a sect closely akin to them.

As I wandered with Père de Vaux among the ruins, the story of the men who lived and worshiped God here for almost two centuries sprang to life.

The sect began in the second century B.C., when the worldly and intrigue-ridden Hasmonaean dynasty ruled Judaea. The founder was a priest called by his followers "the Teacher of Righteousness, to whom God made known all the mysteries of the words of His servants the prophets."

DESERT MONASTERY *of Qumran, overlooking the Dead Sea, offered the Essenes a refuge from the world. Men roll the clay roof after a rain; herdsmen in white garments of the order drive sheep to sparse pasture as dark-clad visitors approach the entrance. Today the ruins and a cemetery to right brood over a landscape little changed since Jesus' day. Openings of two caves that yielded scrolls crown spur at center.*

PAINTING BY PETER V. BIANCHI, NATIONAL GEOGRAPHIC STAFF ARTIST (ALSO PAGE 309). RIGHT: GEORGE R. THOMPSON

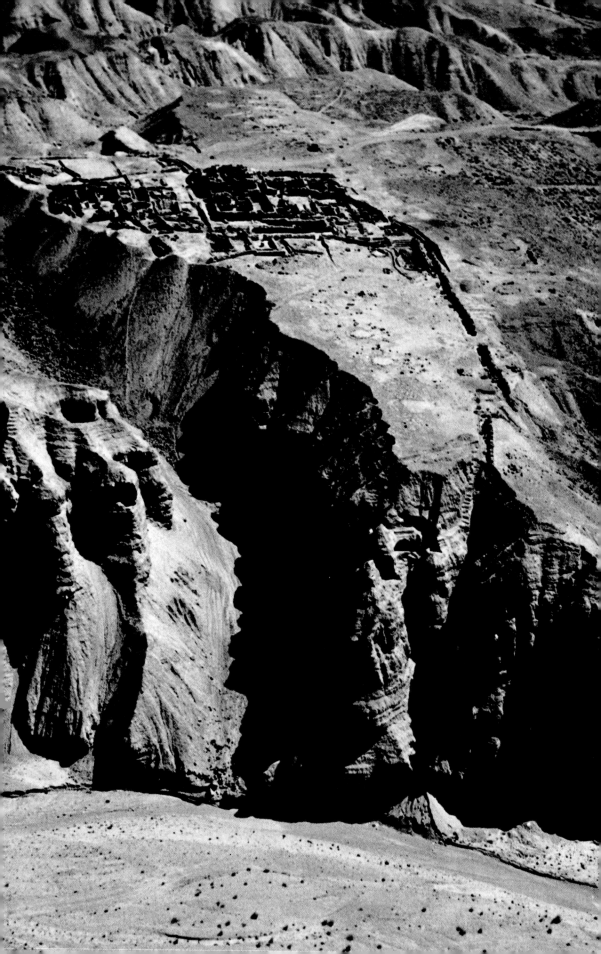

According to this priest, the time of judgment was at hand, when God would come to punish the wicked and reward the just. The crass secularity of Jerusalem finally drove the founder and "the righteous remnant of Israel" to seek a haven in the desert. In their *Manual of Discipline,* this migration fulfilled the prophecy of Isaiah (40:3): "Prepare ye the way of the Lord, make straight in the desert a highway for our God." Confident that they were ushering in the Messianic age, the men of God's "New Covenant" built the monastery at Qumran and retired there to study the law and await the "end of the days."

PÈRE DE VAUX AND I TOURED KITCHENS, bakery, pantry (in which he had found hundreds of dishes, neatly stacked), workshops, pottery, and kilns—with wood ashes and the iron poker in place! A stone-lined depression once contained a potter's kick wheel, duplicated in Hebron to this day. But to me the most arresting feature was the intricate system of water channels leading to the many cisterns and baths. "How do you tell which are which?" I asked De Vaux.

"The finest," he replied with a twinkle, "are for bathing."

An aqueduct brought water from the western highlands. There was also water at a farm established by the Essenes at Ayn Fashkhah, two miles to the south.

Among the Essenes' chief practices was the ritual ablution, a form of baptism enacted perhaps several times a day. And they used water to cleanse and sanctify their buildings. The floor of the main assembly hall, where members of the sect would "eat communally, and bless communally, and take counsel communally," slopes slightly to a low point near one corner. Diagonally opposite lies the opening of a small water channel. This they would open to clean the room.

Another center of community life was the scriptorium. Here scribes made copies of Jewish Scriptures as well as Essene interpretations of them; of the sect's *Manual of Discipline;* and of apocalypses predicting cataclysmic events.

The Essenes were relatively democratic: All full members in the assembly could speak in proper turn. But a council of twelve laymen and three priests guided them. Père de Vaux believed he had found their council chamber—a small room with a bench running around the wall. A basin, set in the wall and filled from the outside through a conduit, allowed deliberators to quench their thirst in the hot, dry climate of Qumran even while maintaining secrecy.

Like the early Christians, the Essenes turned over all worldly possessions to the community. And they apparently scorned private property in death as in life, for the thousand graves in their main cemetery contain none of the jewelry, weapons, tools, and lamps commonly interred with the dead in other Mediterranean cultures. But beads and earrings found with female skeletons in smaller burial grounds nearby

PRIEST IN HEADCLOTH *conducts the ceremonial cleansing of a newcomer. Assistant reads a benediction from a scroll while onlookers offer prayers; one man holds the initiate's white mantle. Unlike Christian baptism, the Qumran ritual immersion was repeated.*

THE WORD OF GOD *flows from pens as scribes in the scriptorium tirelessly copy and* ▶
*recopy treasured works, confident their labors will prepare them for Messianic deliverance.
A reader dictates to two writers; a third cleans his inkwell. Others copy scrolls
propped open with sticks, or ceremoniously wash hands. More scrolls rest in wall niches.*

suggest that asceticism among the women had its limits. Archeological evidence of women and children here supports the statement of Flavius Josephus, Jewish historian of the first century A.D., that not all Essenes were celibate.

Coins found at Qumran and at the Ayn Fashkhah farm indicate that both were built and both abandoned at the same time. We do not know whether the "Doers of the Law" fled political or religious pressures from Jerusalem, or whether a great earthquake in 31 B.C. drove them away. But for a generation, roughly the reign of Herod the Great (37-4 B.C.), a mysterious gap occurs in their history.

The Essenes returned to Qumran after Herod's death. Then, A.D. 66, the Jews rose in bloody revolt against their Roman overlords. No corner of the land, not even the Wilderness of Judah, offered a haven of peace. The men of Qumran began gathering up their precious scrolls, carefully wrapping them in linen, and placing them in large storage jars. But disaster must have come quickly, for they apparently piled many scrolls in the caves at the last minute without protection. Of these, the ravages of time, rats, and worms have left only fragments.

The final fate of the Essenes is unknown. Vespasian's Roman legions captured the monastery A.D. 68. Perhaps the men of Qumran died defending it; perhaps some of them fled south to the anvil-topped rock of Masada, fortified by Herod and now the last redoubt of the Jews. Here, high above the Dead Sea, 960 Zealot rebels made a pact of mutual homicide rather than surrender to overwhelming odds A.D. 73. "Let our wives die before they are abused," exhorted their leader, Eleazer ben Yair, "and our children before they have tasted of slavery."

Warriors "with tears in their eyes," reported Josephus, embraced and kissed their families, then slew them. A group of ten chosen by lot dispatched the rest of the men, each falling by his loved ones. The executioners selected one compatriot, who beheaded them, set fire to the palace, and fell on his own sword.

A scroll found in these ruins during the massive 1963-65 excavations contains a text identical to one discovered in a Qumran cave. Israeli archeologist Yigael Yadin, leader of the expedition, believes this is evidence that some Essenes perished in the last hours of Masada.

While the reconstruction of Dead Sea scrolls by an international team of specialists was still in progress at the Palestine Archaeological Museum in Jerusalem, I visited their workroom there. I was amazed to see a scholar pick up a fragment smaller than a postage stamp, carry it to the other

HISTORY IN HIS HANDS, *Father Jean Starcky (right) deciphers fragments of "the ultimate in jigsaw puzzles" at Jerusalem's Palestine Archaeological Museum.*

Scroll seekers Gerald Harding (wearing hat) and Roland de Vaux sift rubble in a Qumran cave (below) for similar shreds of manuscripts. In 11 caves scientists and Bedouin found parts of some 600 works, including every book of the Old Testament except Esther.

Oxidized copper rolls (above) from Cave 3 remained unread four years until ingenuity triumphed. H. Wright Baker of the Manchester College of Science and Technology in England (opposite, lower) coated the brittle rolls with plastic to prevent shattering, then sliced them into troughlike leaves with a saw used to split pen nibs. Not one letter was lost! The documents revealed enigmatic clues to hoards of gold and silver.

JOHN M. ALLEGRO. LEFT: DAVID S. BOYER, NATIONAL GEOGRAPHIC STAFF
UPPER: J. BAYLOR ROBERTS. OPPOSITE: WILLIAM L. REED

SHRINE OF THE BOOK, *Israel's showcase for scrolls from Cave 1, swells like the lid of a huge jar from its moat on a Jerusalem ridge. Bronze gates open on a manuscript-lined corridor leading to the sanctuary (inset). Scroll of Isaiah, 24 feet long, girdles a jar-shaped fountain that jets water through the dome's top to baptize its white tiles. Red-rock crypt below evokes a cave.*

end of the "scrollery," and casually fit it into its proper niche among hundreds of incomplete documents. With quiet intensity these men labored over texts already bought from the Bedouin. But they suffered agonies of apprehension over discoveries the desert searchers might yet make.

They all remembered with horror the Bethlehem antiquities dealer who buried a basket of fragments for safekeeping and later found an indecipherable mass of glue when he dug them out of the damp ground. And, despite all precautions, manuscript material sometimes went astray. Fragments were even bought and smuggled out of the Holy Land by tourists. Middlemen tried to shoulder their way in, selling something that did not exist or that someone else possessed. They operated on the theory that if they could find a buyer they could produce the goods.

In Jerusalem, I vividly recall, a man once approached me in a devious manner, saying he knew someone who had a scroll for sale. The "someone" turned out to be a member of Jordan's Parliament living in Amman. Since rumor then had it that a complete scroll from Cave 1 was circulating clandestinely, Père de Vaux felt constrained to follow through. He made a special trip to Amman, only to find a comparatively modern scroll of the Torah.

DECADES, EVEN GENERATIONS, may pass before the full import of the scrolls can be assessed. But already those which have been translated and published have filled important gaps in our knowledge of the Bible. We are now certain that the Hebrew text of the Old Testament as it stands today represents a tradition going back to the time before Christ. The scrolls also have pointed up certain striking parallels between the practices and beliefs of the Essenes and of the early Christians.

Both groups believed that the end of the world was imminent. In preparation for the event, both groups practiced a life aimed at salvation from sin and a state of purity symbolized by baptism and ceremonial cleansing. Both joined in a sacred repast, utilizing bread and wine. Both worshiped as a community, praying together, singing psalms, listening to the reading and exposition of Scripture. Both owned all things in common and considered celibacy preferable to marriage. Both preserved the memory of their founders and diligently composed new literature which embodied their beliefs. Both considered themselves the "true Israel" of the New Covenant. Both were persecuted minorities.

These parallels do not suggest, however, that Christianity is only a latter-day "successful" Essenism. Both movements

JOHN C. TREVER

"O ZION, *herald of good tidings; lift up your voice with strength"* (Isaiah 40:9). *Best preserved of the scrolls holds all of Isaiah, cherished by Essenes for its Messianic prophecies. Style of Hebrew letters dates the leather copy about 100* B.C. *Scribe's editor inserted corrections. Cave 1 also yielded a commentary on the Book of Habakkuk; a version of Genesis in Aramaic, the tongue of Jesus; thanksgiving psalms; the Essene's* Manual of Discipline *and a battle order for the final clash between good and evil.*

shared in the Jewish heritage. And few theologians have ever considered Christianity to be unique—without precursors, without affinities to Judaean thought patterns or modes of life. Jesus declared in Matthew 5:17: "Think not that I am come to destroy the law, or the prophets: I am not come to destroy, but to fulfil."

The Dead Sea Scrolls cast a new light on the elements of Judaism that influenced Christian development. They also reveal the hitherto mysterious Essenes, whose spiritual struggle swells out of the past like a mighty hymn.

Khirbat Qumran, high on its blighted terrace, is now a dead ruin in a dead world. Nothing grows in the bitter marl; nothing stirs among the ancient stones. The sky yawns emptily over the strange blue of the Dead Sea, and a lonely wind sighs through the rubble. But here, a long time ago, men strove to find God. And the record they left of their endeavors gives us a better understanding of the religious climate into which Jesus was born.

THE YEARS IN GALILEE

Among shepherds and villagers,
  National Geographic's Howard La Fay seeks the path
of the Nazarene carpenter who became a fisher of men

I WALKED ONE MORNING to a grassy mount overlooking the Sea of Galilee and awaited the dawn. With first light, the bluffs across the sea stood dark against the sky. A faint wind ruffled the sea's pewter face, cut by the wakes of vessels returning from a night's fishing. If luck had been good, they were jammed with small silvery *mousht*. If not, well, it has happened before. The words of Peter echoed across the centuries: "Master, we have toiled all the night, and have taken nothing" (Luke 5:5).

Cocks crow. Tiny birds flit from bush to bush. Suddenly the sun bursts above the hills, bathing in light the land of Jesus. There—along the north shore—the verdant Plain of Gennesaret, where He walked and taught; Capernaum, center of His ministry; Tabgha, traditional site of the Sermon on the Mount. And hidden in hills behind me, His boyhood home, Nazareth.

I had come to trace the footsteps of Jesus in His early years and Galilee ministry. My guidebook would be the Bible. Because the four Gospels—Matthew, Mark, Luke, and John—vary in the selection and arrangement of events in Jesus' life, I would rely for chronology mainly on Mark, believed

Flocks graze as in Jesus' day above Tiberias on the Sea of Galilee; B. Anthony Stewart, National Geographic photographer

to be the first written. I would draw also on scholars' studies and the claims of tradition.

The Galilee of modern Israel seemed much changed from Jesus' day. Buses toil up hills He walked. Tractors chug across fields where yoked oxen labored; jet fighters with Star of David insignia roar across skies where eagles soared. Yet Jesus spoke of "wars and rumors of wars." And here, where endless border clashes between Israeli and Syrian patrols flared into war in 1967, He would find that the centuries had not purged this fairest of Palestinian provinces from violence, blood, and the awkward sprawl of death.

Two thousand years ago the Son of Man was born into a world—like ours—in turmoil. Roman legions had conquered Palestine 60 years earlier. When the Jews revolted, Romans nailed their leaders to crosses from Dan to Beersheba. The Jews—"stiff-necked people"—bore the Roman yoke with smoldering hatred. Self-proclaimed Messiahs, revolutionaries, false prophets arose. Everywhere they and their followers were brutally crushed.

Brigands and guerrillas infested the hills. Fanatical Jewish rebels called Zealots spread terror with their concealed daggers. Tax collectors squeezed the peasantry while Roman-appointed monarchs—Herod the Great and his sons—lived in pagan splendor. Many Jews foresaw "the end of days" and coming of the Messiah, the anointed one promised by the prophets. He would restore Israel's glory.

"AND IT CAME TO PASS in those days, that there went out a decree from Caesar Augustus, that all the world should be taxed.... And all went to be taxed, every one into his own city" (Luke 2:1, 3). Roman records mention tax censuses, though not this one.

The carpenter Joseph, "being of the house and lineage of David," journeyed from Galilee to Bethlehem, David's home city, to be enrolled. With him came Mary, "his espoused wife, being great with child."

The new, the old, the proud, and the humble all meet on the road from Jerusalem to Bethlehem. Gleaming limousines laden with dignitaries swoosh by ancient buses jammed with villagers. Robed women stride along, water jugs on their heads. A shepherd guides his flock by casting stones where he

"NOW WHEN JESUS WAS BORN *in Bethlehem of Judaea in the days of Herod the king, behold, there came wise men from the east. . . . And when they were come . . . they saw the young child with Mary his mother, and fell down, and worshipped him" (Matthew 2:1, 11).*

"THE ADORATION OF THE MAGI" BY FRA ANGELICO AND FRA FILIPPO LIPPI, C. 1445; IN THE KRESS COLLECTION, NATIONAL GALLERY OF ART, WASHINGTON, D. C.

"O BETHLEHEM... *from you shall come a ruler who will govern my people"* (Matthew 2:6). *Thus Herod fearfully heard the Wise Men quote prophecy. Gilt and incense in Bethlehem's Church of the Nativity (left) evoke their gifts: "gold, and frankincense, and myrrh." Star in its grotto marks the spot hallowed as Jesus' birthplace.*

Constantine began this oldest of active Christian churches about 325; Justinian enlarged it two centuries later Beyond a Bethlehem belfry, its squarish tower rises left of center, opposite. On skyline to right of minaret stands flat-topped Herodium, citadel and mausoleum of Herod. He died in 4 B.C., reference point for scholars, who reckon Jesus' birth between 8 and 4 B.C.

Dating events B.C. (before Christ) and A.D. (anno Domini, in the year of our Lord) started with Dionysius Exiguus, abbot of Rome, who around A.D. 525 used the Nativity (which he set at December 25) to begin his chronology. He erred by several years.

THOMAS NEBBIA

wants them *not* to go. Terraced olive groves march up sere hills. Clinging to one ridge is Bethlehem itself, dominating Shepherds' Field (page 9). Here, tradition tells us, an angel appeared and said: "unto you is born this day in the city of David a Saviour ... Christ the Lord" (Luke 2:11).

At the time of that first Christmas, perhaps in the year 6 B.C., Bethlehem was a place where caravaneers plying between Jerusalem and Hebron could stop for provisions. By the 16th century A.D., the town had dwindled to about a hundred souls. Today it flourishes on tourism.

I joined pilgrims unloading from buses in the square facing the massive Church of the Nativity. We stooped to enter. Some say the partly sealed door served to thwart Turkish cavalry, ever fond of clattering through Christian shrines. And in the grotto beneath the church, revered as Jesus' birthplace, I found a lone woman

kneeling. Guttering lamps reflected in gold icons lit her lined face as she read to herself from the second chapter of Luke: "And she brought forth her firstborn son, and wrapped him in swaddling clothes, and laid him in a manger; because there was no room for them in the inn."

On the eighth day the child was circumcised and given a name, a common one then—Jesus in Greek, Yeshua or Joshua in Hebrew, meaning "Yahweh is salvation."

Only Matthew recounts the Holy Family's flight into Egypt and Herod's slaughter of infant boys to remove the One who might replace him on the throne. But the incident vividly reflects the pathological character of the king. He murdered members of his own family—yet scrupulously observed Mosaic dietary laws and would eat no pork. This provoked his Roman master Augustus into jesting: "I would rather be Herod's pig than Herod's son."

"THEY RETURNED into Galilee, to their own city Nazareth. And the child grew, and waxed strong in spirit" (Luke 2:39-40). Galilee did not enjoy a high reputation among Jerusalem sages—too often its farmers seemed to value their crops above the law. "Galilee, Galilee, thou hatest the Torah," one discouraged rabbi cried. But even in Galilee, Nazareth bore a poor name. When told that the Messiah had been found there, Nathanael would reply, "Can there any good thing come out of Nazareth?" (John 1:46).

Present-day Nazareth, swollen by churches, shrines, and monasteries, bears little resemblance to the hamlet known to Jesus. With its steeples, red tile roofs, and cypress-cloaked

"FLEE INTO EGYPT," *said the angel of the Lord, "for Herod will seek the young child to destroy him" (Matthew 2:13). Escaping by night, the Holy Family sojourned there "until the death of Herod."*

"IS NOT THIS THE CARPENTER?"
*(Mark 6:3). People of Nazareth
would recall that Jesus learned
this trade at Joseph's knee.
Artisans in those days were
held in low esteem.*

*Yet a carpenter, adz tucked
in his belt, would proudly teach
time-honored skills to his son.
The boy would learn to saw
and smooth planks of cypress,
oak, olive, perhaps precious
cedar; to cut mortises with a
smack of stone hammer on iron
chisel; to drill with an auger,
holding the beam with his feet.
He would fashion tables and stools
as well as yokes and plows.*

*As builders in a land of little
wood, carpenters also worked
in stone. Jesus' teachings
would reflect this knowledge.*

*Though almost nothing remains
of the Nazareth Jesus knew,
arched old quarter (opposite)
keeps the look of the past.*

"ST. JOSEPH THE CARPENTER" BY GEORGES DE LA TOUR,
C. 1645; THE LOUVRE, PARIS. OPPOSITE: B. ANTHONY
STEWART, NATIONAL GEOGRAPHIC PHOTOGRAPHER

hills, it resembles a northern Italian hill town. Guides cheerfully offer visits to two rival grottoes of the Annunciation (each claiming that here an angel revealed to Mary that she would give birth to Jesus), a cave purported to be Joseph's workshop, and two homes of the Holy Family. To me the most authentic echo of Jesus' world persists in the suq, where peddlers in flowing kaffiyehs prod tiny, heavily laden donkeys, and merchants importune passers-by from booths. The air is loud with haggling, fragrant with the smell of fruit, pressed olives, spices, and new-baked loaves. Fresh-killed lambs dangle from butchers' hooks, and children eye pastries basted with clear, golden honey.

I found carpenters' shops too. Though they hummed with power tools, I could imagine a shop of Jesus' day—father and son, a wood chip tucked behind an ear as a badge of their calling, working with tools easily recognizable today. The bracing odor of new-cut wood filled the workshop as they fashioned plows, wheels, furniture, and saddles. Some of the time young Jesus probably attended a synagogue school and there studied the Scriptures. Luke tells how at the age of 12 Jesus astounded the sages in the Jerusalem temple with His questions (page 298).

In what kind of house did Jesus dwell? Dr. James B. Pritchard, who has been excavating a Biblical city in the Jordan Valley (page 14), showed me a one-room, mud-brick house, roofed with mud-covered reed mats, that he had built atop the

tell. It was copied exactly from 3,000-year-old homes he has unearthed. Yet it rarely draws a second look. Why? Because it differs in no essential from Arab village houses today. Doubtless such was Jesus' home.

Since Jewish maidens were betrothed at puberty, Mary probably was no more than 14 when she bore Jesus. In her daily rounds she would have fetched water, tended the fire, and ground grain. The family dined on a porridge of wheat or barley groats, supplemented by beans, lentils, cucumbers, and other vegetables—with onions, leeks, garlic, and olive oil for seasoning. For dessert came dates, figs, pomegranates. Watered wine was the universal drink. Only on feast days did humble Galileans eat meat.

Ranging themselves around a common bowl, they would dip in with their right hands. With darkness, they unrolled mats and huddled near the fire.

Nazareth preserves one unquestionable link to the Holy Family. The mother of Jesus certainly drew water at Mary's Well; there is no other in Nazareth.

"AND IT CAME TO PASS... that Jesus came from Nazareth of Galilee, and was baptized of John in Jordan" (Mark 1:9). Standing at the traditional site of His baptism, near Jericho, I was struck by the smallness of the Jordan. Compared to rivers like the Mississippi, the Rhine,

"COMING UP OUT OF THE WATER, *he saw the heavens opened, and the Spirit like a dove descending upon him" (Mark 1:10). This 13th-century painting at St. Catherine's Monastery in Sinai portrays Jesus' baptism by John in the Jordan. Greenery fringes the traditional site (opposite), Hijlah Ford, about four miles above the Dead Sea.*

To this day, pilgrims come from all over the world to be "born again" in consecrated waters from the Jordan (above).

FRED ANDEREGG, MOUNT SINAI EXPEDITIONS. LEFT AND OPPOSITE: THOMAS NEBBIA

or the St. Lawrence, it seems puny indeed. Then a rowboat moved into midstream. In it stood a Greek Orthodox priest, prayerbook in hand. With him was an elderly woman in a white linen gown. Reciting prayers in the language of the New Testament evangelists, the priest dipped basil leaves into the water and sprinkled her head and shoulders—rebaptizing her. She wept quietly.

Afterward, I talked to her. She was indeed very old and had journeyed from Australia to cleanse her soul in the waters that had baptized her Redeemer. Her pilgrim's gown would one day serve as her shroud. "Now I am at peace," she said. A radiant smile lit her face. Her tears had been tears of joy.

When I turned again to the stream, I did so with respect. I had learned why the Jordan, to Christians, is the greatest of all rivers.

Jesus was in His early thirties when He came to be baptized by John. The enigmatic figure of the Baptist, crying repentance and garbed "with camel's hair, and with a girdle of a skin about his loins," looms large in all the Gospels. Some scholars have sought to link him with the Essenes, who dwelt only a few miles to the southwest. According to the evangelist John, Jesus gained His first disciples from among the Baptist's followers. In those days of religious tumult, men often attached themselves to rabbis and prophets and at their feet sought instruction.

AFTER BAPTISM, JESUS SOUGHT SOLITUDE in the wilderness. There for 40 days, Mark tells us, He was "tempted of Satan; and was with the wild beasts." I wandered those stark hills west of Jericho and came upon the Greek Orthodox monastery of St. George, sprawling against the wall of the Wadi Qelt. Father Prokopios, white-bearded and in tattered cassock, opened the locked gate and led me down silent corridors.

"A monastery has stood here 1,500 years," he said. "Once hundreds of monks lived here; now we number only seven." Three of the seven, he explained, live in nearby caves. Like the ancient anchorites, they remain in isolation for long periods. For the rest, the day begins with the liturgy at 2 a.m. and ends with another service just before sunset. Like the Essenes, the monks eat no meat, subsisting on vegetables, olives, and water. Once a month they bake bread.

Time collapses in such a setting. In the chapel lay 14 yellowed skulls. Father Prokopios patted one: "Monks martyred by Persian invaders in the year 611"—in his time scale, only yesterday.

Did he miss the secular world? He gestured toward the wilderness: "This is the world of Jesus. I want to know no other."

After the sojourn in the wilderness, the time had come for Jesus' public ministry. In the brief span between A.D. 28 and 30 or 31, He would proclaim a New Covenant between God and man. He returned, not to the hills of Nazareth, but to the shores of the Sea of Galilee. The towns clustered there—Tiberias, Capernaum, Magdala—teemed with merchants, traders, and caravaneers. Roman legionaries wandered through the suqs, along with Germanic mercenaries of the Herods.

"HE WAS THERE IN THE WILDERNESS FORTY DAYS" (Mark 1:13). Hostile hills frown on a lone traveler near Jebel Qarantal, traditional Mount of the Temptation above Jericho. The Arabic preserves the Crusader name for "mountain of the 40 days." Ancients fasted in sorrow; Jesus—like Moses—to gird for a holy mission.

THOMAS NEBBIA

DEAD SEA

• QUMRAN

• BETHLEHEM

• JERUSALEM

J U D A E A

JERICHO •

HIJLAH FORD

• JACOB'S WEL

P E R A E A

"Then were there two thieves crucified
with him" (Matthew 27:38). As Jesus' earthly
life ends "there was darkness over all the land. . . .
and the earth did quake." A centurion cries:
"Truly this was the Son of God."

"There cometh a woman of Samaria
to draw water: Jesus saith unto her,
Give me to drink" (John 4:7).
At Jacob's Well, though "Jews have no
dealings with the Samaritans,"
He reveals Himself as the Messiah.

SCYTHOPOLIS •

"Go thy way; thy faith
hath made thee whole"
(Mark 10:52). Jesus heals
"blind Bartimaeus" near
Jericho on His way to
Jerusalem and the Cross.

JORDAN RIVER

D E C A P O L I S

THE WORLD OF JESUS

*A mere 120 miles spans the journeys of Jesus
during His brief ministry which changed the world.
Born in Bethlehem amid Judaea's hills, raised in Nazareth
of Galilee, He went with His family to Jerusalem for
Passover as a youth; as a man He was baptized in the Jordan
by John the Baptist—probably at Hijlah Ford.*

*After 40 days in the wilderness near Jericho,
"Jesus went about all Galilee, teaching . . . and healing"
(Matthew 4:23). Tiberias, Herod Antipas' capital
of this fertile region, stood on the Sea of Galilee,
a 13-mile lake through which the Jordan flows. Ringing it
were fishing ports like Magdala, home of Mary Magdalene,
and Capernaum, which Jesus made "his own city."
Often He strode the Plain of Gennesaret, and nearby
preached the Sermon on the Mount and worked the
miracle of loaves and fishes.*

*Westward, at Cana, He changed water to wine; at Nain
He raised a widow's son from the dead. Eastward, He bore
His message into Peraea (which means "beyond the Jordan")
and the Decapolis, a league of ten Hellenistic cities.
He journeyed north "to the region of Tyre and Sidon," and
later near Caesarea Philippi asked each disciple to "take up
his cross, and follow me." His Transfiguration, traditionally
atop Mount Tabor, revealed Him as the "beloved Son" of God.
Soon Jesus followed the Jordan's deep corridor to Jericho,
thence to Jerusalem to be "delivered into the hands of men."*

SEA C

N

ILLUSTRATED MAP BY WILLIAM H. BOND, GEOGRAPHIC ART DIVISION

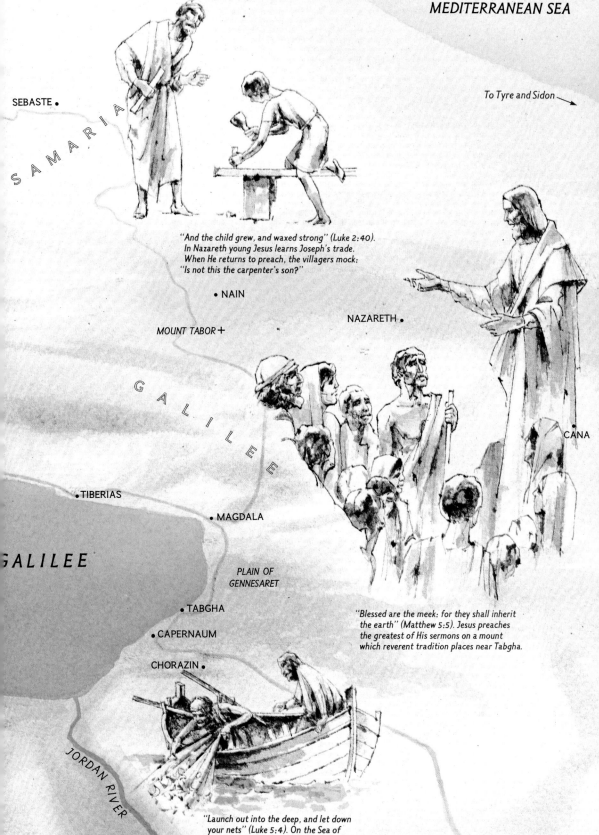

MEDITERRANEAN SEA

SEBASTE •

To Tyre and Sidon →

S A M A R I A

*"And the child grew, and waxed strong" (Luke 2:40).
In Nazareth young Jesus learns Joseph's trade.
When He returns to preach, the villagers mock:
"Is not this the carpenter's son?"*

• NAIN

MOUNT TABOR +

NAZARETH •

G A L I L E E

CANA •

•TIBERIAS

• MAGDALA

GALILEE

PLAIN OF
GENNESARET

*"Blessed are the meek: for they shall inherit
the earth" (Matthew 5:5). Jesus preaches
the greatest of His sermons on a mount
which reverent tradition places near Tabgha.*

• TABGHA

• CAPERNAUM

CHORAZIN •

JORDAN RIVER

*"Launch out into the deep, and let down
your nets" (Luke 5:4). On the Sea of
Galilee, Simon Peter heeds Jesus and hauls in
a net-breaking catch. Then he receives a new
destiny: "henceforth thou shalt catch men."*

To Caesarea
Philippi →

To Damascus →

One heard Aramaic, Greek, and sometimes Latin. Hebrew was so little understood that in synagogues readings from the Torah had to be translated into Aramaic.

Today pilgrims usually come to the Sea of Galilee at Tiberias, modern counterpart of the capital of Herod Antipas—"that fox," Jesus called him. The tetrarch's Hellenized city and the marble palace above it have vanished. But the hot sulphur springs still draw clients who sweat and talk politics in many languages in baths recalling those that scandalized ancient Jews. The streets still bustle—but with jeeps, trucks, buses, and bulldozers that bespeak a young nation's vitality. And on the lake a timeless calling lives on.

"NOW AS HE WALKED BY THE SEA OF GALILEE, he saw Simon and Andrew his brother casting a net into the sea. . . . And Jesus said unto them, Come ye after me. . . . And straightway they forsook their nets, and followed him" (Mark 1:16-18). So too did James and John, sons of Zebedee. The heirs of these four

"I WILL MAKE YOU FISHERS OF MEN"
(Matthew 4:19). Like the disciples,
men of modern Galilee fish at night
with lights and seines, returning
at dawn with their silvery catch.
Gas lamps rather than torches draw
fish to the glow, and outboards
not muscles propel the boats.
But the look of sea and land and
patriarchal beard stays the same.

still cast their nets into the Sea of Galilee. Like the disciples, they are Jews; and they too push out into the darkling waters after the sun has set. But they have their own method of taking the tasty mousht that swarm the lake. In the evening they tow out unmanned boats. Each boat bears a powerful gas-mantle lamp to attract fish. Hours later a launch goes out with an electronic fish finder. Locating a large concentration, it radios the shore. Out comes a purse seiner to lay its long nylon net around the lightboat that has lured the most fish. Small power winches haul in the lake's bounty—a fluttering, glittering netful.

The mousht, about six inches long and with a great mouth, is sometimes called "St. Peter's fish." Legend ascribes to it a place in the Gospels. When the annual tax to support the temple in Jerusalem was demanded of Jesus, He instructed Peter to "cast an hook, and take up the fish that first cometh up." In its mouth, Jesus said, Peter would find a piece of money: "that take, and give unto them for me and thee" (Matthew 17:27).

"AND THEY WENT INTO CAPERNAUM; and straightway on the sabbath day he entered into the synagogue, and taught" (Mark 1:21). A lakeside road looks from Tiberias past the ruins of Magdala, home of Mary Magdalene, through the lush Plain of Gennesaret, to the cypress-shaded ruins of Capernaum. Amid a jumble of stone flour mills, ovens, mortars and pestles, and chunks of columns and porticoes stands an ancient synagogue. It dates from two centuries after Jesus, but the Franciscan priests who preserve it believe it stands on the site, perhaps on the very foundations, of the synagogue in which Jesus taught.

Stone lions crouch at its entrance; walls bear carved date palm trees, olives, grapes, figs, fish, and centaurs. All reflect the Greek influence so strong in ancient Galilee, and a liberal interpretation of Jewish law, which prohibits graven images. As I watched small purplish land crabs scurry among the fallen stones, I thought

THOMAS NEBBIA. RIGHT: CHARLES HARBUTT, MAGNUM

"THEY WERE ASTONISHED *at his doctrine: for his word was with power"* (Luke 4:32). *Empty streets and a gaping basalt grain mortar at Capernaum once echoed the shuffle of sandals, the murmur of multitudes who gathered to hear Jesus. Columned ruin of a third-century synagogue marks the site of an earlier one where He began His ministry. He wrought miracles, healing the blind, the lame, the leprous, but was rejected here in "his own city."*

Right: Faces in a suq, and a wooden plow little changed for centuries, show that time lies lightly on the land of Galilee.

of Jesus' warning to this once-flourishing town that spurned His message: "And thou, Capernaum, which art exalted to heaven, shalt be thrust down to hell" (Luke 10:15). I thought too of Chorazin, its ruins in the hills above, and of Bethsaida, its site now lost—two of the "cities wherein most of his mighty works were done" (Matthew 11:20). They too "repented not."

Vigorously in synagogues, in fields, from fishing boats by the shore, Jesus preached His revolutionary message: "Love your enemies, do good to them which hate you, Bless them that curse you, and pray for them which despitefully use you" (Luke 6:27-28).

Unlike Old Testament prophets, Jesus consorted with sinners—even with publicans, the despised tax collectors. Outraged Pharisees demanded to know why. Jesus answered: "They that be whole need not a physician, but they that are sick" (Matthew 9:12). And at Capernaum He called as a disciple the publican Levi, later known as Matthew.

Always, through the months of teaching on the lakeshore, the crowds demanded miracles. "Except ye see signs and wonders, ye will not believe," Jesus had observed (John 4:48). He cured lepers and paralytics. He raised the dead and, by casting out "unclean spirits," brought lucidity to the insane.

Mark relates that one day, as Jesus taught in a house at Capernaum, four men came bearing a sick man. Finding the door blocked by a throng, they climbed atop the house, uncovered the mat-and-mud roof, and "let down the bed wherein the sick of the palsy lay." When Jesus saw their faith, He said to the palsied one: "Arise, and take up thy bed, and go thy way" (2:1-11). And he did.

Once a multitude surrounded Jesus as He preached beside the lake. When afternoon waned into evening, He asked where bread might be bought for so many. A disciple found a lad with five barley loaves and two fishes. Jesus bade the multitude sit down, then took the loaves and fishes and "blessed them, and brake. . . . And they did eat, and were all filled: and there was taken up of fragments that remained to them twelve baskets" (Luke 9:16, 17).

In a church in Tabgha, a village nestling by the lake a mile from Capernaum, I found the remains of a fourth-century basilica—a beautiful mosaic floor. One detail, depicting loaves and fishes, recalls the early tradition that here Jesus fed the multitude. As I studied it, a group of South African pilgrims raised their voices in an Afrikaans hymn. Then they moved outside to picnic on the grass. Fittingly, the box lunches packed by their Tiberias hotel included bread and fish.

Many believe that a gentle slope above Tabgha is where Jesus preached the Sermon on the Mount—the heart of His teaching. Comfort

"WHERE HE MADE THE WATER WINE" *(John 4:46): Olive and cypress trees border Kafr Kanna, village with ancient claim to be the Cana of the miracle (page 305). Highway speeds cars to nearby Nazareth; laden camels tread it at age-old pace. Some scholars place the event at Khirbet Qana, a ruin five miles to the north.*

KENNETH MACLEISH, NATIONAL GEOGRAPHIC STAFF

for the afflicted, the impoverished, the persecuted. Mercy, charity. Peace. I thought of the years of armed patrols—Arab and Israeli—playing their lethal game of hide-and-seek near the Sea of Galilee, where Jesus taught. I thought of wars around the globe. Many have heard the Sermon on the Mount. Ironically, few seem to have listened.

"AND HE BEGAN AGAIN TO TEACH BY THE SEA SIDE: and there was gathered unto him a great multitude, so that he entered into a ship, and sat in the sea; and the whole multitude was by the sea on the land. And he taught them many things by parables" (Mark 4:1-2).

The subjects of these short allegorical narratives evoke the fields and skies and humble dwellings of Galilee: the farmer with his mustard seed, the housewife with her leaven, the birds of the air, the lilies of the field, the vineyard, the fig tree. Jesus spoke of stony places and good ground, of sowing and reaping, of wheat and tares.

He likened the joy in heaven at the saving of a soul to the rejoicing of a father at the return of his prodigal son, or a shepherd at finding his lost sheep. God's kingdom is like a drag net cast into the sea gathering fish of all kinds—the good to be saved, the bad to be discarded. "All these things spake Jesus unto the multitude in parables" (Matthew 13:34). His listeners could look about them and understand.

Today the green patchwork of Galilee's cultivated fields crowns the highlands above the sea. Grain nods plumply in the breeze; clouds seldom mar the blue sky; all the earth seems an endless harvest. I envisioned Jesus and the disciples swinging lightheartedly through these fields one long-ago Sabbath, plucking and eating new ears of grain. Reproached for violating strict Sabbath precepts, Jesus answered, "The sabbath was made for man, and not man for the sabbath" (Mark 2:27).

Jesus' public ministry centered in Galilee. But John recounts a journey to Jerusalem which presaged the majesty of His teaching. Returning from the Holy City through Samaria, Jesus stopped at a well and asked a Samaritan woman for a drink. She was astonished. Rabbis cautioned Jews not to address any woman in the street, even their wives, lest they cause scandal. Above all, as the woman remarked, "Jews have no dealings with the Samaritans." They had shunned the schismatic group since the days of Ezra, for the Samaritans had intermarried with pagans during the Assyrian and Babylonian conquests. Since then, the Samaritans claimed their own holy mount—Gerizim—as a rival to Zion in Jerusalem, and accepted only the first five books of the Bible.

In an act pregnant with symbolism, Jesus—according to John—first revealed Himself as the Messiah not to His family nor to His disciples nor even to His fellow Jews, but to this woman of a despised sect.

"AND THERE AROSE A GREAT STORM OF WIND, *and the waves beat into the ship"* (Mark 4:37). "Lord, save us: we perish," the disciples cry; Jesus calms them, then stills wind and wave (Matthew 8:25-26). Normally placid, the Sea of Galilee sometimes churns in six-foot billows as tempests swoop down from encircling hills.

DAVID S. BOYER, NATIONAL GEOGRAPHIC STAFF. OPPOSITE: THOMAS NEBBIA

"And he...taught then.
saying, Blessed are
the poor in spirit"

Matthew 5:2-3

From Capernaum, watched over now by a Franciscan monastery (opposite), Jesus carried His messa along the shores of Galilee. Above its waters He preached: "Ye have heard that it hath been said, An eye for an eye, and a tooth for a tooth: But I say unto you ... whosoever shall smite thee on thy right cheek, turn to him the other also" (Matthew 5:38-39)

Words such as these from the Sermon on the Mount lured "great multitudes." And once, to feed a multitude, hungry and far from home, He multiplied five loaves and two fishes into food for all. This miracle, the only one recorded in all four Gospels, inspired the fourth-century mosaic below, preserved in a church at Tabgha.

Fish became a symbol of Christ, for the Greek letters that spell it (ichthys) form the initials of the phrase translated as "Jesus Christ Son of God Saviour." Applying the term Christ to Jesus signified belief that He was the Messiah, for the terms are synonymous.

Jacob's Well (above), near Nablus, still refreshes travelers as it did in Jesus' day.

At Jacob's Well I drank where Jesus had quenched his thirst. In a dry land, a precious water source survives. So do the Samaritans. I visited them in nearby Nablus, climbed their sacred mount, talked with their high priest, tall and eagle-faced. He told me of the sect's desperate poverty.

"Our young people cannot afford to marry. I fear that we can only diminish. But at Passover, we keep God's command in the ancient way" (page 92). I asked if the Samaritans still expect a Messiah. "We wait," he said softly. "We wait."

IN THE SYNAGOGUE at Nazareth, Jesus stood up and read from the Scriptures, as is a Jew's right. He took as text Isaiah 61:1: "The spirit of the Lord God is upon me; because the Lord hath anointed me to preach good tidings unto the meek; he hath sent me to bind up the broken-hearted, to proclaim liberty to the captives, and the opening of the prison to them that are bound."

Closing the book, He announced: "This day is this scripture fulfilled in your ears" (Luke 4:21).

His astonished listeners raged at His messianic claim. "Is not this the carpenter's son?" They rushed Him to the brow of a hill "that they might cast him down headlong." But

Jesus passed "through the midst of them." How apt His words: "A prophet is not without honour, save in his own country" (Matthew 13:57).

Jesus met increasing resistance. He learned too that John the Baptist had been beheaded by Herod Antipas to fulfill a drunken pledge to his sensual stepdaughter Salome. Jesus journeyed north toward Phoenician Tyre and Sidon. Then He and the disciples set out toward the town of Caesarea Philippi. Somewhere near this now-ruined Syrian city He asked His disciples, "But whom say ye that I am?" Peter answered, "Thou art the Christ"—the Messiah.

"JESUS TAKETH WITH HIM Peter, and James, and John, and leadeth them up into an high mountain apart by themselves: and he was transfigured before them" (Mark 9:2). According to the Gospels, the three disciples watched terrified as Jesus changed in appearance and spoke with Moses and Elijah. From a cloud that overshadowed them came a voice, "This is my beloved Son: hear him."

348

Long ago, pilgrims climbed Mount Tabor on their knees; now a road hairpins to the top. There I found the crumbling walls of a 13th-century Saracen fortress enclosing a large basilica. Within the church, a massive mosaic depicts Jesus transfigured. I paid it little heed. Mosaics are, after all, but colored stones.

Yet I soon noticed a shaft of light pouring through a stained-glass window. The light crept up the wall and caught the mosaic. Suddenly the image of Jesus shimmered with dazzling brilliance, exploding into tiny, blinding bits of gold. Then the light moved on. The moment passed.

Outside, long shadows raced across the Plain of Esdraelon, and lights flickered on in the hills above Nazareth. A distant glimpse of blue marked the Sea of Galilee, beyond the fields so often crossed by Jesus. His preaching in Galilee had been but prelude. Now the Son of Man had a dread rendezvous to keep in Jerusalem, at a place called Calvary.

"THEY SAW HIS GLORY, *and the two men that stood with him"* (Luke 9:32). Radiance from the transfigured Christ dazzles disciples; Moses and Elijah represent the law and prophets. Tradition sets this scene on 1,929-foot Mount Tabor in Galilee (opposite).

Ancients sought their gods on high places. Lacking heights, Mesopotamians built ziggurats. Moses received the law on Sinai. And on a mountain in Galilee, Matthew 28 relates, the risen Christ would tell his disciples, "Lo, I am with you alway."

In the Footsteps of Jesus: Part II

JERUSALEM AND THE LAST DAYS

Joining fervent throngs during Holy Week,
John Putman walks the way of the Teacher
from triumphant entry to death on the Cross

"AND WHEN they came nigh to Jerusalem, unto Bethphage and Bethany, at the mount of Olives, he sendeth forth two of his disciples, And saith unto them, Go your way into the village . . . ye shall find a colt tied, whereon never man sat; loose him, and bring him. And if any man say unto you, Why do ye this? say ye that the Lord hath need of him" (Mark 11:1-3).

The Lord hath need of him . . . This simple, unpretentious phrase came to mind as I joined hundreds of pilgrims gathering in the garden of the Franciscan church at Bethphage on Palm Sunday. In a few moments we would begin the annual procession commemorating the entry of Jesus into Jerusalem some 1,900 years ago: over the Mount of Olives, down the path past Gethsemane, across the Valley of Kidron, and through St. Stephen's Gate into the walled Old City. In the following days of Holy Week, each step of His journey toward Calvary—and the fulfillment of His promise to "give his life as a ransom for many"—would be remembered in scores of ceremonies and rites, in a babel of tongues.

Now our great throng begins to move—nuns in black habits and sunglasses, Americans in sport jackets, Syrian children in sparkling white robes, Lebanese schoolgirls in jaunty blue berets, all clasping palm fronds. As we crest the Mount of Olives, the ancient city lies spread before us. Voices rise in solemn song: *"Ho-san-na . . . Ho-san-naaa,"* and from somewhere someone reads:

"And they that went before, and they that followed, cried, saying, Hosanna; Blessed is he that cometh in the name of the Lord . . . Hosanna in the highest. And Jesus entered into Jerusalem" (Mark 11:9-11).

"PEOPLE . . . TOOK BRANCHES OF PALM TREES, *and went forth to meet him" (John 12:12-13). Bearing swaying standards of joy, a Palm Sunday procession enters the Holy City. Priests, monks, nuns here accompany the Latin Patriarch of Jerusalem, in bright biretta. Through St. Stephen's Gate looms the Mount of Olives, where Gethsemane awaited Jesus.*

DAVID S. BOYER, NATIONAL GEOGRAPHIC STAFF

351

CHARLES HARBUTT, MAGNUM. BELOW: BRITISH MUSEUM. OPPOSITE: "CHRIST DRIVING THE MONEY CHANGERS FROM THE TEMPLE" BY EL GRECO, 1605-14; IN SANTO CHRISTO DE SAN GINÉS, MADRID

"AND WHEN HE HAD MADE A SCOURGE *of small cords, he drove them all out of the temple" (John 2:15). Jesus accused the money changers (opposite) of making the house of prayer "a den of thieves." To pay the half-shekel temple tax, Jewish pilgrims had to change their money into the trusted coinage of Tyre:* tetradrachm *(bottom) is a shekel weight — half an ounce — of silver. Taxes to Rome called for the* denarius, *or silver penny. Jesus looked on one of Tiberius (upper) when He said, "render to Caesar the things that are Caesar's" (Mark 12:17). Widow's mite was bronze* lepton *of Pontius Pilate (left). Only the "Wailing Wall" (top) remains of Herod's Temple. For centuries Jews came here to mourn the temple's destruction* A.D. *70. June 14, 1967: They return by tens of thousands to the shrine barred to them 19 years by Arab Jordan. Many tuck prayers in niches.*

Jesus had come from Galilee, where He had revealed to the disciples that He was the Messiah and must go to Jerusalem to be "delivered into the hands of men" (Mark 9:31).

This last journey had taken Him down into the Jordan Valley. And there I picked up His footsteps at Hijlah Ford, traditional site of His baptism by John. Surely as Jesus passed here by the Jordan He thought of that now-stilled "voice crying in the wilderness" and of the event which had begun His ministry.

"And they came to Jericho" (Mark 10:46). I clambered atop a mound, site of the winter residence of Herod, and looked down on the stone bones of New Testament Jericho. Here Jesus restored the sight of Bartimaeus, saying, "Go thy way; thy faith hath made thee whole" (10:52). And here the despised tax collector Zacchaeus climbed a sycamore to catch a glimpse of Jesus over the heads of the crowd. Jesus called him down, "for to day I must abide at thy house" (Luke 19:5). Zacchaeus received Him joyfully.

To the west a dusty track, remains of the old Roman road to Jerusalem, rises swiftly into the stark Judaean hills. This lonely way, the setting for Jesus' parable of the Good Samaritan, remains a dangerous route to travel alone. With an Arab student I followed the footsteps of Jesus into these hills. Soon we were enveloped by wilderness and sky, the only sound the scuff of our shoes.

Across a wadi we heard the tinkling of sheep bells and the haunting notes of a shepherd's flute. We watched the flock spill down a slope. A lamb balked. The shepherd picked it up and carried it on his shoulder.

"I am the good shepherd: the good shepherd giveth his life for the sheep," said the Teacher who walked here on His way to Jerusalem and the Cross (John 10:11).

"AND HE ENTERED THE TEMPLE and began to drive out those who sold and those who bought . . . and he overturned the tables of the money-changers and the seats of those who sold pigeons" (Mark 11:15).

There are still money changers in Jerusalem, though not in the holy places; and men who sell pigeons, but not for sacrifice. I passed them in the crowded streets of the Old City one morning as I walked toward the Haram Esh Sharif, the great enclosure that girds the Dome of the Rock (pages 226-29). Where this Moslem shrine now stands, Herod's Temple rose. In Jesus' time, what is now the Haram was the temple esplanade.

I purchased a ticket, required of non-Moslems, and entered the Haram. The bustle of the city receded behind me. The brilliance of the shrine before my eyes startled me. How like Jesus' day! The temple then sat on a raised platform and was faced with gold and costly marble. It "dazzled the eye like sunlight . . . it shone from afar like a snow-clad mountain," observed Josephus. "Master," the disciples exclaimed, "see what manner of stones and what buildings are here!" (Mark 13:1).

THE GREAT FEAST of Passover was approaching as Jesus walked here, fervent crowds surging around Him. During my visit the Old City lay within the Arab sector of a divided Jerusalem, and Passover was not celebrated there. Still I sensed an air of religious excitement, for hajis—Moslem pilgrims—were streaming through on their return from Mecca. Weeks before I had seen them on the roads of Syria and Turkey, barreling southward in convoys of buses, with water bags, pots, and pans dangling from windows, followed by trucks laden with baggage and tents. In the Haram, second only to Mecca as a holy place, they reappeared in their robes and baggy pants.

I followed one group of hajis. They stopped first for the ritual ablution at the sunken fountain called The Cup, washing hands, faces, and feet. I took off my shoes and padded behind them as they entered the Dome.

A world straight from *Arabian Nights* surrounded me. Virtually every surface has been gilded, molded, painted, mosaicked, or inscribed with graceful arabesques and verses from the Koran in flowing Arabic script. Through windows set with translucent tile grilles came a soft and diffuse light. Below the dome itself lay the massive rock on which Solomon built his temple. And there, most probably, had stood the altar where the priests of Jesus' time offered sacrifices.

In the temple Jesus taught the people, debated with priests, elders, and scribes, and castigated those proud scribes who "desire to walk in long robes, and love greetings in the markets, and the highest seats in the synagogues, and the chief rooms at feasts . . . and for a shew make long prayers" (Luke 20:46, 47). He saw the rich give much money to the temple, whereas a poor widow gave but two mites— a farthing. And He said to His disciples that she had cast more into the treasury than the rich did, for they "cast in of their abundance; but she of her want did cast in all that she had" (Mark 12:44). And here He was asked which was the first commandment of all. He replied (12:29-31): ". . . The Lord our God is one Lord: And thou shalt love the Lord thy God with all thy heart. . . . And the second is . . . Thou shalt love thy neighbor as thyself. There is none other commandment greater than these."

"DAUGHTERS OF JERUSALEM, *weep not for me,*" Jesus told the women who "bewailed and lamented him" on the way to Calvary (Luke 23:27, 28). A pilgrim prays at the Sixth Station of the Cross, where tradition says Veronica wiped Jesus' brow, retaining the imprint of His face on her veil.

RUSSIAN CHURCH
AND MONASTERY

CHURCH OF
THE PATERNOSTER

MOUNT OF OLIVES

CHAPEL OF
THE ASCENSION

JERICHO ROAD

CHAPEL OF
DOMINUS FLEVIT

TOMB OF
ZACHARIAH

CHURCH OF
ST. MARY MAGDALENA

TOMB OF
ABSALOM

BASILICA OF
THE AGONY

GARDEN OF
GETHSEMANE

CHURCH
OF THE TOMB
OF THE VIRGIN

GOLDEN
GATE

HARA

ESH

ST. STEPHEN'S
CHURCH

SHARIF

ST. STEPHEN'S GATE

JERICHO ROAD

CHURCH OF
ST. ANNE

POOLS OF
BETHESDA

MONASTERY
THE FLAGELLATIO

TOWER OF
THE STORKS

HEROD'S
GATE

PALESTINE
ARCHAEOLOGICAL
MUSEUM

N

"Behold, we go up to Jerusalem"

Mark 10:33

Here Jesus fulfilled His mission "to give his life
as a ransom for many." On Palm Sunday He rode
down the Mount of Olives and entered the city
near where St. Stephen's Gate now stands.

Suleiman the Magnificent built Jerusalem's
crenellated walls in the 16th century; these
follow in part the line laid in Herod's day.
Dome of the Rock stands on site of Herod's Temple.
Tradition places Last Supper in Coenaculum on the
mount early Christians called Zion; excavations
now locate "the city of David, which is Zion" on
Mount Ophel to east (page 225). Seized in Garden
of Gethsemane, Jesus was scourged, probably in
Antonia Fortress, which lies beneath Monastery of
the Flagellation and Convent of Our Lady of Zion.
Via Dolorosa, "Way of Sorrows," leads to Church
of the Holy Sepulcher, hallowed as the place of Jesus'
crucifixion and entombment. Doves perching there
(below) symbolize the Holy City's hope for peace.

Chapel of Dominus Flevit, "the Lord wept," looks
from Mount of Olives on view (opposite) Jesus beheld
when He foretold, "they shall not leave in thee one
stone upon another" (Luke 19:44). Jewish revolt,
A.D. 66-70, led to Roman destruction of Jerusalem.
Church of St. Anne and Church of the Dormition
suffered damage in the 1967 Arab-Israeli war.

BRIAN BRAKE, MAGNUM. OPPOSITE: THOMAS NEBBIA. ILLUSTRATED MAP BY
ROBERT W. NICHOLSON, RESEARCH BY JEAN B. McCONVILLE; GEOGRAPHIC ART DIVISION

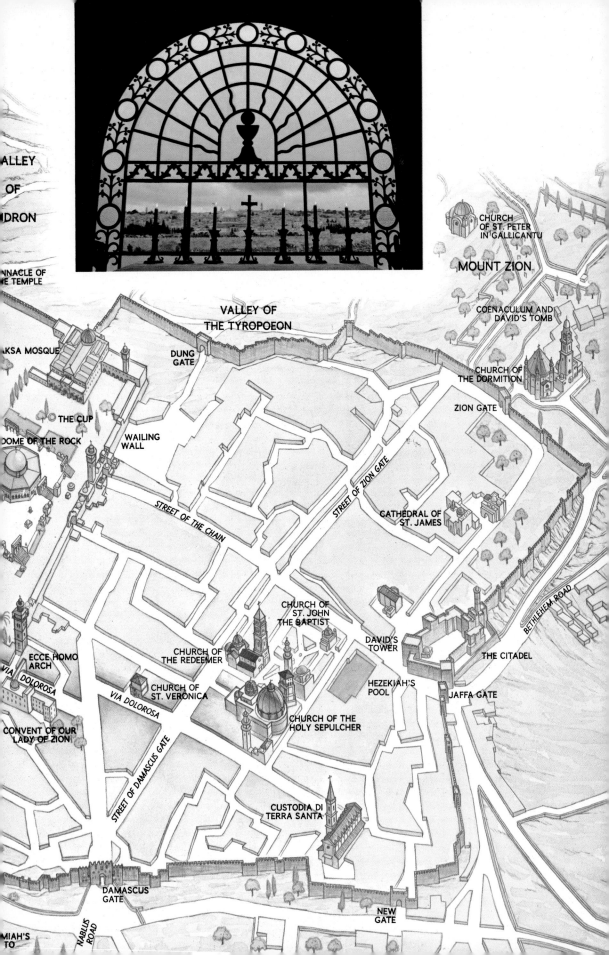

STREETS OF JERUSALEM, *like galleries
in a living museum, preserve timeless
sights and savors. Lad at right learns
the art of haggling as aproned merchant
and coin-pinching buyer bargain before
an array of Arabic sweets. Mountains
of cakes and confections loom over
trays of crescent pancakes filled with
walnuts and cinnamon, and pastries
flavored with goat cheese and honey.*

*Folded headdress (bottom) pillows
a sweetmeat seller's tray, laden with
nut-studded cakes and chunks of* halvah
*laced with sesame oil. He totes his
stand on his back.*

*Bustling, shop-lined Via Dolorosa
(below) belies its doleful name.*

As I left the Dome of the Rock a group of local Arabs moved swiftly across the Haram, led by a tall man who bore in his arms a bundle wrapped in a carpet. Near The Cup, on the porch of the Aksa Mosque, he laid down the bundle, and he and his companions dropped to their knees. They rose, the tall man picked up and cradled the bundle, and they quickly moved off toward St. Stephen's Gate.

The doorkeeper answered my unspoken question: "It was a small dead boy. When a boy dies, they must wash his body and wrap him in white and bring him here for prayers. Then they take him outside the walls and bury him."

I asked who carried him. "An uncle or close family friend. Not the father. It would hurt too much." Tourists who only minutes ago had been chattering and taking snapshots now stood silent and shaken. Just beyond the city wall, in timeless ritual, a beloved son, wrapped in white, was being laid in a grave.

JESUS DID NOT STAY THE NIGHTS in Jerusalem, thronged with Passover pilgrims, but in Bethany, just over the Mount of Olives. Here, John tells us, Jesus raised Lazarus from the dead, and I was shown the traditional tomb from which the brother of Martha and Mary emerged "bound hand and foot with graveclothes: and his face ... bound about with a napkin" (11:44). Bethany's Arabic name, Al Ayzariyah, derives from "Lazarus."

Here, too, in the house of Simon the Leper, a woman broke open a costly jar of ointment and poured it over Jesus' head. Onlookers complained: The ointment should have been sold and the proceeds given to the poor. "Let her alone," Jesus rebuked them. "For ye have the poor with you always ... but me ye have not always. She hath ... come aforehand to anoint my body to the burying" (Mark 14:6-8).

Even as He spoke of impending death, "Judas Iscariot, one of the twelve, went unto the chief priests, to betray him unto them."

The disciples asked Jesus where they should prepare the Passover meal. He instructed them to go into the city and meet a man bearing a pitcher of water. Following him, they would come to a house whose master would show them "a larger upper room furnished and prepared" (Mark 14:15). Custom decreed that pilgrims might request of a host the use of a room for the Passover meal.

As they sat together that evening, Jesus spoke: "One of you which eateth with me shall betray me ... one of the twelve, that dippeth with me in the dish."

The disciples protested. But Judas slipped out of the room into the night.

The traditional room of the Last Supper, the Coenaculum, lay in the Israeli part of Jerusalem. I could not visit it during Holy Week, for once I crossed through the Mandelbaum Gate into Israel, I could not re-enter Jordan. So it was days later when I climbed the long stairway up the hill called Mount Zion amid groups of chattering Israeli schoolchildren in blue uniforms bound for the tomb they believe to be David's, elsewhere in the same multidomed complex of buildings.

I walked up a flight of stairs and suddenly found myself standing alone in a bare room. I heard the laughter of children outside; inside there was only the cold silence of stone walls. Was it here, I wondered, that Jesus "took bread, and blessed, and brake it, and gave it to them, and said, Take, eat: this is my body. And he took the cup, and .... said unto them, This is my blood" (Mark 14:22-24).

Franciscans, I later learned, built the room in the 14th century. But the site's tradition as a holy place goes back at least a thousand years before that.

I climbed to the roof of the venerable building. Before me stretched the Old City, and, beyond, the Mount of Olives. Almost below me, in what Israel and Jordan called No Man's Land, lay the hulks of houses blasted in the 1948 war, mocking symbols of cruel passions that again in 1967 were to bloodstain the Holy City.

MAUNDY THURSDAY commemorates the day of the Last Supper. "Maundy" stems from *mandatum,* "command." For after Jesus washed the disciples' feet He gave "a new commandment . . . That ye love one another" (John 13:34). Now as night fell on Maundy Thursday, a column of pilgrims wound from Zion Gate in Jerusalem across the Valley of Kidron and to "a place which was named Gethsemane." There, in the great basilica of the Franciscans, they observed in solemn ceremony the agony of Jesus: "Father, if thou be willing, remove this cup from me; nevertheless not my will, but thine, be done" (Luke 22:42).

I walked one day in the small but beautiful garden, pausing by ancient olive trees so gnarled and twisted they seemed to reflect Jesus' suffering. Fruit from the groves that gave the Mount of Olives its name was gathered and pressed here in the fall; Gethsemane may mean "oil press." In the spring season of Passover, however, the place would have been deserted.

In the garden Jesus awaited betrayal. Suddenly, "a great multitude with swords and staves" arrived. At Judas' signal, a kiss, they moved in. Jesus' followers fled, one in such panic that he tore out of his clothes when someone grabbed him. But one disciple—John identifies him as tempestuous Peter—hacked off a temple servant's ear. "Put up again thy sword," Jesus commanded, "for all they that take the sword shall perish with the sword" (Matthew 26:52).

Not far from where that sword flashed, the Russian Orthodox Church of St. Mary Magdalena now stands, its seven onion domes seeming to float above the

"ONE OF YOU SHALL BETRAY ME," *says Jesus, breaking bread with the disciples for the last time
(Matthew 26:21). In Leonardo da Vinci's masterpiece, Judas, clutching moneybag at middle left, recoils;
Peter grasps the shoulder of drowsing John. Farther to left, Andrew, James the Younger,
and Bartholomew sit shocked. To right, Thomas raises a doubting finger; James the Elder spreads
hands in disbelief; Philip leaps up; Matthew, Thaddaeus, and Simon eye each other.*

*Soon after Leonardo finished this fresco on an Italian monastery wall, his tempera began flaking
from the damp plaster. Monks cut a door through the painting. Retouchers marred it. Napoleon stabled
horses in the monastery; World War II bombs unroofed it. Seven years' labor restored "The Last Supper."*

Below: Across twilit Jerusalem, double-domed Church of the Holy Sepulcher enshrines Cross and Tomb.

THOMAS NEBBIA. UPPER: "THE LAST SUPPER" BY LEONARDO DA VINCI, C. 1495-98, IN SANTA MARIA DELLE GRAZIE, MILAN

"Then cometh Jesus ...unto a place called Gethsemane"

Matthew 26:36

Basilica of the Agony stands beside a walled garden revered as the place where Jesus told the disciples, "Sit ye here, while I go and pray yonder." They fell asleep, and He chided: "the spirit indeed is willing, but the flesh is weak" (26:41).

A Franciscan monk (opposite) meditates amid centuries-old olive trees that may have sprouted from roots of trees that witnessed Jesus' arrest.

The first basilica rose here in the fourth century. Gifts from many lands completed the present shrine in 1924, inspiring a name, Church of All Nations. Above, on the Mount of Olives, onion domes mark Russian Orthodox Church of St. Mary Magdalena.

trees. I rang the bell at the gate and a nun led me to Mother Mary, the Scotswoman who leads this community.

"Our church was dedicated in 1888 by Czar Alexander III," she said, pointing to a faded photograph taken during a visit to Jerusalem by the royal family. "This young girl, the future Grand Duchess Elizabeth Feodorovna, expressed a wish to be buried here. Oddly, when revolutionaries murdered her family years later, they allowed her body to be transported here.

"She has been an inspiration to us," Mother Mary said.

In a wooden cottage tucked away behind pine and cypress trees—a tiny patch of Russia in the Holy Land—I watched nuns keeping alive the art of the icon. Sister Natalie, her broad face framed in a shawl, showed me samples of her work—saints and Madonnas. "I mix pigments with egg yolks, vinegar, and water," she told me. "First I apply a dark base coat to the wood, then build on the lighter colors. When it's finished, I varnish it.

"I am very busy these days," she added. "So many bishops are visiting, and we give them icons as gifts."

As I wound down the path to the gate, I fell in step with a novice, daughter of a Christian Arab family. I asked her name. "When I entered the convent they gave me a new name; it means resurrection," she said. "Anastasia."

"**A**ND THEY LED JESUS AWAY to the high priest: and with him were assembled all the chief priests and the elders and the scribes" (Mark 14:53). After many had borne false witness against Jesus, the high priest asked: "Art thou the Christ, the Son of the Blessed?"

Jesus said, "I am." For this seeming blasphemy, Mark records, Jesus was sentenced to death.

He was then taken before Pontius Pilate, who as Roman procurator bore the responsibility of confirming or rejecting a death sentence. Pilate had come to Jerusalem at Passover to be on hand for just such matters.

"Art thou the king of the Jews?" he asked.

"Thou sayest it," Jesus replied.

Baffled, the procurator offered to release Jesus under the traditional Passover amnesty, which provided that one of a group of prisoners might be spared. But the crowd demanded instead the release of Barabbas, described as a revolutionary and murderer. Pilate thereupon "delivered Jesus . . . to be crucified."

This brutal method of execution, reserved for slaves and non-Romans, took place outside a city's walls. The victim usually carried the crossbeam to the site, where he was

362

stripped and nailed or lashed to the beam. This was fitted onto a post and the victim set astride a peg, which helped support his weight. Death might take days; a soldier sometimes broke the victim's legs with a club to hasten the end.

So, at Pilate's order, Roman soldiers led Jesus to the Praetorium. "And they clothed him with purple, and platted a crown of thorns, and put it about his head, and began

to salute him, Hail, King of the Jews!" (Mark 15:16-18).

I knocked on the great door of the Convent of Our Lady of Zion. The convent stands on the site of the Antonia Fortress, built by Herod and used by Pilate's soldiers. The door opened, and one of the sisters led me along a corridor into the chapel. Here I joined an American family.

Sister Mary took us down to the cellar where lie the

MASS IN A GROTTO *draws faithful beneath the Church of St. Peter in Gallicantu (Latin for cock's crow). Here, some believe, stood the house of the high priest Caiaphas, where Jesus was accused of blasphemy and where, as He had prophesied, Peter said: "I know not the man."*

great paving stones that once formed the courtyard of the Antonia, believed by many to be the Praetorium of the Gospels. For centuries the stones lay buried, forgotten, until excavated by a French archeologist in the 1930's.

"Here we are walking on the very stones where Jesus trod," Sister Mary said. "Here He was scourged, mocked, condemned, and sent to His death. It is not possible to fix the precise location of these events. However, it is extremely probable that the exact place of the crowning with thorns is denoted by the Game of the King, engraved on the flagstones there." We looked down at the Roman game incised, perhaps by soldiers' weapons, on the shiny stone.

I lingered. From an adjoining room came the echo of voices, sounding like voices from this cellar's haunted past. I closed my eyes and imagined the courtyard as it was in the year 30 or 31: Roman soldiers lounging on the shaded galleries, the rattle of an occasional chariot, the shout of a centurion as he leads in yet another religious agitator, followed by an angry mob and perhaps by a second mob protesting his innocence. Roman soldiers in the Jerusalem of Christ's time no doubt were baffled by the swirling passions of the city's conquered and frustrated populace.

But the soldier ghosts here are not all Roman. Plaques cover the low walls. Sister Mary explained: "Just before World War II Australian soldiers stationed here visited the convent and found Sister Marie Godeleine continuing to excavate this floor almost alone. They gave her money to hire

"AND HE BEARING HIS CROSS
went forth" (John 19:17).
Pilate sat in judgment
"in a place that is called the
Pavement...." Crude marks of a
game played by Roman soldiers
grave the paving stones of
Herod's Antonia Fortress (above),
now in the Convent of Our Lady
of Zion. Many consider the
fortress to be the Praetorium
where Pilate washed his hands
of Jesus' blood, and soldiers
crowned Him with thorns and
mocked, "Hail, King of the Jews!"

On Good Friday, pilgrims
form in the street outside, some
bearing heavy crosses (opposite).
They retrace the Via Dolorosa,
Christ's sorrowful way to
Calvary. Marked since the
Middle Ages by Stations of
the Cross, now numbering 14,
the route stands on centuries
of rubble some 20 feet above
first-century levels. But the
devout pilgrim at right views
the procession as one of the
disciples would—with clenched
fist and anguished face.

THOMAS NEBBIA

workmen. She thought of thanking them with a plaque. It started a tradition." Now the words engraved on brass and marble seemed to join the cadence of voices from the past: "To the glorious dead of the 1st Battalion; they shall grow not old. . . . To those of the Royal Tank Regiment who so nobly gave their lives. . . ."

"AND WHEN THEY HAD MOCKED HIM, they took off the purple from him, and put his own clothes on him, and led him out to crucify him" (Mark 15:20). On Good Friday in Jerusalem, pilgrims, tourists, and spectators swarm down every narrow, twisting street toward an Arab school, site of the first of 14 Stations of the Cross. Shortly after noon, the great procession spills into the Via Dolorosa, "the Way of Sorrows," traditional route of Jesus to His crucifixion.

Since the first century, Jerusalem has been destroyed and rebuilt time and again so that present streets may lie 20 feet above the level of Jesus' day. Yet today's stones may well follow the course of His tortured footsteps.

At each station, which marks an event on Jesus' path to Calvary, a priest reads an appropriate devotion, often into a portable loudspeaker.

Jesus Receives the Cross, Jesus Falls the First Time . . . As we move from station to station, the various groups—French, Syrian, Lebanese, English, German—melt into one vast throng. Weeping women in black toll their rosaries. Puzzled children perch on parents' shoulders. Great wooden crosses swirl and bob in the sea of fervent faces. The curious watch from roofs, windows, walls, unheeded by the faithful, who are caught up in the drama they are reliving.

I find myself toward the rear of the procession, marching with Ethiopian

CRUCIFIX BY CIMABUE, C. 1265; SCALA

"WHEN THEY WERE COME *unto a place called Golgotha . . . they crucified him"* (Matthew 27:33, 35). *Planted in hate, the Cross took root in men's hearts as the emblem of Christ's love. Brandished by Constantine, it emerged from the catacombs to crown cathedrals and emblazon Crusaders' shields. The agony of the Crucifixion inspired artists through the centuries. The Florence flood of 1966 defaced Giovanni Cimabue's masterpiece, "Crucifix." But this great twin endures in Church of San Domenico in Arezzo.*

there was . . . a new sepulchre"
(John 19:41). Christendom's
holiest shrine, the Church
of the Holy Sepulcher, stands
where Constantine's mother
Helena claimed to find the
True Cross at Calvary in 326,
and where Jesus' tomb also
was said to be discovered.
On each site the emperor built
a church. Crusaders, arriving
in 1099, enshrined both
in a great cathedral.

On Maundy Thursday,
third day before Easter, throngs
fill the forecourt (opposite) to
witness the lesson in humility
Jesus taught at the Last Supper
when He "poureth water into
a bason, and began to wash the
disciples' feet" (John 13:5).
The Greek Orthodox Patriarch
(in gold below), who "took a
towel, and girded himself,"
washes the feet of 12 priests.

Orthodox pilgrims. We pass St. John's Hospice, then rows of coffee shops and souvenir stalls until we reach the steps leading into the once-columned Street of Damascus Gate.

Now the crowd before us has grown so huge that we must stop. But the pilgrims behind us do not understand. They push. Crushed on the steps, shoulder to shoulder, chin to ear, we begin to sway. Amid screams and shouts, police work desperately to untangle us.

The last five stations—*Jesus is Stripped of His Garments, Jesus is Nailed to the Cross, Jesus Dies on the Cross, Jesus is Taken Down From the Cross,* and *Jesus is Laid in the Sepulcher* —lie within the Church of the Holy Sepulcher. Here, on Good Friday, an effigy of Jesus is taken from a cross, borne to the Stone of Unction, there anointed, spiced, and censed, and laid to rest in the Holy Tomb.

The placing of these events rests on hallowed tradition. The Gospels locate Jesus' crucifixion on Calvary—Golgotha, "the place of the skull"—outside the city walls of His day, and put the entombment nearby. Fourth-century Christians reported discovery of the tomb beneath a pagan shrine. On the site the emperor Constantine built "a church of wondrous beauty." Nearby he raised another commemorating

the Crucifixion. Both were dedicated in 335. Bits of these churches endure in the existing structure, built by Crusaders and restored after a fire in 1808. Now within the Old City, the site was outside the walls of Jesus' time.

Early Saturday I entered that ancient and somber church, whose earthquake-weakened walls went unrepaired for years because of disagreements among the religious communities that share it. Finding a place alone, I read by candlelight from the 15th chapter of Mark: "And when the sixth hour was come, there was darkness over the whole land until the ninth hour. And at the ninth hour Jesus cried with a loud voice, saying . . . My God, my God, why hast thou forsaken me?"

I noticed groups of people huddled in the shadows. Others were entering the church. Already in the cold dawn they were gathering for the ceremony of the Holy Fire, the most spectacular Easter ritual of the Eastern churches.

IT IS PAST NOON NOW. For hours a crowd has jammed the rotunda of the church, pressing round the ornate Chapel of the Holy Sepulcher, revered as the site of Jesus' tomb. From time to time ushers bear out a limp and gasping pilgrim. Now enter the prelates of the four religious communities that share in the ceremony: Copts in turbans and purple-lined robes; Armenians in pointed black hoods

"Then took they the body of Jesus and wound it in linen clothes with the spices"

(John 19:40)

Widows mindful of Jesus' mother weeping over her slain son caress the Stone of Unction in the Church of the Holy Sepulcher. Worn with kisses and washed by tears, the slab proclaims in Greek that here mourners anointed the body of Christ.

John tells us that Nicodemus, a Pharisee but also a secret follower of Jesus, "brought a mixture of myrrh and aloes" —a fragrant resin from India— to put in the burial wrappings. Haste was necessary, for custom decreed that the body be entombed before the Sabbath.

The Jews had no undertakers and no formal cemeteries. Family or friends would wash a body, anoint it with oils and scents, bandage hands and feet, shroud the corpse in linen, cover the face with a cloth. Burial might be in a family garden or in one of Palestine's abundant caves—but at least 50 cubits from a house and not along a main road. The person was laid on his back, to rest while awaiting resurrection.

THOMAS NEBBIA

373

and pastel vestments; Syrians in skullcaps; Greek Orthodox priests in golden robes and brimless hats — all paced by the metronomic *thump thump* of maces wielded by the prelates' guards. From the pilgrims come thunderous clapping, cries, rhythmic chants.

The Greek Orthodox and the Armenian Patriarchs step into the chapel. Suddenly, from small oval windows on opposite sides of the chapel, appears the Holy Fire — torches held by the prelates — symbol of Christ rising from the tomb.

A deafening cry springs from the pilgrims, church bells peal wildly, and the fire springs to life as laymen runners rush it toward their communities. Hundreds surge forward, seeking to light their own bundles of candles from the runners' torches. The fire spreads like a woodland blaze whipped by the wind. The smell of burning wax fills the air, and a blue cloud of smoke ascends slowly into the dome.

Policemen shoulder through the crowd, opening the way for a Coptic priest. A car will speed him to the airport, where a plane waits. Soon the Holy Fire will flare in Egypt.

T HAT NIGHT I returned to the church. Instead of entering the rotunda I climbed a dark stairway and groped along a corridor until I stepped out onto the roof of the Chapel of St. Helena. The yellow light of gasoline lanterns revealed a lofty courtyard, its centerpiece the chapel's dome. Friendly hands helped me onto a wall. Around me women slipped off their shoes, and sleepy children cuddled in their parents' laps. We had gathered to watch the Ethiopians celebrate their Easter rites beneath the stars. This Christian community had been denied a place in the Church of the Holy Sepulcher 300 years ago, so they worship on the roof.

To the thump of a drum, they emerged from a tent near the dome: gaunt priests in dark cloaks and light jodhpurs, lovely girls swathed in gowns of

"**I AM COME TO SEND FIRE ON THE EARTH**" (*Luke 12:49*). *Holy Fire, kindled over the Holy Sepulcher, leaps from taper to taper as pilgrims reach for this symbol of the risen Christ. In the bedlam (a shortened form of the word Bethlehem) many scramble on scaffolding that has braced the rotunda since an earthquake in 1927. The rite flares on the Easter Eve of Eastern churches, whose religious calendar can date Easter the same day as the West's, one week after, or five weeks later.*
THOMAS NEBBIA

375

gossamer white. All bore tapers. Three times, behind the drummer, clergy, and acolytes bearing velvet umbrellas, a river of fire circled the dome. Then they all re-entered the tent. We observers clustered about the entrance.

The bishop read in Geez (the liturgical language of Ethiopia) from the 28th chapter of Matthew—"I know that you seek Jesus who was crucified"—and then gave a prayer. Beside him stood a young man, his son, who translated his words into English: "He died for us, and we believe He will return again . . . and in the coming world there will be no unhappiness, only happiness . . . and that is why we revere Christ. . . ." The bishop retired. Four aged and bent men rose and, forming a circle, began to chant, raising and lowering their tall staffs in unison.

As the night wore on, the crowd outside the tent melted away. At last I too sought the darkened stairs, leaving behind the rhythmic tattoo of great Ethiopian staves.

"AND WHEN the sabbath was past, Mary Magdalene, and Mary the mother of James, and Salome, had bought sweet spices, that they might come and anoint him. And . . . they came unto the sepulchre at the rising of the sun. And they said among themselves, Who shall roll us away the stone from the door of the sepulchre?" (Mark 16:1-3).

Easter Sunday came bright and sunny to Jerusalem. Even vacant lots blossomed with red poppies. I rose early and walked streets now strangely quiet after the fervor of the preceding days. But, as I passed a walled garden outside the Old City, I was startled to hear voices raised in a familiar old Protestant hymn.

I entered lovely Gordon's Calvary, named for the 19th-century British general, who believed Jesus was entombed here. The pine trees, the flowers, the people seated on wooden benches, the modest little organ, all transported me back to my childhood in the Deep South. Here, in Jesus' own land, was a pine woods "meeting on the ground."

The preacher stood by a little table near the entrance to an ancient rock-cut tomb. "We have many groups here today. Friends from Norway, a group from Elkhart, Indiana. I know there are others here. Would you just call out where you're from?" Many voices answered: "India . . . Denmark . . . Canada . . . Australia."

Now the preacher prayed: "Our Father, we thank You for the Gospel, the Good News. . . ." The song leader asked all to stand and sing the hymn beginning, "I serve a risen Saviour." The organ swelled, voices rose, and finally over the Garden Tomb soared the chorus: "He lives, He lives!"

"And when they looked...the stone was rolled away"

(Mark 16:4)

Three who had wept at the Cross— Mary Magdalene, Mary the mother of James, and Salome—come at sunrise after the Sabbath to complete the hasty burial. Sorrow turns to fear, for the tomb stands open. Inside, they find "a young man . . . clothed in a long white garment," the garb of a heavenly messenger.

"Be not affrighted," he says. "Ye seek Jesus of Nazareth . . . he is risen. . . . But go your way, tell his disciples. . . ."

Thus Mark recounts the resurrection of Jesus.

Jesus' tomb, "hewn out of a rock," was closed by rolling "a stone unto the door of the sepulchre." It probably had two chambers; bodies were placed in niches along the inner chamber's walls. The entrance must have looked much like this; here a huge stone slab rolled in a groove. Built in the first century B.C., this tomb offered shelter to the living during the Arab-Israeli wars of 1948 and 1967. It stands outside the Old City walls near Mount Zion.

EFREM ILANI

By Emil G. Kraeling

The World of Paul

"**As I made my journey**, and was come nigh unto Damascus about noon,
suddenly there shone from heaven a great light round about me."
Thus, on the barren plateau east of snowy Mount Hermon, Saul of Tarsus,
a young Pharisee zealot up from Jerusalem on a mission of terror against
the Christians, bolted onto the stage of destiny. "And I fell unto the ground,
and heard a voice saying unto me, Saul, Saul, why persecutest thou me?
And I answered, Who art thou, Lord? And he said unto me, I am Jesus of Nazareth,
whom thou persecutest. . . . And I said, what shall I do, Lord? And the Lord said unto me,
Arise, and go into Damascus; and there it shall be told thee of all things
which are appointed for thee to do" (Acts 22: 6-10).

Only several years after the Crucifixion, this astonishing about-face by a Jew
from the Roman province of Cilicia, along the southern coast of modern Turkey,
had an impact on history second only to the birth of Christ. For the things
Saul was appointed to do as Paul, Apostle to the Gentiles, changed the course
of Christianity, and with it, the course of the world.

Before Paul's far-ranging missionary journeys planted congregations across
Asia Minor and Greece, the new sect centered around Jerusalem as little more than
a Jewish religious society. These early followers of Christ, called Nazarenes,
observed the Mosaic law, worshiped in the temple, made vows, fasted, and performed
good works while waiting for the return of Jesus.

Heading this congregation were the twelve apostles, mainly humble villagers
of Galilee drawn to Jesus by His spiritual force and His teachings.
These leaders, Peter at first pre-eminent among them, surely traveled from Jerusalem.
Mark relates that "they went forth, and preached everywhere" (16:20).
In the second chapter of Acts we are told that on the day of Pentecost, when
Jews celebrated the harvest fete, the apostles gathered to await the Holy Spirit
that Jesus had promised them. "And suddenly there came a sound from heaven

"*I AM A JEW, FROM TARSUS in Cilicia, a citizen of no mean city," Paul proclaims
in Acts 21. Though no contemporary portrait of the apostle survives, the pride of a man
of Paul's world here shines across the centuries in the vigorous realism of Hellenistic art.*

PORTRAIT FROM COFFIN LID OF EL FAIYUM, EGYPT, 2ND CENTURY A.D.; ROGERS FUND, METROPOLITAN MUSEUM OF ART, NEW YORK

"THE CONVERSION OF ST. PAUL" BY MICHELANGELO, 1542-45, IN THE VATICAN; SCALA

as of a rushing mighty wind, and it filled all the house where they were sitting. And there appeared unto them cloven tongues like as of fire, and it sat upon each of them." Thus each apostle received the ability to speak in a different language, revealing the area in which he was to preach.

But it was Paul, the self-proclaimed "apostle"—from the Greek *apóstolos*, for "one sent" as plenipotentiary—who sowed the seeds of a world religion. He wrested from the leaders in Jerusalem the right for gentiles to embrace the faith without becoming Jews. This crucial step opened Jesus' message to every man.

"I COULD NOT SEE for the glory of that light" (Acts 22:11). Blinded by his vision of Christ on the road to Damascus, Paul, come to torment Christians, would leave as an apostle of the faith he had sought to destroy.

Who was this persecutor turned missionary? His personality leaps across the centuries with startling vividness. Though Paul is not mentioned in the four Gospels and almost certainly never met Jesus, more than a third of the New Testament—most of the Acts of the Apostles and the Epistles—involves what he said and did and wrote. His epistles to his congregations, letters which rank next to the words of Jesus in spiritual power, reveal him as Christianity's most creative exponent.

Paul could be warm and gentle: "Love is patient and kind; love is not jealous or boastful; it is not arrogant or rude" (I Corinthians 13:4). No stained-glass saint, however, he could when challenged give vent to fiery anger: "I wish those who unsettle you would mutilate themselves!" (Galatians 5:12). An illness he called "a thorn in the flesh" plagued him, and detractors described his appearance and speech as unimposing. Yet the high-strung evangelist, depressed one minute, joyous the next, faced hostility with confidence. "For the sake of Christ, then, I am content with weaknesses, insults, hardships, persecutions, and calamities; for when I am weak, then I am strong" (II Corinthians 12:10).

O N THE APOSTLE'S EARLY LIFE we have little firsthand information. But from knowledge of the social and religious background of the times we can reconstruct the forces that molded his youth. His native Tarsus, with access to the Mediterranean as well as to a gap in the Taurus Mountains used by camel caravans from the heart of Asia Minor, long reigned as queen city of the fertile Cilician plain, cultivated by slave labor. Famous conquerors had marched this way: Ashurbanipal of Assyria, Cyrus of Persia, Alexander of Macedon, Julius Caesar. The Tarsus of Paul's time belonged to the Roman world, which preserved many fruits of Hellenistic civilization—in engineering, architecture, city planning, education, and athletics. And within this handsome city, standing somewhat apart from the mainstream of Hellenistic and Roman life, was a Jewish community.

Sometime between A.D. 5 and 14, in the reign of Caesar Augustus, the wife of a Jewish citizen of Tarsus bore a son. Eight days later, the babe was circumcised and named Saul—fitting for a descendant of the tribe of Benjamin, which had given the Hebrews their first king, Saul. But the infant's father was also a Roman citizen. And gentiles would call the boy by his Roman name, Paulus.

Julius Caesar, passing through on his way from Egypt to the Black Sea in 47 B.C., may have granted Roman citizenship to Paul's grandfather. Or the favor may have come several years later from Mark Antony, who made Tarsus a free city—self-governing and with the right to duty-free export and import—as a reward for its loyalty to the Caesarean cause. And here Antony met Cleopatra, Egypt's beautiful queen. Plutarch, the Greek biographer, describes how she "came sailing up the river Cydnus, in a barge with gilded stern and outspread sails of purple, while oars of silver beat time to the music of flutes and fifes and harps. She herself lay all along under

a canopy of cloth of gold, dressed as Venus. . . ."
The populace, in haste to see the enchanting sight,
rushed out of the marketplace, leaving Antony
"alone sitting upon the tribunal."

The Cydnus starts high in the snow-capped Taurus;
its name means "cold river," and its waters almost
cost Alexander the Great his life. The young king,
weary, overheated, and feverish, plunged in to cool
himself. For days he lay at death's door. The fever
broke, but for a time history's clock stood still.

Paul and his boyhood friends would frolic in that
river during the steamy Cilician summer, while
a heat haze hung over the plain and water buffaloes
lazed in the shallows with only their horns, eyes,
and nostrils showing. To escape summertime's worst,
many families took refuge in the hills to the north,
returning to Tarsus in autumn.

Paul would sleep in the courtyard of his father's
house, upon a raised platform like the ones still used
in this region. Against the starry sky he could
see V-squadrons of wild geese winging south toward
the open sea. Tarsians claimed that each migrant

bird carried a stone in its bill to prevent it from honking and thus betraying
the passage of the flock over the Taurus to eagles infesting these heights.
Plutarch cited such behavior as a prudent example for human babblers to follow.

*T*HE ROMAN WORLD OF PAUL'S TIME stretched from the Rhine and the Danube
to the sands of North Africa and Arabia, from the Atlantic to the Euphrates.
With a professional army of 300,000, the emperor guarded the frontiers.
Governors, extracting as much in taxes as they could, administered the provinces,
though a Roman citizen had the right to appeal directly to the emperor.

Rome looked mainly to Egypt as the granary of the empire. The round ships
of commerce also brought rugs and tapestries, linens and glassware from Syria and
other eastern provinces. Augustus had established the pax Romana—the stern
Roman peace—and highways and sea lanes were safer than ever before. Delegations

ANATOLIAN VILLAGERS *herd their flocks along dusty, sun-scorched roads. Paul, pushing inland through*

traveled to festivals and games. Merchants converged at the large cities. Teachers wandered from town to town, giving orations, seeking fame and employment. Missionaries of mystery cults, wonder workers, and charlatans were on the move.

Roman roads, constructed now at an unprecedented rate, went straight as possible over hill and dale, using cuts and fills, spanning rivers on massive bridges of arched stone. Paved with polygonal stones, punctuated by milestones to facilitate troop movements and the courier service, these curbed thoroughfares six to ten feet wide linked many of the principal capitals in the East Paul knew.

An average day's journey on foot took him perhaps 16 miles, mostly during the cooler morning hours. Shelter sometimes might be had at the *mansiones*, or caravansaries, where a courier would end his day's travel, and the *mutationes* where he changed horses. Severe weather discouraged travel through the Cilician Gates into the heart of Asia Minor except from May till November. Winter storms also limited Mediterranean navigation. Late-summer winds could speed a vessel from Italy to Egypt in a week or two; the return voyage took 50 days or more. A grain ship from Egypt, like the one in which Paul sailed for Rome, would not have left Alexandria until September, and would arrive shortly before the close of navigation. But Rome's need of Egypt's grain was so great that the government insured shipowners against loss of vessels, thus later voyages sometimes were risked.

THOMAS NEBBIA

the Cilician Gates, trudged the stark uplands of Asia Minor during his arduous missionary journeys.

BUFFETED by the pagan winds of Greece and Rome, Jews of Paul's day found it difficult to abide by the multitude of laws and restrictions of Judaism. Four out of five lived outside Palestine. Some of these Jews of the Diaspora— Greek for "dispersion"—were assimilated and disappeared into the melting pot of Roman cities. To avoid jeers at the public baths, a few even suffered an operation to undo circumcision. But most remained true to the law and even sought converts.

In his youth, Paul probably stood by the athletic field on the banks of the Cydnus, watching with envy his gentile friends in games and races. Alas, he could not compete, for sports evoked pagan rituals honoring Zeus and Apollo. Yet the regimen of training and the zeal to win impressed Paul, for he would write in I Corinthians 9: "Do you not know that in a race all the runners compete, but only one receives the prize? So run that you may obtain it. Every athlete exercises self-control in all things."

Paul's father taught him his religious duties. The boy picked up his craft, which, literally translated from the Greek, means "tentmaker." Such words often have broad connotations. Although tents of goat's hair were made by nomad women, leather was the basic tent material of the Greco-Roman world. Paul would have seen fierce-looking Pisidian mountaineers bring in the hides by camel caravan. From the processed hides men made saddles, harnesses, sandals, and tents. In the synagogue school Paul would have studied the Old Testament in Greek—

385

for even in a long-established Jewish community
such as that at Tarsus, services were in Greek.
But Roman citizens were expected to know Latin.
So the boy probably learned that tongue as well
as the *koinē,* the common Greek which people spoke.

Tarsus then ranked next to Athens and Alexandria
in the reputation of its scholars. Ever since
the aging Stoic, Athenodorus, tutor to Augustus,
wrested control from corrupt politicians, philosophers
had governed the city. Athenodorus was succeeded by Nestor,
a follower of Plato. Paul surely heard him in the marketplace.
And he must have heard traveling philosophers speak there, for he sometimes
follows their methods — the *diatribē* — especially in raising and answering questions.

His father would not have permitted him to join Greek lads in studying
rhetoric, philosophy, and science under the Tarsus teachers. But Paul probably
eavesdropped on student-tutor discussions in the colonnades. He evidently thought
much of the wrangling inconsequential. For later, in I Corinthians 1, he cried:
"Where is the wise man? Where is the scribe? Where is the debater of this age?
Has not God made foolish the wisdom of the world?"

*D*URING THE FESTIVAL of the city's god, whom every citizen was obligated to honor
Tarsian Jews found it wise to lie low. This festival resembled a Mardi Gras
in which the population — especially descendants of Canaanite and Hittite elements —
went wild. They carried about a statue of the "Lord of Tarsus," equated by the
Greek element with Heracles (the Roman Hercules), and burned it.
This symbolized the death of the god. In frenzied procession back to the temple,
they dramatized his restoration to life, token of the renewal of nature's fertility.

Paul's world was a hothouse of competing pagan cults. Astrologers with their
globes and planetariums proclaimed men's fates by reading the stars. Deification
of the emperor was being fostered as a state religion. Mystery cults, so named

because of their secret rites, flourished. The worship of Mithras, god of Persian and Roman soldiers, would take place in a grotto which held a sculpture of Mithras killing a bull. Initiates underwent a baptism, passed through degrees of membership as in Freemasonry, and partook of a sacred meal of bread and water mixed with wine, commemorating Mithras' meal with the sun god before ascending to heaven. Mithraism was to become Christianity's chief rival and subtly to influence its ritual. Also prevalent in Paul's day was the veneration of Isis, Egyptian goddess who reigned over heaven, and Osiris, her husband and brother whom she had raised from the dead.

*P*AUL'S FATHER decided to send him to Jerusalem, to imbibe Judaism at its fount and perhaps to arm him against such influences. Arriving in the Holy City, Paul visited the temple after the seven-day period of purification, required of all Jews coming from foreign lands. At the terrace before the women's court, he would see a posted warning: "No heathen shall enter within the hedge and wall about the sanctuary. Whoever is caught can only blame himself, because death will follow." Years later, when he was indicted for bringing gentiles into the temple, these words would haunt him.

After exploring various Jewish sects, Paul chose the Pharisees, as his father had before him. And he must have followed a radical group: "I advanced in Judaism beyond many of my own age among my people, so extremely zealous was I for the traditions of my fathers" (Galatians 1:14). For a while he even fasted twice a week rather than the Pharisee's minimum requirement of once a year. Later Paul found most social contacts among the Sadducees, the sophisticated governing clique around the high priest. They saw in the early Jewish followers of Christ peril for themselves and for all Judaism. After all, these Nazarenes proclaimed a Messiah who, though crucified by a Roman governor, would return as king of kings! Alarmed at the rapid progress of the new sect, Sadducee politicians suggested to impressionable young men like Paul that the people would be served if somebody

SCENES PAUL KNEW
survive in stone and metal. Stubby ships carried grain, goods, and intrepid passengers. Wagons clattered over paved roads. Rome gathered taxes in coins honoring the emperor— here Nero, A.D. *54-68. Cutlers and other craftsmen made and sold wares in home shops. Crowds roared at the spectacle of gladiators and wrestlers.*

would move to stifle the dangerous propaganda. Forming a band of adventurers, Paul commenced his reign of terror. Outside the temple these men baited Stephen, a leader of the Greek-speaking element of Nazarenes. A screaming mob hauled Stephen beyond the city gates and smashed him with stones. "And he kneeled down, and cried with a loud voice, Lord, lay not this sin to their charge. . . . And Saul was consenting unto his death" (Acts 7:60, 8:1).

Paul apparently feared that the new sect would prove particularly dangerous for the Jews in foreign lands. He aimed his Jerusalem attack almost exclusively at Greek-speaking Christians who could spread the faith across the Hellenized world. Yet, as his band went from house to house, lashing and torturing, demanding recantation, he promoted what he sought to prevent. He scattered the Christians, and new groups rose elsewhere, just as new fires arise from wind-carried sparks. Paul tracked the Nazarenes down in cities like Ashdod and Ashkelon on the coast, and perhaps across the Jordan. Eventually, convinced he had broken the back of Christianity, he returned to Jerusalem. Here he received a final task. At dawn one spring day a few weeks after the Passover pilgrims had departed from the Holy City, Paul set out on the road to Damascus—and his date with destiny.

AFTER HIS BLINDING CONVERSION, perhaps during a sudden tempest on that windswept plateau, Paul was led by his guide and muleteers into Damascus. Here, on the Street Called Straight, the Tarsian recuperated in the house of a man named Judas. Yet he refused food and drink for three days. Suddenly came a knock at the courtyard gate. A stranger to see him! Ananias, a Nazarene who lived nearby, touched Paul's eyelids. Paul felt a sensation of power; then his vision returned, as night yielding to day.

The Tarsian, baptized into the new faith, returned home with Ananias. His host revealed that the Lord, appearing, had said of Paul: "he is a chosen vessel unto me, to bear my name before the Gentiles, and kings, and the children of Israel: For I will shew him how great things he must suffer for my name's sake" (Acts 9:15-16).

His awesome mission stood revealed. Over the empire's busy trade routes, in synagogue and marketplace, he would spread a message of universal brotherhood: "For ye are all the children of God by faith in Christ Jesus. . . . There is neither Jew nor Greek" (Galatians 3:26, 28).

We can imagine Paul, at dawn outside the walls of Damascus, pausing a moment to watch the spectacle in the heavens. In the east the first red flush starts up. "Hind of the morning," Palestinian Jews called it, perhaps imagining it a doe fleeing a hunter, the sun. Paul's eyes sweep the green oasis that clasps the city like a jewel, and looks down the dusty road toward the mountains and the cities to the south. He faces a difficult path, a hostile world. But in his darkest hours a voice will sustain him: "Be not afraid . . . For I am with thee" (Acts 18:9, 10).

WEIRDLY SCULPTURED CAPPADOCIA, *scoured by grit-laden winds, provided fertile soil for the faith Paul preached. Thousands of Christian hermits found haven in its caves and cones. Here Turkish villagers bring in precious wood.*

THOMAS NEBBIA

In the Footsteps of Paul

FROM DAMASCUS TO CAESAR'S ROME

Through mountain passes
and over ancient sea lanes,
National Geographic's David S. Boyer
tracks the great missionary
whose "good news" changed history's course

LUIS MARDEN AND (LEFT) B. ANTHONY STEWART, BOTH NATIONAL GEOGRAPHIC STAFF

"God," wrote Paul in II Corinthians, "hath made us able ministers of the new testament." No more able minister ever lived than this inspired man who bore the gospel of Christ to all who would hear it. Preaching, teaching, writing, healing, he traveled 12,000 miles on his epic mission. In four great journeys he traversed Asia Minor, crossed the Aegean Sea to Greece, and voyaged on the Mediterranean to Crete, Malta, to Rome itself.

The most ardent traveler of his time, Paul trod Roman roads and sailed Roman seas. In the empire of the Caesars he encountered no frontiers, needed no passport. As I sought Paul's footsteps, I would cross the borders of nine countries

DROWNED SEAWALLS *outline
the principal port of Palestine
in Paul's day. Herod the Great
spent 12 years building a regal
city, dedicating it in 10 B.C.
to his patron, Caesar Augustus.
Paul tarried among the faithful
at Caesarea during his journeys;
later Caesar's minions held him
in custody here two years.*

*Dime-size token (left), found
on the harbor floor, shows
ships sailing toward the twin
towers at the port entrance.
Soaring arches frame a Crusader
citadel raised with stones from
this capital of Roman Judaea.*

in a strife-torn era. But I was spared the perils of Paul:

"Thrice was I beaten with rods, once was I stoned, thrice I suffered shipwreck, a night and a day I have been in the deep; In journeyings often . . . in perils of robbers, in perils by mine own countrymen, in perils by the heathen, in perils in the city, in perils in the wilderness . . . In weariness and painfulness, in watchings often, in hunger and thirst . . . in cold and nakedness" (II Corinthians 11:25-27).

In Damascus, where Paul found Christ, I began my quest. As I drove into town from Damascus airport I realized that I could not be far from the spot "nigh unto Damascus" where Paul's blinding vision had turned persecutor to apostle.

Syria's bustling capital bulges far beyond the Roman walls that ringed it in Paul's day. Handsome apartments climb like steps up a mountainside. But a great deal remains

unchanged within the ruined walls of the old city. The Roman highway Vicus Rectus, the Street Called Straight, still bisects the city from east to west. My Arab guide called it Suq et Tawil, the Long Bazaar, for it is lined with shops selling brassware, Persian carpets, brocades, and inlaid furniture.

Along this street Paul was led, sightless, his mind throbbing with "the glory of that light" (Acts 22:11). An underground chapel marks the site revered as the home of Ananias, who restored Paul's sight and told him: "The God of our fathers hath chosen thee."

As a hunted turncoat, Paul had to escape his erstwhile friends: "And through a window in a basket was I let down by the wall" (II Corinthians 11:33). A recent restoration purports to show the kind of window from which he was lowered. But it opens over a gate—a poor place to escape, for gates would be guarded. Houses of the old Jewish quarter are built into and atop the present wall. From one of these windows I could envision an escape more likely to succeed.

A Syrian professor I met refuted this idea. "The walls," he said, "had been built for

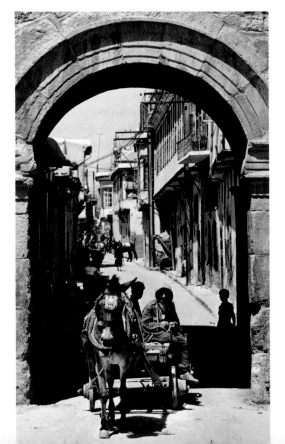

"THE RICHES OF DAMASCUS," *chronicled in Isaiah 8:4, gleamed in Paul's day as they do today (opposite). Threads of silver and gold mingle with silk in brocades that cascade in a Damascus showroom. Cocoons dangle from the hands of a manufacturer of silk thread for the city's fabled looms. Since antiquity this Syrian oasis has flourished on the trade of its famed products. Its name shines in fine damascene steel and is woven into damask.*

Christianity found fertile soil here within a few years after the Crucifixion. To stamp out the new faith came Paul, "breathing out threatenings and slaughter." But after his searing conversion on the road to Damascus, Paul preached of Jesus in the city's synagogues and "all that heard him were amazed" (Acts 9:21). In the Street Called Straight (left), a colonnaded avenue in Roman times, he found rest and shelter among the hounded sect.

395

defense. Desert marauders were near at hand. Can you imagine the Romans allowing houses to be built along the top of a wall? St. Paul's 'window' must have been an opening in the crenellated guard walk."

A FTER PAUL'S ESCAPE from Damascus, a hiatus occurs in his history. In a letter written years later, he says he "went into Arabia." Some scholars believe his path led into the realm of the Nabataeans, an ancient tribe that had evolved into a monarchy; in Paul's time they had not yet been incorporated into the Roman province of Arabia.

The Nabataeans, rulers of the desert east of Damascus and southward into present-day Saudi Arabia, had their capital in Petra, a rock-girt citadel south of the Dead Sea. Here sheer gorges cut the mountains of Old Testament Edom, near the route Moses followed to the Promised Land. And here, his reputation unknown, Paul would have found a welcome in the little Jewish colony in the pagan stronghold carved from rose-red rock.

In earlier days Nabataeans had plundered caravans laden with gold, incense, and spices from Arabia, India, and East Africa. When their victims sent out punitive expeditions, the brigands cached their loot in caves and retreated to the desert, surviving on water drawn from hidden cisterns in the rock. Parched, their pursuers would turn back.

Once in control of the caravan routes, Nabataean kings adopted a wiser policy. They exacted protection money from the merchants, guaranteeing them safe conduct. The nomadic desert marauders became warehousemen and brokers. Petra developed into a thriving commercial capital, with thousands of warriors to garrison its outlying settlements and guard its trade routes.

I rode into Petra through the Siq—Arabic for "pass." A canyon whose sheer walls tower 300 feet high, the Siq at places narrowed to a few yards, while overhanging masses of bright sandstone almost shut out the sky. On the canyon's dark floor sparks glinted from the hoofs of my weary horse. Then, abruptly, the Siq opened into a broad, transverse chasm. There, framed through what is almost a tunnel,

"ROSE-RED CITY, HALF AS OLD AS TIME," *Petra glows at the end of the mile-long Siq, cleft—Arab legend says—by the mighty rod of Moses. Nabataeans ruled a caravan empire from this stronghold in southern Jordan. Perhaps Paul watched stonecutters chisel out the "Treasury" (opposite), proudest of Petra's tombs and temples. Lost to the world for centuries, the cliff city's wonders were rediscovered in 1812 by John Lewis Burckhardt, a Swiss adventurer disguised as a Bedouin.*

LUIS MARDEN, NATIONAL GEOGRAPHIC STAFF

rises the first in a series of rock-hewn monuments: El Khazneh, the Treasury, perhaps the tomb of a Nabataean king. Carved in the lower part of a cliff, its 130-foot-high façade retained the luminosity of the dying sun. Paul may have seen stonecutters shaping this colossal cameo in living rock.

I climbed to the Great High Place. Here I could picture priests gathering at the open altars to feast and conduct sacrificial rituals. Black stones—emblems of Dusares, the Nabataean sun god—probably were smeared with blood. Huge, plaster-lined cisterns nearby provided water to wash away the gore.

Later, as I watched a desert moon cast shadows down into the deserted city in its rocky fastness, I wondered how Paul would have felt in this strange community. I could imagine him as he climbed to some rock ledge, avoiding the pagan high places, to commune with the God of Israel and the Redeemer.

In the morning, sounds of the camp broke the eerie silence of old Petra and brought me back through time from the days of Paul. Now I must again pick up his trail—so faint and uncertain in this fortress, which is deserted but for tourists and a few Bedouin.

The Book of Acts tells us that Paul appeared in Jerusalem and helped the apostles preach. But when Paul again was threatened, they sent him to Tarsus.

I found Tarsus unchanged in name, but Paul's city had been smothered by silt and rubble. Though he might recognize a few Roman ruins, the grandeur of his day is gone. Only in the marketplace would he feel at home. Here, among color- fully garbed buyers and hag- gling merchants, I recalled his warning that "the love of money is the root of all evil" (I Timo- thy 6:10).

ROME

ITALY

PUTEOLI

THESSALONICA

BEROEA

MACEDONIA

GREECE

ATHENS

CORINTH

CENCHREAE

ACHAIA

RHEGIUM

CAPE
SALMONE

CRETE

PHOENIX

FAIR HAVENS

CLAUDA

SYRACUSE

MEDITERRANEAN

MALTA

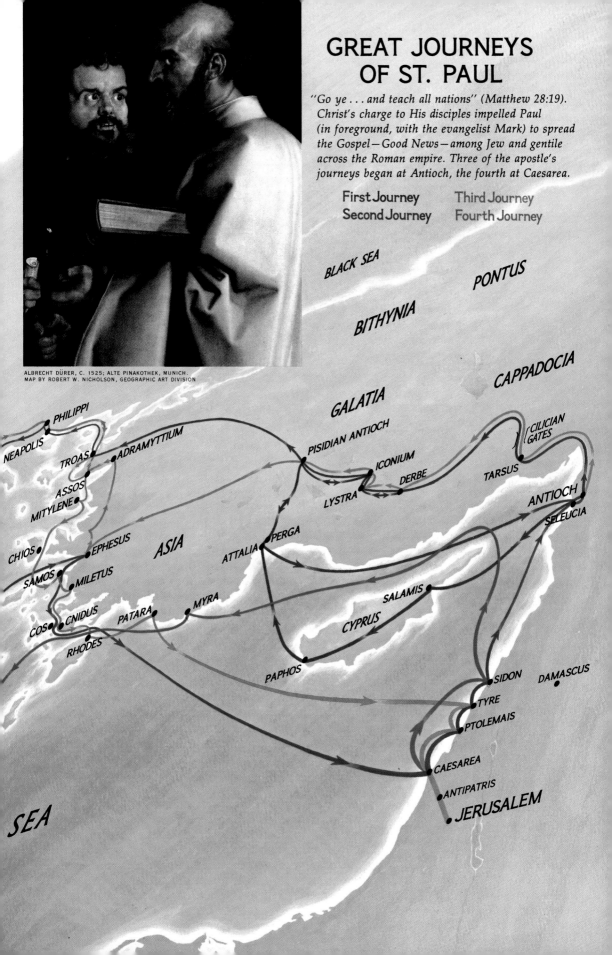

GREAT JOURNEYS OF ST. PAUL

"Go ye . . . and teach all nations" (Matthew 28:19).
Christ's charge to His disciples impelled Paul
(in foreground, with the evangelist Mark) to spread
the Gospel—Good News—among Jew and gentile
across the Roman empire. Three of the apostle's
journeys began at Antioch, the fourth at Caesarea.

First Journey   Third Journey
Second Journey   Fourth Journey

BLACK SEA

PONTUS

BITHYNIA

CAPPADOCIA

GALATIA

ALBRECHT DÜRER, C. 1525; ALTE PINAKOTHEK, MUNICH.
MAP BY ROBERT W. NICHOLSON, GEOGRAPHIC ART DIVISION

PHILIPPI

NEAPOLIS

TROAS   ADRAMYTTIUM

PISIDIAN ANTIOCH

ICONIUM

CILICIAN GATES

ASSOS

MITYLENE

DERBE

TARSUS

LYSTRA

ANTIOCH

SELEUCIA

CHIOS

EPHESUS

ASIA

ATTALIA   PERGA

SAMOS

MILETUS

SALAMIS

COS   CNIDUS

PATARA   MYRA

CYPRUS

RHODES

PAPHOS

SIDON   DAMASCUS

TYRE

PTOLEMAIS

CAESAREA

ANTIPATRIS

JERUSALEM

SEA

I T WAS IN ANTIOCH, then the largest city in the Mediterranean world after Rome and Alexandria, that Paul's apostolic mission really began. Peter, probably the first of the apostles to visit Antioch, had preached there in a cave believed to be the first Christian church. "And the disciples were called Christians first in Antioch" (Acts 11:26). As the congregation grew, the mother church at Jerusalem sent Barnabas, a Cypriot Jew, to preach there. Barnabas brought Paul from Tarsus.

On the Orontes River at the southern tip of Turkey, a day's drive from Tarsus, today's Antakya occupies only a fraction of the site where paved boulevards and colonnades once graced ancient Antioch. Little remains visible: an aqueduct that once carried water to villas, baths, fountains, hippodromes, and theaters; lively floor mosaics that Paul might have seen, now displayed in a museum. To reach St. Peter's cave, I climbed a hillside through olive groves, leaving behind the city and its brass workers hammering out pots and pans.

At Antioch's ancient port, Seleucia, I saw shipwrights building broad-beamed vessels much like those that sailed the Roman seas Paul knew so well. Piles of

HELEN AND FRANK SCHREIDER, NATIONAL GEOGRAPHIC STAFF. LEFT AND UPPER: THOMAS NEBBIA

"THESE HANDS HAVE MINISTERED *unto my necessities,"*
said Paul (Acts 20:34). Trained in toil since boyhood
and proud of it, he would recognize the craft of
the saddlemaker (above) sewing straw-stuffed donkey
saddles in Antalya, on Turkey's southern coast.
Paul embarked here, when it was Attalia, during his
first missionary journey. The tireless apostle followed
the rabbinic tradition of earning his living
and teaching without fee. "If any would not work,
neither should he eat," he bluntly commanded
in II Thessalonians 3:10.

The Bible calls him a tentmaker, though the
original Greek word may also mean leatherworker.
In the Greco-Roman world tents were usually of hide;
some, however, were still made of cilicium,
a goat's wool from Paul's native Cilicia.

Donkey-led camel caravan wades a watery shortcut
off Latakia (left), Syria's doorway to the sea.
Famed as Laodicea in Roman times for its wine and
fruit, Latakia today ships choice leaf tobacco bearing
its name. Kaffiyeh (upper) shielded travelers' heads
from sun and sand long before Paul's day.

401

timber, yellow in the sun, lay beside each cradled skeleton ship. Along the roads near here, peasants rose to offer—for a price—Roman coins they had dug from the soil.

On his first great missionary journey—probably from A.D. 45 to 49—the apostle and Barnabas sailed from Seleucia for the island of Cyprus. At Salamis, the ancient commercial capital, "they preached the word of God in the synagogues of the Jews" (Acts 13:5), then crossed the island to Paphos.

Sergius Paulus, the Roman proconsul at Paphos, sent for them "to hear the word of God." When a sorcerer heckled them, Paul called down the wrath of God, and the tormentor was blinded. The proconsul, "when he saw what was done, believed. . . ." Paul's first recorded triumph, with Sergius Paulus, may have spurred him to preach the new faith to gentiles as well as to Jews.

I too crossed the island to Paphos, traversing the Troodos Mountains by car. Their highest peak is called Olympus, one of several in the classical Greek world to bear the name of the home of mythological gods and goddesses. The mountain route turned out to be a forest ride of primeval majesty. Through writhing mist we climbed, my driver and I, at times sheeted in storm and cuffed by squalls of slashing rain. Clouds would dip and swirl through the valleys, revealing Olympian views of purple summits lashed by jagged tongues of lightning. I half expected to come face to face with Zeus or Apollo.

At Paphos I wandered among the ruins of Sergius Paulus' provincial seat of Roman government. A few miles farther along the shore, watching seafoam whiten the waves, I reflected on the legend that tells how Aphrodite, Greek goddess of love, rose out of seafoam here off the coast of Cyprus. The pagan sex worship surrounding her must have shocked the apostle Paul.

With Barnabas, Paul sailed from Paphos to Asia Minor, present-day Turkey. They made their way to Pisidia, a rugged, mountainous part of the Roman province of Galatia. In the rich city of Pisidian Antioch (not to be confused with the Antioch to the south), they established a church. There Paul preached that by Christ "all that believe

ANTIOCH "THE BEAUTIFUL" —*modern Antakya—nestles below terraced Mount Silpius in southernmost Turkey. Gaiety and wit sparkled in this luxurious capital of Caesar's Syria; by night thousands of lights glinted like a moonlit sea. The music of the flowing Orontes charmed the Romans, who bridged the river here. Amid the splendor Christ's word flourished. Paul's missionary journeys began here, where the term "Christian" was coined, perhaps in scorn. In a cave on Silpius (right) tradition places Christianity's oldest church, the Grotto of St. Peter.*

JOHN J. PUTMAN, NATIONAL GEOGRAPHIC STAFF

are justified from all things, from which ye could not be justified by the law of Moses'' (Acts 13:39). Many gentiles came to hear Paul preach. But the Jews, envious of Paul's success, began ''contradicting and blaspheming.'' And ''Paul and Barnabas waxed bold, and said . . . lo, we turn to the Gentiles'' (13:46).

The temples, colonnades, and public squares of Pisidian Antioch are long since gone; I found instead the village of Yalvac in the foothills of the Sultan Mountains. Its houses were patched together of wood, mud, and stone. A classic column had been thrust into the hodgepodge construction of a stable. An open aqueduct, far less grand than the Roman one Paul saw, brought cool water from the snow-clad heights. Water still dribbled through a worn and broken fountain stone set in place by the Romans.

I remembered a passage from H. V. Morton's book, *In the Steps of St. Paul:* ''I cannot understand how any traveller . . . can see a Corinthian capital lying in the mud without feeling that such things hold a lesson and a warning and, perhaps, a prophesy.''

Expelled at last by the Jews of Pisidian Antioch, Paul and Barnabas ''shook off the dust of their feet . . .

BURROS AND BALANCES *at Bodrum evoke a market scene from the Asia Minor Paul knew. Here women dress as he urged: "in modest apparel," not with "gold, or pearls, or costly array" (I Timothy 2:9). In this Turkish port, ancient Halicarnassus, the historian Herodotus was born and King Mausolus buried. His tomb, one of the Seven Wonders of the World, gave us the word "mausoleum."*

JONATHAN S. BLAIR

"To comprehend...what is the breadth, and length, and depth, and height" *Ephesians 3:18*

Paul the traveler knew the Roman mile, for the empire was reckoned by its length. Yet the Bible mentions it but once: "whosoever shall compel thee to go a mile," taught Jesus, "go with him twain" (Matthew 5:41). Highway markers, some of them ten feet tall, gave distances to major centers. Milestone below also proclaims titles of Emperor Trajan and reminds passers-by that Trajan's money built the road from Benevento to Brundisium (Brindisi).

Romans fixed the mile—and its name—at *mille passus*, 1,000 Roman paces, double steps of about five foot-lengths; hence a 5,000-foot mile close to today's. Paces measured Palestine's short distances; long trips were estimated in days' journeys, the span depending on terrain and traveler.

Paul heard seamen sound depths in fathoms—the spread of a man's arms, model for today's six-foot unit. Jesus as a carpenter would use His arm for a ruler, laying out finger-widths, palm-widths, the span of a spread hand, the cubit from elbow to fingertip. The thumb-width lives as our inch, the double cubit as our yard.

BARLETTA MUSEUM; SCALA

Ancients sold food by volume, precious items by weight, sometimes using kernels of grain to even the scales. Chemists still weigh in "grains." The shekel, from a Hebrew verb for "weigh," equaled about half an ounce; 50 shekels made a *mina*, 60 minas a *talent*. The shekel later denoted value, as did the talent: some $2,000 for a talent of silver, perhaps $30,000 for one of gold. Some scholars trace the talent to the Egyptians' weight of a cubic foot of water.

Romans split this weight into hundredths called *librae*, then each libra into *unciae*, or "twelfth parts," that named the ounce.

Mesopotamians judged a field's size by the seed it needed. Hebrews measured by the "yoke," what an ox team could plow in a day; our acre originated the same way. The load of grain an ass could carry became the Hebrew "homer."

Some merchants toted a light set of weights for selling, a heavy one for buying. Measures often varied with the country, as did calendars. Israel's twelfth month, *Adar*, was Egypt's seventh and Greece's sixth. Romans had tinkered with their twelvemonth, adding days to pad terms of office. By Julius Caesar's time January fell in autumn. He added 90 days, pushing March into spring and fixing the Julian calendar, little changed today.

and came unto Iconium" (Acts 13:51). Again they preached in the synagogues; again devout Jews resisted the new faith and "stirred up the Gentiles, and made their minds evil affected against the brethren" (Acts 14:2). Today, scarcely a handful of Christians—Armenians—live in Konya, a Turkish city of some 120,000 on the site of Iconium.

The missionaries sparked riots in Iconium and had to flee. They headed for Lystra, a Roman colony 18 miles southwest of Iconium and home of Timothy, a disciple of Paul. Iconium troublemakers followed Paul to Lystra, where he was stoned and left for dead. But "he rose up" and went on to Derbe, now a mound west of modern Karaman. Here at last Paul was able to gather a small group of believers without being persecuted.

Later, when some Christian congregations in Galatia—so named because Gauls had invaded the region three centuries earlier—argued over whether non-Jewish converts should observe the law of Moses, Paul answered: "O foolish Galatians. . . . the law was our schoolmaster to bring us unto Christ. . . . But after that faith is come, we are no longer under a schoolmaster. . . . There is neither Jew nor Greek, there is neither bond nor free, there is neither male nor female: for ye are all one in Christ Jesus" (Galatians 3:1, 24-28).

I turned southward into the present province of Antalya and, to wash off a coating of dust, went swimming among Corinthian capitals fallen into the Mediterranean. I sat in the Roman theater and climbed the half-buried stadium Paul must have known at Perga. And I imagined his revulsion, in Roman cities, at hearing the screams of men and beasts dying in the arenas.

At the end of his first mission, Paul sailed back to Antioch from the port of Attalia, now *(Continued on page 412)*

PORTAL FOR PAUL *as he "went through Syria and Cilicia, strengthening the churches" (Acts 15:41), the Cilician Gates here give passage to Turkish goat herders. Threaded by Alexander, this defile in the Taurus Mountains linked ancient East and West.*
THOMAS NEBBIA

406

Faith carved a niche in a land of rock

Early Christians hollowed cells and chapels
in fantastic cones that stud the Goreme Valley
in the heart of the Anatolian highland.
Turkish farmers now dwell in these pinnacles
where Christianity found roots, perhaps from
seed sown by Paul in Galatia. Peter, writing
to dispersed brethren, saluted "the strangers
scattered throughout . . . Cappadocia" (I Peter 1:1),
as this land was then known.

Frescoes a millennium old embellish vaultings,
domes, and columns of Elmah Kilise, tiny Apple
Church (below), named for dwarf apple trees
that grew outside its cone. In another,
monks burrowed a ten-story monastery
whose chimneylike hall linked tiers of cells
with a kitchen, church, and burial rooms.

Eons ago 12,848-foot Erciyas Dagi, loftiest
peak in Asia Minor, spewed ash and lava,
building a vast layer hundreds of feet deep.
As this cooled and cracked, rain and melting
snow gouged chasms around surviving towers
of tuff, a crumbly rock of volcanic ash.
Winds honed the towers into cones.

CAVE DWELLERS *at the public fountain in rock-hewn Urgup enact a Cappadocian tableau evocative of Paul's time: A balky donkey, bearing all its mistress' possessions, tarries at the trough, inspiring goads and grins.*

Antalya, which crouches in the lee of the snow-covered Taurus Mountains. I found three vessels riding at anchor in Antalya's teacup-sized harbor. Forgoing a voyage on a creaking old merchantman—surely a descendant of the craft that carried Paul—I pushed on overland.

PAUL'S SECOND JOURNEY, originating in Antioch, sent him through the Cilician Gates, north of Tarsus, into the high country of Asia Minor. Accompanied this time by Silas, another missionary from the Jerusalem church, Paul swung off on a mountain trek to "visit our brethren in every city where we have preached the word of the Lord, and see how they do" (Acts 15:36).

It is often difficult, when following the apostle's footsteps, to feel you have found his exact path. So it is that his passage seems excitingly real as you walk the very miles he walked to thread the Cilician Gates—a defile through the mighty Taurus cliffs where ancient Tarsus engineers carved a road 80 miles long. Here passed conquering armies of Alexander the Great and, more than a thousand years later, the Crusaders. And here, 1,900 years ago, one might have sat to rest and been passed on the road by Paul, staff in hand, striding to his destiny.

Paul and Silas preached as they walked westward, reaching the coast not far from where the current of the Dardanelles floods into the Aegean. Here I tried to reach the ruins

"AN IDOL IS NOTHING," *said Paul (I Corinthians 8:4). His words echo amid a rubble of fallen gods atop Turkey's 7,000-foot Nemrud Dagh, above a bend in the Euphrates.*

Antiochus I of Commagene carved this "throne room of all the gods." Tiny buffer between East and West, Commagene drew from the religions of Persia, Greece, and Anatolia. Worshipers fused Greece's Apollo and Persia's Mithras into this sun deity (opposite), toppled from the terrace where Antiochus sat as a fellow god with deities of fertility, thunder, strength.

In a major dig American scholar Theresa Goell unearthed the East Terrace (above). Stars, planets, and a crescent moon arrayed on a relief apparently date the shrine to 61 or 62 B.C. *The National Geographic Society supported Dr. Goell's excavations.*

At Derbe, Paul turned away from the border of Commagene's realm, whose king, a vassal of Rome, guarded its cults.

of Alexandria Troas and Assos, ports well known to Paul. Once he chose to walk from one to the other while his companions sailed. I should have done the same. After three flats and a blowout on the "highway," my driver gave up.

In Troas, Paul had a vision. A "man of Macedonia" appeared before him and pleaded: "Come over into Macedonia, and help us" (Acts 16:9). Perhaps this was Luke, evangelist, "beloved physician," and traditional author of the Acts of the Apostles. Apparently Luke now joined Paul, for at this point in the narrative the author writes in the first-person plural: "And after [Paul] had seen the vision, immediately we endeavoured to go into Macedonia. . . ." Sailing across the Aegean, Paul now for the first time set foot in Europe. Accompanied by Silas, Luke, and Timothy, who had joined the apostle at Lystra, he landed at the little Roman port of Neapolis, now Kevalla, in Macedonia.

I wondered if Neapolis was as charming as the modern harbor I visited. In Paul's time the waterfront would not have had its present warm, snufflike perfume. Kevalla today is the heart of the Greek tobacco industry. In its warehouses men and women sort and bale tiny leaves of "Turkish" for shipment all over the world.

414

MINARETS *stab the sky over Konya, which Paul knew as Iconium. Mevlana Mosque (left) entombs Jalal-ud-din Rumi, Persian poet and mystic who founded the order of Mevlevis—whirling dervishes.*

The apocryphal Acts of Paul *tells how he converted Thecla in this Turkish oasis. Doomed to stake and arena, she survived with divine help. As a missionary, she later met Paul in Myra.*

There a spinster (opposite) follows Paul's precept, "to be quiet, and to do your own business, and to work with your own hands." Nicholas, a 4th-century bishop of Myra, became the saint we call Santa Claus.

The first Macedonian I met bore the improbable name of Romeo. Naturally, he had a sister named Joulietta. Romeo, an impassioned guide, insisted on our viewing the dozens of Greek and Roman tombstones along the route from Kevalla to Philippi. We trod Paul's very steps, for we walked a stretch of Roman road, Via Egnatia. It is a remnant of Rome's efficient highway system, which served Paul so well. The ruts of wagon and chariot wheels still scar it, three or four inches deep.

Philippi, some nine miles from the coast, now lies in ruins that sprawl over several acres. The huge Roman forum, dating from after Paul's time, stands completely excavated. Its rain gutters still work.

Outside Philippi's walls Paul and his missionaries baptized a well-to-do woman named Lydia, together with her household—Paul's first Christian converts in Europe. The

415

MISSION TO MACEDONIA *took Paul first to steep-hilled Neapolis, today the Greek port of Kevalla (opposite). Treading Europe's roads for the first time, he founded churches, was jailed, "feet fast in the stocks," but trekked on, for "we had courage in our God" (I Thessalonians 2:2).*

In Athens (left) the curious gathered to hear him preach. "Ye men of Athens," he declared, "I perceive that in all things ye are too superstitious" (Acts 17:22). Quoting Greek poets, orating like a Greek philosopher, Paul won such converts as Dionysius, a member of Athens' supreme council whom a tradition names as the city's first bishop.

crystal stream in which the ceremony took place today bubbles through tobacco fields. Inside this city, after exorcising a half-demented slave girl, Paul and Silas were whipped and flung into prison. "And suddenly," Luke writes in Acts 16, "there was a great earthquake, so that the foundations of the prison were shaken: and immediately all the doors were opened, and every one's bands were loosed."

Thessalonica, some 75 miles southwest, was Paul's next target. Here he ran into trouble again, for his opponents marshaled the authorities against him, charging: "These that have turned the world upside down are come hither also" (Acts 17:6).

IN MODERN Thessaloniki I found one of Paul's most devoted disciples: Father Pangratios, archimandrite of the Monastery of Vlatadon. The rotund abbot told me that Paul had very probably preached on the exact site of this monastery. The pagan temple that stood here was a likely place to draw a crowd.

The old priest lay grimacing with pain in bed, for he had twisted an ankle on the steps of his garden. But, as the stories of Paul's life and the fiery language of the epistles came flooding back to memory, Father Pangratios thrashed about beneath his quilt in a fit of oratory. He swept the air with passionate gestures; he tossed his head, his hair flying like a horse's mane. Only when he struck his sore foot with the other did he wince and fall back on the pillow, giving Romeo a chance to translate. As we left, he sank back in his rumpled bed and called imperiously for his Bible. He wanted to read again the two Epistles to the Thessalonians, Paul's "children of light," his "glory and joy."

Hounded out of town, Paul and Silas went to nearby Beroea, now Veroia. Here I saw the stones on which they may have stood to preach. The Jews of Beroea "received the word with all readiness of mind" (Acts 17:11). But enemies from

416

Thessalonica, hot on his trail, forced Paul to flee again, this time to Athens, Greek in spirit though ruled by Rome.

In modern Athens Greeks turn to politics rather than philosophy for their conversation. Every citizen, Greeks told me, considers his own opinions on the subject to be of magisterial weight: "If I could just run this country for 24 hours!" In sidewalk cafes on Constitution Square, amateur politicians chatter as they sip Turkish coffee and consume uncounted glasses of cold water.

The Athens of Paul's day lived amid the glories of its past. It remained a famed center of the arts, a fountainhead of philosophy, a showplace of architecture and sculpture. This sophisticated metropolis did not give Paul much of a hearing. He spoke in the agora, or marketplace—the Constitution Square of his time—with anyone who would listen. But the Athenians still clung to the teachings of Socrates, Plato, and Aristotle. The Bible says that "certain philosophers of the Epicureans, and of the Stoicks, encountered him. And some said, What will this babbler say?... He seemeth to be a setter forth of strange gods" (Acts 17:18).

"I HAVE PLANTED," *said Paul,*
"... but God gave the increase"
(I Corinthians 3:6). The faith
still flourishes where he sowed.
At Thessaloniki a coppersmith
toils as Paul taught, "working
with his hands the thing which
is good" (Ephesians 4:28).

Near Philippi (left), founded
by Philip of Macedon, villagers
transplant tobacco by a stream
where Paul baptized Lydia, the
"seller of purple" (probably
dyed goods). Here Paul and Silas
were jailed. Freed by a quake,
they converted their jailer.

A spiritual descendant of Paul's
Greek Christians, the abbot of
St. Panteleimon Monastery
blesses his monks (opposite).
Here, on a 30-mile peninsula
crowned by Athos, Holy Mountain
of Greece, monastic communities
gathered a thousand years ago.
Monk-ruled Mount Athos
bars women—and female livestock—
and uses the old Julian calendar.

"Paul… saw the city wholly given to idolatry"

Acts 17:16

On the rock called Areopagus, or Mars' Hill, Paul gave his famous speech to the Athenians. He told them of seeing an altar inscribed TO THE UNKNOWN GOD. "Whom therefore ye ignorantly worship, him declare I unto you" (Acts 17:23), he said. Then, probably staring up at the Parthenon, with its gold-and-ivory statue of Athena, he told them: "God

that made the world and all things therein . . . dwelleth not in temples made with hands. . . ."

The apostle went from Athens to Corinth, which stands on the northeastern tip of the Peloponnesus, beside the isthmus that links that peninsula to the mainland. To avoid a 200-mile circumnavigation of stormy Cape Malea, the

THE PARTHENON, *shrine of Athena, jewels the Acropolis in sprawling Athens as it did when Paul urged Athenians to worship his God— not one of "gold, or silver, or stone, graven by art" (Acts 17:29). Beyond thrusts Mount Lycabettus.*

421

"I beseech you, be ye followers of me" I Corinthians 4:16

"I speak to your shame," Paul admonished in I Corinthians 6:5. Columns of Apollo's temple (left) once overlooked tavern tipplers draining cups labeled Love while 1,000 slave girls cavorted at notorious Aphrodite's temple nearby.

Paul penned his first epistle, I Thessalonians, in Corinth, about A.D. 50. In 66, Nero dug with a golden spade to start a canal, then left the job to 6,000 Jews, captured in a revolt against Rome. Engineers' doubts killed the project. Not until 1893 was the four-mile canal cut (opposite).

southeastern finger of the Peloponnesus, small vessels were hauled from sea to sea on rollers over the *diolkos,* or slipway. Slaves and oxcarts transferred the cargoes of larger ships across the four-mile-wide isthmus.

At Corinth, Paul founded a congregation that was at once his pride and despair. For though faith flourished here, so did sin. Rendezvous of sailors and traders, Corinth came to symbolize wealth, high living, night life, and immorality. The apostle's two letters to the Corinthians tell how he suffered on behalf of this cluster of sinners who had accepted Christianity.

Paul apparently had not intended to stay long. But while he was awaiting the arrival of Timothy and Silas from other cities, winter closed the mountain passes and sea lanes. And so it was that, about A.D. 50, he "tarried there yet a good while" (Acts 18:18). His sojourn lasted 18 months.

When Paul finally embarked for Syria, he left behind a promising church at Corinth. Later, however, he was to discover that quarreling had broken out and members of the congregation had split into factions. In a magnificent evocation of Christian love—rendered in the King James Bible as "charity," from the Latin

caritas—he wrote these immortal words to his troubled flock:

"Though I speak with the tongues of men and of angels, and have not charity, I am become as sounding brass, or a tinkling cymbal. And though I have the gift of prophecy, and understand all mysteries, and all knowledge; and though I have all faith, so that I could remove mountains, and have not charity, I am nothing.... And now abideth faith, hope, charity, these three; but the greatest of these is charity" (I Corinthians 13:1-2, 13).

Returning from Europe, Paul stopped briefly at Ephesus, in what is now western Turkey. His pause here, at the greatest Roman city in Asia Minor, set the stage for his third mission, which began about A.D. 53 and lasted some five years. After a short rest he set out again from Antioch, passed again through the Cilician Gates,

THE BLUE AEGEAN, *coursed by Paul on his second great journey, frames a church on Mikonos. The Greek island, only nine miles long, has nearly 400 churches built by fishermen to fulfill vows made while in peril at sea. Woman on Mikonos (opposite) ignores an inquisitive pelican as she knits near a dockside display of curios, bait for Mikonos' biggest catch: tourists.*

A visitor to Patmos (right) scans a tenth-century manuscript. Here, in banishment, St. John may have composed Revelation after hearing "a great voice, as of a trumpet, Saying ... What thou seest, write" (1:10, 11).

WINFIELD PARKS AND (BELOW) GILBERT M. GROSVENOR, BOTH NATIONAL GEOGRAPHIC STAFF

"All...cried out, Great is Diana of the Ephesians" Acts 19:34

Rioting against Paul and his Christianity, screaming mobs swarmed on the marble-paved Arcadian Way and poured into the Great Theater of Ephesus. Soon the chant of Diana's worshipers rolled like thunder through the vast sweep of seats—66 rows that terrace Mount Pion.

Ruins now litter the slope (right) where 25,000 watched dances and rites honoring the goddess. Weed and water pave the Arcadian Way, which marched 1,735 feet, flanked by columns and torchlit at night. But Diana—Artemis, "the many-breasted Mother of Asia"—survives in life-size marble (below). Animal images invoke her as goddess of nature and guardian of wildlife.

ARCHAEOLOGICAL MUSEUM, EPHESUS; JONATHAN S. BLAIR
RIGHT: JOHN J. PUTMAN, NATIONAL GEOGRAPHIC STAFF

revisited his congregations in Asia Minor, and, reaching the Aegean, settled down for an important and successful two-year stay at Ephesus.

According to Greek legend, the city had been founded by Amazons — mythical female warriors. Greeks had lived there for a thousand years, suffering conquest by Croesus, King of Lydia; by Cyrus of Persia; and by Alexander the Great. The Romans acquired the city in 133 B.C. and made it the capital of the province of Asia.

Located a few miles up a navigable river from the Aegean coast, near the island of Samos, Ephesus sat athwart the main line of communication between Rome and the East. Merchants and traders flocked to it.

From all over Asia Minor pilgrims came to Ephesus to worship. Under Roman influence, the city's Greek goddess, Artemis, became identified with the Roman's Diana. An awesome effigy of Diana lured the devout to a marble temple that stretched longer than a modern football field. More than a hundred Ionic columns 60 feet high surrounded the temple. Here stood masterpieces of the foremost sculptors of Greece. Ancients called the temple one of the Seven Wonders of the World.

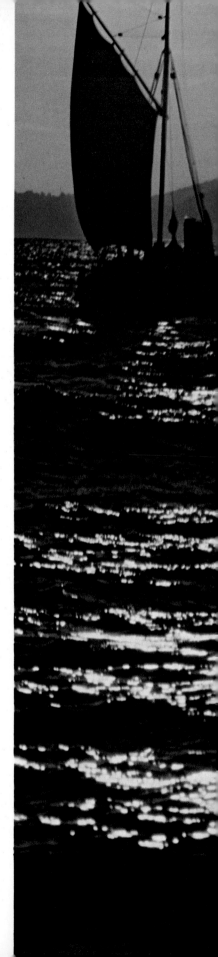

T O ALL THE CITIZENS and transients of Ephesus, Paul preached the new faith — with such impact that he caused a riot. Local artisans had long grown rich selling amulets and votive images of Diana to her hordes of followers. But Christians would not buy charms and tokens. And, as the number of converts grew, sales declined. The silversmiths, led by one Demetrius, decided to end the sales slump by driving the troublemaking apostle from their city.

Soothsayers, stargazers, and magicians joined the tumultuous demonstration. A mob seized two of Paul's companions. Clamoring throngs chanted: "Great is Diana of the Ephesians!" Dissuaded by his friends from debating with the angry crowd, Paul stayed hidden until the uproar died, then slipped away.

The Temple of Artemis, or Diana, was built upon a marsh where frogs croaked. Today the water has reclaimed it. I gazed at the huge sink where it stood, now only a pond in the Turkish farmland. Children mounted the bank beside me and tossed pebbles into the stagnant water. Myriad frogs sang in the sun where thousands of pilgrims and Ephesians had once chanted in worship. Near the site a modern museum guards beautiful statues of Diana. And all about, stretching

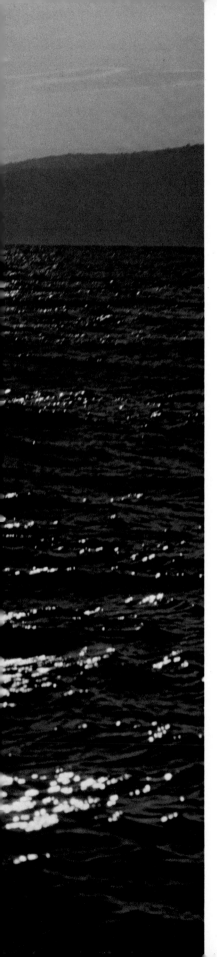

over hills and across level land, stand white-columned relics of the old city, silent monuments to past glory.

Farmers till the soil around the city's skeletal remains. I watched one pair, astride flea-bitten donkeys, clatter across a path of stone—the avenue, about a third of a mile long and 35 feet wide, that once ran from the center of Ephesus to the harbor, now but a marsh. The stream that once brought shipping to Ephesus has long since silted up. At the other end of the marble avenue stood the theater where Demetrius' mob "rushed with one accord" to howl down Paul and his comrades with shouts of fury. Tourists now ramble through the reconstructed theater. I discovered a little shed where I could buy brown bread and white cheese and drink cups of sweet black coffee while I looked out on the heart of one of the world's largest ruined cities.

Christian pilgrims now roam the ruins of the Church of St. John and visit a tiny chapel on a hillside site revered as the place where the Virgin Mary was taken after the Crucifixion. From the Cross, Jesus had entrusted His mother to a beloved disciple, who "took her unto his own home" (John 19:27). Local tradition maintains that the disciple John brought her to Ephesus to escape persecution in Jerusalem.

After leaving Ephesus, Paul visited Macedonia, then sailed along the eastern Aegean coast, stopping at Alexandria Troas, Assos, Mitylene, Chios, Samos, and Miletus. Here, at the mouth of the winding Meander (whose name became a verb), he summoned the elders of the Ephesus church to say farewell: "I go . . . unto Jerusalem, not knowing the things that shall befall me there: Save that the Holy Ghost witnesseth . . . that bonds and afflictions abide me" (Acts 20:22-23).

So it was that, after journeying thousands of miles and establishing congregations all the way to Athens and Corinth, Paul returned to the Holy City. His premonition of afflictions proved true. For angry Jews accused him of defiling the temple by taking gentiles into the sacred inner confines. Arrested, he avoided scourging by declaring to the authorities his Roman citizenship. To foil a murder plot against Paul, they

IN GOLD-FLECKED WATERS *of Turkey's Gulf of Kerme, a fishing boat sails seas plied by Paul on his voyage to Cos. A fertile island famed for its wheat, wine, silk, and ointments, Cos revered Asclepius, god of healing. Fittingly, Hippocrates was born here. His students on Cos took the oath physicians still swear.*

JONATHAN S. BLAIR

429

placed him in custody in Caesarea. I followed Paul to the ruins of Caesarea, on the coast of Israel between Tel Aviv and Haifa. Here I saw excavated a lavish marble city built by Herod the Great and fawningly dedicated to Caesar Augustus. An 18th-century Turkish pasha, however, had beaten the archeologists to much of Herod's marble. In Acre, farther north on Israel's coast, it decorates the pasha's mosque and baths, which now serve as an unusual museum.

Paul exercised his full rights as a Roman citizen: "I appeal to Caesar" (Acts 25:11). With a companion or two, and under the charge of a centurion, he took ship for Rome. He voyaged to Myra in Asia Minor, there transferring to a grain ship from Alexandria. South of Crete she ran into a savage Mediterranean storm, and for a fortnight a maddened sea battered the craft. Her crew despaired. But Paul had a vision and told his shipmates: "there shall be no loss of any man's life among you. . . . we must be cast upon a certain island" (Acts 27:22, 26).

During the 14th night the weary sailors dropped anchor over an unknown shoal. When day dawned they saw waves

"The ship was caught, and could not bear up"

Acts 27:15

For 14 days the tempest pounds Paul's ship, blotting out sun and stars. Only he has hope, "For there stood by me this night the angel of God" (Acts 27:23). Sailors jettison the cargo, grain destined for Rome. The ship runs aground off Melita, now Malta. All 276 aboard survive.

In Valletta, modern capital of Malta, the storm rages in a painting on the ceiling of the Church of St. Paul Shipwrecked (opposite). Across Grand Harbour the Three Cities—Senglea, Cospicua, and Vittoriosa—crowd the shore with medieval forts and baroque churches (below).

ITALY'S "DIVINE COAST" *rises from the Tyrrhenian Sea.*
Paul sailed past this coast on his journey to Rome.
Atrani, a suburb of Amalfi, glistens along twisting
Almalfi Drive. Ravello, high on its rocky promontory,
perches above terraced, lemon-scented gardens.

LUIS MARDEN, NATIONAL GEOGRAPHIC STAFF

crashing on a nearby shore. Had they not anchored when they did, they surely would have been wrecked in the dark.

Now, spying a bay, they cast off the anchors, hoisted the foresail, and ran for it. The ship grounded off a beach, and all abandoned her to the pounding surf. Struggling ashore, Paul and the others set foot on Malta at what is now called St. Paul's Bay.

Friendly islanders lighted a fire to warm passengers and crew. Paul laid some sticks on it—and a viper suddenly fastened on to his hand. He shook it off and suffered no ill effect. The incident probably paved the way for his conversion of everyone on Malta.

The diminutive island was the happiest surprise of my entire trip. Malta is fiercely proud that the apostle converted it. Half the men I met, it seemed, bore the name Paul. So did church after

church. And nowhere did I see more mosaics, frescoes, statues, and portraits honoring the saint. On a high altar in Valletta's richly decorated Church of St. Paul Shipwrecked stands a relic revered as an arm bone of Paul.

When winter storms abated and springtime came to the Mediterranean, Paul, still under guard, embarked for Italy. He landed at Puteoli, near today's Naples. He probably saw the cone of Vesuvius innocent of even a plume of smoke; in a few years the volcano would explode and bury Pompeii.

P AUL walked north along the Via Appia, "queen of the long roads," as it was then called. Approaching Rome, the ribbon of cemented stone blocks spanned the low plain of the Campagna di Roma. Nearby loomed the aqueduct Claudia, borne on arches 110 feet high. On the plain, suburbs sprawled, flecked with gardens and grandiose villas.

Nearer the city, smaller houses clung closer together. Beyond the Porta Capena, a city gate now long in ruin, the heart of Rome spread over its famed seven hills. Balconies ranged above narrow, undulating streets. Passing through these streets, Paul must have wondered at the maze they

"We came the next day to Puteoli" Acts 28:13

Shadows tread the amphitheater at Puteoli (opposite), where Paul finally debarked upon Italian soil. Now Pozzuoli, the town exported sulphur—its foul smell may have given Puteoli its name—and was Rome's port. When Alexandrian grain ships came in the spring, throngs cheered the arrival of "Rome's bread." After tarrying a week with brethren here, Paul went to Capua, then followed the Appian Way for 132 miles to Rome. Tourists still see scars of chariot wheels on the road (above). Fragments of grave markers pattern a wall beside Casal Rotondo, largest tomb along the route, once lined by cemeteries for Roman noblemen.

formed—and at the noisy press of horsemen, pedestrians, and chair bearers who picked their way past piles of refuse. On his way to the Forum, the center of the Roman world, the goal of all roads, he would have passed the eastern edge of the edifice-crowned hill called Palatine, related to our word "palace." Along the Via Sacra he would have seen the temples of Nero's Rome. Paul "dwelt two whole years in his own hired house" in Rome (Acts 28:30), under surveillance, but allowed to preach and write.

Tradition tells of the martyrdom of Paul, along with Peter, A.D. 67—Peter in the Circus, Paul outside the city's walls. The Church of St. Paul of Three Fountains hallows the place where, legend says, water sprang up as his severed head struck the ground thrice. The Basilica of St. Paul's-Without-the-Walls enshrines what many believe to be the apostle's final resting place. A priest there allowed me to open a grille and read PAULO, Roman letters said to have been inscribed on the pavement by order of the emperor Constantine.

But the man who taunted, "O death, where is thy sting? O grave, where is thy victory?" (I Corinthians 15:55) left more than his dust. "I have fought a good fight," he wrote to Timothy, his young disciple, "I have finished my course, I have kept the faith" (II Timothy 4:7). The faith was the same that had led men through all the Bible epic, from the wanderings of Abraham to the journeys of Paul. Now the faith would live on, for the end of Paul was but a beginning.

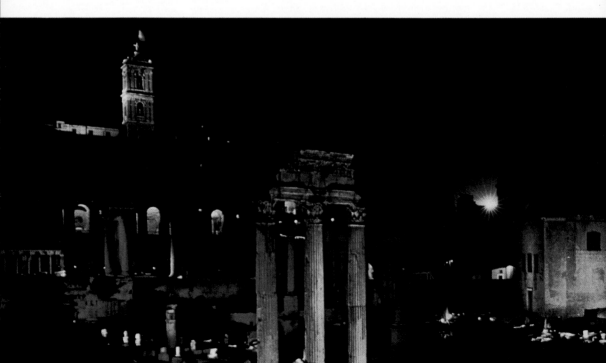

"I have kept the faith" II Timothy 4:7

In these humble words to a trusted follower,
Paul the militant evangelist summed up his life.
Sword in one hand and Scripture in the
other, he stands before Rome's
Basilica of St. Paul's-Without-the-Walls.
A Roman blade is said to have killed him.
Opposite him on the church's pediment sits Peter
at Jesus' feet, holding the keys to the Kingdom.

On summer nights, sound and light revive
scenes of the past in the Roman Forum (below).
As Rome burns, lights bathe the triple columns
of the Temple of Castor and Pollux, the restored
Senate Building at center, and the Temple
of Antoninus and Faustina, right.

Here walked Paul—"a servant of Jesus Christ,
called to be an apostle" (Romans 1:1).

Index

Text references are indicated in roman *type; illustrations and illustrated text in* **boldface.**

*Designates map.

EYE OF HORUS, *god of the sky, stares from pendant (above) found in Tutankhamun's tomb; Egyptian Museum, Cairo. Swimming girl (opposite) brought perfume to a New Kingdom lady in a compartment covered by bird's wings; the Louvre, Paris. A queen of Thutmosis III sought beauty in the silver mirror with gilded handle; Metropolitan Museum of Art, New York.*

Italicized Biblical events show their relationship to other historical dates. Years in this chronology reflect a consensus of scholars, who do not always agree on dates in ancient times; many dates, especially for earlier periods, are approximations.

EGYPT

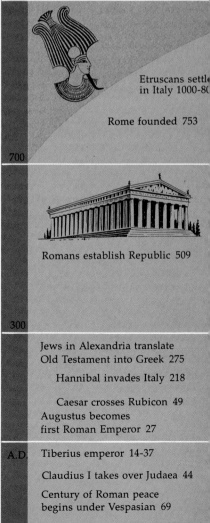

7000	
	Farm villages rise along Nile 5000
	Kingdoms of Upper, Lower Egypt 3500
	Rise of Old Kingdom; Djoser builds step pyramid 2650
	Old Kingdom falls 2200
	Rise of Middle Kingdom 2050
1700	Hyksos invade with horse and chariot 1700
	Rise of New Kingdom, Age of Empire begins 1567
	Joseph enters Egypt 1550
	Akhenaten worships single deity, Aten 1367
	Amarna letters mention *habiru* 136(
	Israel's bondage in Goshen begins 13(
	Moses leads Exodus from Egypt 1240
1200	Egyptian power begins decline 120
	Etruscans settle in Italy 1000-8(
	Rome founded 753
700	
	Romans establish Republic 509
300	
	Jews in Alexandria translate Old Testament into Greek 275
	Hannibal invades Italy 218
	Caesar crosses Rubicon 49
	Augustus becomes first Roman Emperor 27
A.D.	Tiberius emperor 14-37
	Claudius I takes over Judaea 44
	Century of Roman peace begins under Vespasian 69

The BIBLE STORY weaves through early civilizations

PALESTINE AND SYRIA

MESOPOTAMIA AND PERSIA

Earliest known date in history; Egyptians adopt calendar 4241

Jericho oldest known walled town 7000

Oldest cities rise in "land between the rivers" 4500

Menes unites Egypt, founds Memphis 3000

Frescoes at Teleilat el Ghassul 3500

Sumerian civilization flourishes 3500

Invention of writing 3100

Cheops builds Great Pyramid 2600

Growth of Canaanite cities, trade with Egypt 3000-2200

Gilgamesh summons first "congress" 2700

Semites invade Fertile Crescent 2300

Ziggurat of Ur built 2000

Amorites invade Canaan 2000

Hammurabi of Babylon codifies law 1750

Abraham sojourns in Egypt 1720

Abraham enters Canaan 1730

Abraham journeys from Ur 1750

Ahmosis I of Thebes expels Hyksos 1567

Hittites, first to develop iron industry, invade Mesopotamia from Asia Minor 1590

Hatshepsut's expedition to Punt 1482

Frequent foreign invasions keep Mesopotamia in turmoil

Tutankhamun restores ancient gods 1347

GREECE AND ROME

Ramesses II begins 67-year reign 1304

Ramesses II battles Hittites at Kadesh 1300

Greeks destroy Troy 1250

Joshua invades Canaan 1200

Dorians invade Greece 1100

Judges rule Israelites 1200

"Sea Peoples," probably from Aegean Isles, invade Palestine 1175

Philistines invade Canaan 1175

Assyrian power grows under Tiglath-pileser I 1100

Samuel anoints Saul king of Israel 1020

David captures Jerusalem, builds kingdom 1000

Solomon erects first temple 950

Greeks hold first Olympiad 776

Solomon dies, empire splits into northern kingdom of Israel and southern kingdom of Judah 922

Ashurnasirpal II expands Assyrian empire, builds palace at Calah 880

Homer composes "Iliad," "Odyssey" 750

Assyrians conquer Israel and carry its people off to oblivion 721

Sargon II destroys northern kingdom of Israel 721

Isaiah of Judah preaches against alliance with Egypt 710

Draco codifies Athenian law 621

Assyria at zenith under Ashurbanipal 688

Nineveh falls to Babylonians 612

Nebuchadnezzar rebuilds Babylon, creates Hanging Gardens 600

Nebuchadnezzar destroys Jerusalem, takes people into Babylonian captivity 587

Cyrus the Great founds Persian empire 546

Persians enter Babylon, end Hebrew exile 539

Athenians stand off Persians at Marathon 490

Persian King Cyrus returns Jews to Palestine; they rebuild temple 520

Darius invades Europe 513

Athens' Golden Age under Pericles 460-430

Alexander invades Persia 334

Alexander captures Jerusalem 332

Alexander defeats Darius III at Gaugamela 331

Seleucus I, a general of Alexander, founds dynasty 312

Ptolemies rule Palestine 275

Punic Wars begin 264

Judas Maccabeus leads revolt against Seleucids, occupies Jerusalem, cleanses temple 167

Romans destroy Carthage 146

Essene community founded 150

Caesar murdered 44

Pompey conquers Jerusalem for Rome 63

Herod the Great made king of Judaea by Roman Senate 37

Battle of Actium 31

Birth of Jesus of Nazareth 8-4   Death of Herod 4

Praetorian guard assassinates Caligula 41

Jesus, baptized by John the Baptist, begins His ministry 28

Crucifixion of Jesus 30-31   Conversion of Paul 36

Term "Christian" first used in Antioch 41   Paul begins first journey 45

Nero 54-68

Paul's second journey 49   Paul's third journey 53   Paul sails for Rome 60-61

Paul arrives in Rome 60-61

Jews revolt; Romans destroy Jerusalem 70

441

WINGED LION *in the University
of Chicago's Oriental Institute,
fashioned some 24 centuries ago,
probably came from Ecbatana.
Reverse side of the gold ornament
has 16 loops for attachment to cloth.
Bronze stag found at Alaca Huyuk
rode the top of a pre-Hittite
standard about 2200 B.C.; Museum
of Archaeology, Ankara, Turkey.* 443

ROUND CAMPFIRES flickering in the desert night, bards of the ancient Hebrews chanted of the mighty works of the Lord. Centuries later, around the glorious time of David and Solomon, scribes began putting brush to leather, recording the revered narratives of the creation, the great flood, their ancestors' deeds. They wrote as if heeding the command that Isaiah would hear: "inscribe it in a book, that it may be for the time to come as a witness for ever" (30:8).

The Bible evolved, not as a single book, but as a whole library by scores of authors. After the Babylonian Exile in the 6th century B.C., the Pentateuch, or first five books of the Old Testament, came to be regarded as the Hebrews' supreme Law, or Torah. By the 2nd century A.D., 24 books—comprising the Law, the Prophets, and the Writings (such as Psalms and Proverbs)—had been accepted as inspired by God.

The first Bible in everyday language—translated from Hebrew into Greek—appeared in Alexandria as early as the third century B.C. One Greek narrative traces its origin to some 70 scholars from Jerusalem, requested to work on it by Ptolemy II; hence its name, Septuagint.

Reports of Jesus' ministry spread by word of mouth for a generation after the Crucifixion. With the passing of the leading eyewitnesses to His teaching, the accounts of the evangelists, Matthew, Mark, Luke, and John, were set down in Greek. Mark's, considered the earliest, probably appeared before A.D. 70.

Early copyists wrote on rolls of brownish papyrus. By the 2nd century A.D., the codex, or book, with pages of papyrus and parchment, began replacing scrolls. Thus began the splendid craft of rendering rich Biblical manuscripts, which reached a climax in the Middle Ages. Some texts appeared in silver on purple vellum with divine names blazoned in gold.

Bibles lettered by scribes, one copy at a time, suffered from errors. So varied were early Latin translations that Pope Damasus in 382 sought a revision. To draft it he named his secretary, Jerome, who had studied under St. Gregory of Nazianzus (above) at Constantinople. Jerome labored for years, first in Rome, then in a rock-hewn cell in a monastery at Bethlehem. His masterpiece is still the official Bible in Latin for the Catholic Church.

St. Jerome's Vulgate, or "common," version figured in printing history. In the 1450's, Germany produced long-sought "artificial script"—movable type. Texts were standardized: Ten copies of a printing, or a thousand, all looked alike. First large volume so printed was the Gutenberg Bible in Vulgate text. A billion Bibles have since been printed in more than a thousand tongues. Font of literacy for Western man, it has shaped his character, his noblest public institutions. Men have lived by it; men have died for it. No other book approaches its influence.

In 1382 followers of John Wycliffe finished a translation of "Goddes lawe"—first complete Bible in English. But Bibles in everyday language were unwelcome; clerics condemned Wycliffe for heresy. In 1522 Luther's classic New Testament in German appeared. Within a decade William Tyndale brought out another English edition. Copies were put to the torch. So was he.

A copy of Tyndale's New Testament was inscribed to "Ane" Boleyn, second spouse of Henry VIII, "dearest juste wyfe and most virtuous princess." When Henry had her beheaded and married Jane Seymour, other copies kept the citation, changing "Ane" to "Jane."

The Geneva Bible of 1560, used by Shakespeare, was called the "Breeches Bible" for its translation of a passage in Genesis 3—"they sewed fig-leaves together and made themselves breeches."

Sixteenth-century reformers separated a group of disputed books. Such books are called apocryphal—from the Latin apocryphus—"secret." Most Protestant Bibles accept 66 books as authoritative Scripture. The Counter-Reformation's Douay version of 1582-1610 kept the 73 books accepted by Catholics.

In 1604, at a conference in Hampton Court, James I named 54 scholars to translate the Bible for use in all English churches. Drawing heavily on Tyndale, they completed in 1611 the King James, or Authorized, Version. For the ringing vigor and glorious music of its Elizabethan style, men cherish it as the "noblest monument of English prose."

By 1885 usage and new sources led to the Revised Version with more than 35,000 changes. The American Standard and Revised Standard Versions came in the 20th century. In 1917 the Jewish Publication Society of America issued an Old Testament in English based on the medieval Masoretic texts. Catholic scholars in the 1940's began the Confraternity English edition, using Greek and Hebrew sources. New finds like the Dead Sea Scrolls bring fresh insights to the study of Holy Writ and help us to heed the prophet's call: "Seek and read from the book of the Lord" (Isaiah 34:16).

Composition by National Geographic's Phototypographic Division, HERMAN J.A.C. ARENS, Director; JOHN E. McCONNELL, Manager Color separations by Beck Engraving Company, Philadelphia, Pa., Graphic Color Plate, Inc., Stamford, Conn., and The Lanman Company, Alexandria, Va. Printed and bound by Fawcett-Haynes Corporation, Rockville, Md. Paper by Oxford Paper Company, New York

Acknowledgments and Reference Guide

THE EDITORS are grateful to many individuals and organizations for the wealth of information they provided. We especially wish to thank William Stevenson Smith, Curator of Egyptian Art, Museum of Fine Arts, Boston; Henry G. Fischer, Curator, Department of Egyptian Art, Metropolitan Museum of Art, New York; Arabic linguists N. E. Habib of the Library of Congress and John G. Mutziger, Board on Geographic Names, U. S. Department of the Interior; Professor Hans Goedicke, hieroglyphic writing expert, Johns Hopkins University; Rabbi Oscar Groner, authority on Jewish history, B'nai B'rith; Monsignor Patrick W. Skehan of the Semitics Department, Catholic University of America; Theresa Goell of Nemrud Dagh Excavations, Turkey; and James A. Cox, who helped in writing and editing.

We used many translations of Holy Scriptures: King James Version, Revised Standard Version, Confraternity-Douay Version, and *The Holy Scriptures According to the Masoretic Text*. Also helpful were *The Oxford Annotated Bible, The Interpreter's Bible, The Jerusalem Bible*, the Anchor Bible series, and the Jewish Publication Society of America's modern translation of *The Torah*. We regularly turned to the *Dictionary of the Bible* by John L. McKenzie, S.J., *A Dictionary of Life in Bible Times* by W. Corswant, *The Interpreter's Dictionary of the Bible, Analytical Concordance to the Bible* (King James Version) by Robert Young, and *Nelson's Complete Concordance of the Revised Standard Version*.

Books of general scope frequently consulted were: *Biblical Archaeology* and *The Bible and the Ancient Near East* by G. Ernest Wright; *Light from the Ancient Past* by Jack Finegan; *At the Dawn of Civilization*, edited by E. A. Speiser; *Ancient Near Eastern Texts Relating to the Old Testament*, edited by James B. Pritchard; *Archaeology in the Holy Land* by Kathleen M. Kenyon; *The Archaeology of Palestine* by William F. Albright; and *Illustrated World of the Bible Library*, edited by Michael Avi-Yonah and others.

These histories provided insights: *History Begins at Sumer* and *The Sumerians* by Samuel Noah Kramer; *The Greatness that was Babylon* and *Everyday Life in Babylonia and Assyria* by H.W.F. Saggs; *Ancient Mesopotamia* by A. Leo Oppenheim; *The Culture of Ancient Egypt* by John A. Wilson; *A History of Egypt* by James Henry Breasted; *Everyday Life in Ancient Egypt in the Days of Ramesses the Great* and *Eternal Egypt* by Pierre Montet; *Dictionary of Egyptian Civilization* by Georges Posener; *Tutankhamen: Life and Death of a Pharaoh* by Christiane Desroches Noblecourt; *The Pyramids* by Ahmed Fakhry; *Ancient Israel* by Roland de Vaux; *Palestine Before the Hebrews* by Emmanuel Anati; *The Canaanites* by John Gray; *The Hittites* by Oliver R. Gurney;

"MONA LISA OF NIMRUD," *8th-century* B.C. *ivory, adorns the Iraq Museum in Baghdad; Hirmer*

A History of Sinai by Lina Eckenstein; *The Other Side of the Jordan, Rivers in the Desert, Deities and Dolphins*, by Nelson Glueck; *The Antiquities of Jordan* by G. Lankester Harding.

We sampled high adventure in narratives of the giants of archeology: *Nineveh and Its Remains* and *Early Adventures in Persia, Susiana & Babylonia* by Austen Henry Layard; *Seventy Years in Archaeology* by Flinders Petrie; *Excavations at Ur, Digging Up the Past*, and *Dead Towns and Living Men* by Sir Leonard Woolley; *The Tomb of Tut-Ankh-Amen* by Howard Carter and A. C. Mace. More recent accounts are: *Digging Up Jericho* by Kathleen M. Kenyon; *Gibeon, Where the Sun Stood Still* by James B. Pritchard; *Shechem, The Biography of a Biblical City* by G. Ernest Wright; *Masada* and *Hazor* by Yigael Yadin; plus handy surveys: *Signs and Wonders upon Pharaoh* by John A. Wilson; *The March of Archaeology* by C. W. Ceram; *The World of the Past*, edited by Jacquetta Hawkes; also books on the Dead Sea Scrolls by Millar Burrows, J. M. Allegro, Edmund Wilson, Theodor H. Gaster, and *The Ancient Library of Qumran and Modern Biblical Studies* by Frank Moore Cross, Jr.

Specialized volumes referred to included: *Art of Warfare in Biblical Lands* by Yigael Yadin; *Writing* by David Diringer; *They Wrote on Clay* by Edward Chiera; the volumes *Sumer* and *Nineveh and Babylon* by André Parrot, in the Arts of Mankind series; and *The Jewish Wars* by Josephus.

An earlier National Geographic book, *Everyday Life in Ancient Times*, contains much on the Bible period, as does *The Bible Companion*, edited by William Neil.

In preparing the special maps we consulted: *Westminster Historical Atlas to the Bible* by G. Ernest Wright and Floyd V. Filson; *The Atlas of the Bible* by L. H. Grollenberg; *Atlas of Mesopotamia* by Martin A. Beek; and the *Rand McNally Bible Atlas* by Emil G. Kraeling.

Today's traveler will still find Baedecker's *Egypt* and *The Sudan* and *Palestine and Syria* accurate guides to the antiquities of those regions. More recent are *The Middle East*, in Hachette's World Guides; *Guide to Egypt* by Hermann Ziock; and *New Israel Guide* by E. and M. Talmi.

Our editors studied art works and everyday objects from Bible times in the Metropolitan Museum of Art, New York; the Museum of Fine Arts, Boston; the Oriental Institute, Chicago; the Smithsonian Institution, Washington, D. C.; the University Museum, Philadelphia; the Walters Art Gallery, Baltimore; the British Museum, London; the Egyptian Museum, Cairo; the Iraq Museum, Baghdad; the Louvre, Paris; the National Museum, Damascus; the Palestine Archaeological Museum and the Israel Museum, Jerusalem.

National Geographic Society staff members in many departments contributed to this book. See listing on following page. Some 900 issues of NATIONAL GEOGRAPHIC contain a treasure of information, illustrations, and first-hand accounts of Biblical archeology and life in Bible lands. Consult the National Geographic Index.